DOPE GIRLS

The Birth of the
British Drug Underground

Marek Kohn

LAWRENCE & WISHART
LONDON

Lawrence & Wishart Ltd
144a Old South Lambeth Road
London SW8 1XX

First published in 1992

© Marek Kohn, 1992

ISBN 0 85315 772 3

Cover and text designed by
Jan Brown Designs, London.
Photoset in North Wales by
Derek Doyle Associates, Mold, Clwyd.
Printed and bound in Great Britain by
The Cromwell Press, Melksham, Wilts.

CONTENTS

ACKNOWLEDGMENTS

My thanks go to all the individuals and organisations who have helped with this book, including: Rosemary Ashbee at the Savoy Hotel; Virginia Berridge; J. Blakey, Governor, H.M. Prison, Parkhurst; the Newspaper Library, British Library, Colindale; Michael Goss; the Greater London Records Office; Dr John Henry, Consultant Physician at the National Poisons Unit; Mrs Connie Ho; Bob Little; the Local History Archive of Tower Hamlets Central Library; Mrs Rose Maudesley; the Museum of London; the Public Record Office; John Ramsey of St George's Hospital Medical School; Andrew Rose; David Skinner; Bing Spear; the Theatre Museum; Keith Parker at the Wellcome Museum of the History of Medicine; the staff of Maida Vale Library, the Archives and Local Studies Department of Victoria Library, and other branches of Westminster City Libraries; and John Witton at the Institute for the Study of Drug Dependence.

Most of all, my thanks go to my wife, Sue Matthias Kohn, for her love and constant support throughout the time I spent working on *Dope Girls*. This book is dedicated to her.

'Blighters', by Siegfried Sassoon, is reproduced by permission of George Sassoon.

INTRODUCTION

Drugs have lost their history. A few antique episodes remain in popular consciousness: opiate use among Romantic poets, Freud's unwise dalliance with cocaine, Britain's Opium Wars against China, the drug fever of pre-Hays Code Hollywood. But there is little sense of how certain drugs came to assume their special role, corrosive and Dionysiac, in twentieth-century culture. Despite the political and social saliency of the issue today, public understanding of drugs rests on unsophisticated assumptions. Principal among them is the belief that drug laws reflect a sort of natural law; that the illegality of a number of chemicals is the necessary consequence of their inherent pharmacological properties. Indeed, drugs that remain within the law, like alcohol and tobacco, often go unrecognised as drugs at all. (For the sake of convenience, this book generally accepts the everyday usage of the word.)

Until recently, the prohibition of certain drugs has been taken as axiomatic. In the past few years, however, a vigorous challenge to this principle has arisen. It is empirical in essence, arguing that the present regime of drug control is not working, and therefore what has hitherto been unthinkable must now be thought. In starting from the current crisis and trying to plot a way out, it is not overly concerned with the roots of that crisis, put down seventy-five or a hundred years ago. One of the originating premises of this book was the idea that, to help understand our current position, it would be worthwhile to take a look at where the journey began and the course it subsequently followed. *Dope Girls* is about how drugs acquired their modern meaning in one particular place and time: Britain – which is to say London, since the phase was dominated by developments in the capital – during the First World War and its aftermath.

That doesn't mean this is simply a book about drugs, though. I believe that the history of illegal drugs has to have a place in the debate on what to do about them today, and contributing a perspective to the discussion is a specific purpose of this book. But that is not the main reason for writing it. Its fundamental premises are that the modern discourse about drugs is about far more than drugs, and that these other themes are far more interesting than drugs themselves. Drugs permit the terrors of the social subconscious to be voiced. It is an eloquent panic.

It begins when 'drug' becomes 'dope'. In the nineteenth century, it was understood that certain middle-class women and professional men had the 'drug habit'. These were seen as individual burdens, though; the unfortunate by-products of medical treatment, or unwise attempts to cope with the demands of brain-work. Private weaknesses like these did not lead to serious restrictions on the availability of opiates or cocaine, let alone the criminalisation of their non-medical use. Once the 'dope fiend' was identified as a species, however, drugs came to be regarded as properly a police matter. The outlawing of drugs was the consequence not of their pharmacology, but of their association with social groups that were perceived as potentially dangerous.

The process began in the United States, in the 1870s, when white gamblers, delinquents and prostitutes took up the Chinese practice of smoking opium. Thousands of Chinese men had been imported, as indentured labourers, to build the railroads; recreational enterprises such as gambling, prostitution and opium 'dens' accompanied them. The early protests about the dens expressed what was to become a persistent and dominant theme in the drug discourse: the idea that the worst thing about drugs was that they dissolved boundaries between the races, and positively encouraged sexual contact across the colour line. The San Francisco physician Winslow Anderson described 'the sickening sight of young white girls from sixteen to twenty years of age lying half-undressed on the floor or couches, smoking with their 'lovers'. Men and women, Chinese and white people, mix in Chinatown smoking houses.'[1] Variations on this scene set the tone of the British drug panic in the 1920s, firing on the potent juxtaposition of young white women, 'men of colour' (the term was current), sex and drugs. If the ultimate menace of drugs had to be summarised in a single proposition, it would be that they facilitated the seduction of young white women by men of other races.

Britain's introduction to 'dope' was the result of processes that had been underway in the United States for the best part of half a century. In the late 1880s or early 1890s, New Orleans stevedores began to use cocaine. It was a work drug, for men toiling through seventy-hour shifts, as the coca leaf was in the Andes. By the end of the century, the white underworld had discovered the drug. The American political establishment was also beginning to discover the drug issue. It was a colonial acquisition: in taking the Philippines after winning the war against Spain, in 1898, the United States inherited responsibility for controlling the local use of opium. The Spanish had segregated it on ethnic lines, permitting the Chinese to use it, but barring its sale to Filipinos. American missionaries successfully pressurised the authorities to phase the trade out altogether, and then began to lobby the government to take an international stand against the traffic.

The man who orchestrated the campaign, Hamilton Wright, believed that the major obstacle to moral leadership in the international arena was the absence of order in America's own house. To further the cause of domestic drug control legislation, Wright inflated statistics and spread scare stories. It was said that cocaine triggered outbursts of violence in black men; there was talk of Southern police officers acquiring larger calibre guns to counter this individualised version of the spectre of black rebellion.[2] Wright himself conjured up the most terrible negro menace of all, with his claim that, in their cocaine frenzy, black men were apt to rape white women.

The first result of his endeavours was a national ban on opium in smokable form, under which the possession of the drug was criminalised. Smokers switched to morphine and cocaine; the latter, known as a drug of 'bohemians, gamblers, high- and low-class prostitutes, night porters, bellboys, burglars, racketeers, pimps, and casual laborers', was restricted under a series of state laws – an inevitable development, given the prevailing official wisdom that 'the negroes, the lower and criminal classes, are naturally most readily influenced.'[3]

The 1900s also saw the spread of heroin use in New York and other Eastern cities (the drug had been commercially introduced in 1898). The source was the concentration of pharmaceutical factories in the New York area, and the main customers were youths belonging to the street gangs of the slums. In short, urban America had a modern drug scene by 1914, complete with subcultures, hysteria, politics and prohibition laws.

On the international front, several conferences had taken place, and the United States had secured agreement in principle from participating countries that they would pass laws restricting opium, heroin, morphine and cocaine to medical and other reputable uses. In late 1914, the Harrison Narcotic Act established Wright's long-sought exemplary regime at national level.

Britain was lukewarm about implementing the international

agreements, partly because it did not want to impede its own pharmaceutical industry. It certainly did not see any domestic need for an equivalent to the Harrison Act. Anybody was free to walk into a chemist's shop and buy cocaine or morphine, subject to one or two formalities, but almost nobody chose to do so. There was no detectable drug scene, even in the capital. In its economic importance, London could stand proud alongside New York, and comfortably above Paris; politically, the British metropolis could lord it over both. It had the righteous steam and clangour of an imperial capital; it had the commotion of its fly, self-possessed proletariat. It was cosmopolitan enough for a European city, with its substantial migrant population and its great port. But in its pleasures, its libido, it was provincial – a city of threepenny beer and five-shilling brothels. In Paris, loucheness aspired to the status of art. New York had skyscraping modernity and syncopation, as well as street gangs. Until the middle of the Great War, most Londoners would probably have viewed the 'drug habit' as a phenomenon confined to such hothouse cities, in which exotic species of vice were cultivated.

London never did lead the world in drug culture. As a case study, the interest of the British drug scene lies in the attractive neatness of its sudden mushrooming on virgin soil. It has a deeper fascination, as a symptom of a crisis in Britain's evolution as a modern society. Drug panics derive their electric intensity from a concentration of meanings: in Britain, the detection of a drug underground provided a way of speaking simultaneously about women, race, sex and the nation's place in the world. It was a symbolic issue in which a larger national crisis was reworked in microcosm.

Dope Girls considers the birth of the drug underground as a cultural encounter with external influences, taking place under conditions of unprecedented national trauma. The Great War jolted Britain's relationship with the rest of the world into a new shape. 'Dope' was partly a symptom of that impact, and partly a way to express anxieties about it. The drug traffic immediately gave rise to a rich folklore, in which conspiracy theories and the evil influences of other races were prominent. These tales were closely related to the xenophobic spy stories which flourished during the war.

They were also clearly descended from the mythology, already well evolved, of the white slave traffic. The archetypal white slave story involves the seduction of an innocent young white woman, or girl, her abduction by a secret foreign syndicate, and its use of other women as agents. These elements were easily reworked into the mythology of the drug syndicate which employed female agents to lure young women, who would then spread the vice further in turn. One of the most striking features of the British discourse on drugs, which arose in 1916 and reached a peak in the mid-1920s, was its emphasis on women. Actresses, chorus girls, 'night club girls', 'bachelor girls', 'flappers', 'women of the unfortunate class'; whether they played the part of victim or harpy, the women of the drug underworld were of the uncontainable class. Theirs was not a political radicalism, but they all laid claim to an independence that was highly disturbing to orthodox commentators. No form of journalism, popular literature or film is more didactic than the drug story, and contemporary narratives were indefatigable in their efforts to impress the folly of drugtaking upon the public. In continually retelling the story of the downfall of young women, these narratives also asserted that, without protection and dependence, women were in deadly danger.

This was a classically reactionary discourse, and one whose hysterical tone belied its impotence. Possibly the most important social change of the First World War was the transformation of the position of women. As Sandra M. Gilbert argues, a generation of sons seemed to have been sacrificed; the enthusiasm with which the daughters took their place 'suggested that the most crucial rule the war had overturned was that of patrilineal succession, the founding law of patriarchal society itself'.[4]

The destructive capacity of modern warfare consumed manpower at an unprecedented rate; women moved *en masse* to occupy the vacuum. Half a million of them abandoned servants' quarters and sweatshops for munition factories and offices, and women's average wages doubled. With their menfolk away at the war, women controlled the household economy; in public, they acquired an unprecedented visibility. They became bus conductors and ticket collectors: a uniform, even a low-ranking civilian one, was significant. The women's movement created and promoted women's auxiliary services to demonstrate their capacity for full citizenship. The movement's claim was acknowledged in 1918, with the enfranchisement of women over thirty.[5]

While the donning of uniform placed in question one of the boundaries between male and female domains, women's everyday dress and behaviour began to confuse the distinction between respectable women and those 'of a certain class', as the press referred to them. Wearing make-up, smoking in public, eating out or walking the streets unchaperoned were no longer the sole prerogative of prostitutes. For thousands of ordinary women, especially young ones, these signs of independence came with their jobs. As far as they were concerned, their right to occupy public space was no longer in question.

In one domain of society, there actually was no border between prostitutes and socially acceptable women, between demi-monde and monde – and it was here that the drug subculture sprang up. There was a continuum in West End society, from the street prostitutes and petty criminals at the bottom, through the chorus girls and actresses who might work as prostitutes between engagements, to those whose success in the entertainment world allowed them to mix with the social elite.[6] The night world of the West End was a vertical section through the strata, elsewhere rigidly segregated, of British society. It was by no means a modern phenomenon – indeed, its basis was just the sort of sweated casual female employment that the war had enabled women to escape. But it was an elective community made up of people who disregarded traditional conservative values and espoused hedonism. There may have been an artistic or literary element affiliated to it, but it was a more organic – and therefore more interesting – community than the small avant-garde cliques who, from the 1890s, had experimented with drugs as part of their self-conscious rejection of the norm.[7] In the West End, the drug habit was untheoretical; but, as the focus of a subculture that spanned the classes, it was much more subversive than drugtaking performed as a gesture within the enclosed circles of high bohemianism. As the subjects of history, these category-defying people make a refreshing change from, on the one hand, the upper classes, with their lives and letters, and the salt-of-the-earth proletarians on the other.

The West End was also the nursery for jazz, a culture simultaneously of modernity and otherness. Like the opponents of rock'n'roll a few decades later, conservative commentators could not get a purchase on the music. 'Niggers surrounded by noise'[8] might be amply contemptuous, but it was the fogeyish snort of a culture which could not comprehend what was overtaking it. Jazz was the sound of the Aftermath; a revivifying breath from America – and, radically, from Africa – after Europe's bout of self-destruction. It threatened an inversion of the cultural order, with its paradoxical combination of the modern and the 'primitive'.

Victory had taken too long and cost too much to enhance British self-confidence. The fact that American intervention had been needed to turn the tide was a sign of a change in the world order; the revolutionary chaos in Europe and Russia was disturbing. Europe was in crisis; European values had been thrown into doubt; these instabilities encouraged fears about the future of the race. The xenophobia of the war years persisted, and one of the ways in which it found expression was in a demonology of dope. Two individuals in particular, one Chinese and one black, were identified as 'dope kings', and invested with a highly sexualised menace. It was claimed that the main attraction of cocaine for men like Brilliant Chang, a Chinese restaurant proprietor, and Edgar Manning, a jazz drummer from Jamaica, was as a means of seducing and enslaving white women. Along with women like the actress Billie Carleton and the nightclub dancer Freda Kempton, both of whom were killed by drugs, Chang and Manning became characters in a rich dope folklore, which ranged from highly fictionalised journalism to novels and films. The relations between these texts were close. There was a strong hint of Billie Carleton in Sax Rohmer's *Dope*, published a few months after her death. A Cardiff cinema drew protests from the local Chinese community by displaying cuttings about Freda Kempton's death and Chang's alleged role in it, to promote *Cocaine*, a film featuring a caricature portrayal of a Chinese cocaine trafficker.[9]

Dope Girls pays particular attention to this folklore, and to the relationship between these texts. It also focuses on the individuals themselves – for romantic reasons, as much as any. I have done what I can to recover the traces of their lives; apart from their representation in newspapers, however, these are scanty. They were just the sort of people who leave little after them, not even descendants; the period itself has by now receded to the outer edges of living memory.

For a long time I saw this as a flaw in the book's constitution. Then, acknowledging that much of the period's special fascination for me lies precisely in its distance, I came to see it as a vital ingredient of the book's character, both romantically and historically. In the latter respect, I felt that this intuition was vindicated when I read transcripts of oral history interviews made in the mid-1980s with a woman who, probably uniquely, could remember the drug underground first hand. They illustrated how memory is a bird's nest of experience, reinvention, and interpolation from all sorts of sources, from relatives to old newspapers. Her recollections contained just the same narrative fictions, about a supposed relationship between Billie Carleton and Brilliant Chang, that had been a prominent feature of the written dope folklore of the time. It would have been enthralling to have had access to more oral accounts, but they would not necessarily have illuminated a special truth.

The period is also something of a theoretical backwater, which is more surprising. Though specific themes such as the suffrage movement and the social impact of the war have, of course, been extensively researched and discussed, the culture and events explored in *Dope Girls* have remained almost entirely invisible. The exceptions to this neglect are in the work of Virginia Berridge, whose writing sets the terms for any consideration of the history of drugs in Britain, and of Terry M. Parssinen. I gratefully acknowledge these as inspiration and points of departure for this book.

The crisis that Britain experienced during the War and its Aftermath was one of modernity, in which a declining imperial power was confronted at all points with the harbingers of a new era, from the effects of industrialised warfare to the boom in cinemas and dancehalls. The transformation would have happened anyway, but the war caused it to be convulsive rather than gradual. Women, especially young women, were sensed to be the agents and beneficiaries of this transformation. Young women became exceptionally clearly defined as a distinct group in society, and drugs became one way in which anxieties about them could be articulated. Drug use was understood as a crisis of young womanhood; cocaine, especially, was a young women's drug.

The creation of a drug underground was a specific instance of cultural modernity. It disrupted several highly sensitive social boundaries, of sex, class and race, and packed these destabilised ingredients into a confined space. This inevitably provoked a reaction, both legal and textual. After Billie Carleton's death in 1918, two people were jailed, and Carleton herself was 'rewritten'. The court evidence depicted a worldly, materialistic, manipulative young woman. A typical commentary spoke of her 'frail beauty and delicate art ... all of that perishable, moth-like substance that does not last long in the wear and tear of this rough-and-ready world'.[10] Carleton's vigorous modernity was denied; instead, she was reborn as a Victorian waif. Over the next few years, the idea of frailty recurred again and again in representations of the 'dope girls'.[11] The moral drawn from their deaths and degradation was that the pre-modern notion of womanhood had been right after all.

Most of the ideas which emerge from the contemporary texts would nowadays be generally regarded as laughable at best, and repulsive at worst. The vehemence with which they are articulated would be unthinkable in public discourse today. Yet, although they have been erased, or at least diluted, the rhetoric that directly concerns drug use itself has survived more or less unmodified. The same imagery and the same level of hysteria can be found in British newspapers of the 1920s and the 1980s – two decades in which notable drug panics occurred; there seems no reason to suppose that they will not recur in the future, when the connotations of drugtaking once again offer a way to speak about more profound social anxieties.[12]

It is a remarkable cultural spasm, this discourse that has remained immune to the passage of three-quarters of a century, but its persistence is aberrant. The contradictions of drug prohibition may eventually end in a catastrophic reversal of strategy, and the rhetoric of the drug panic will evaporate in the way that of its contemporary, Bolshevism, did in Russia. But under the present regime, it is a paralysing discourse which obstructs the reappraisal that the drug issue needs today. That the themes which formerly accompanied it are now anathema is not, in itself, proof that prohibition is the wrong way to control drugs – it is possible to make the right decision for the wrong reasons – but it is certainly evidence that public debate should take into consideration.

Reading the newspapers of the 1920s, the very familiarity of the drug theme is incongruous. Everything else has changed. Racism and sex have swapped places. Nowadays, sexual acts are routinely described in explicit, often pornographic detail, but racist messages are covert or implicit. In the 1920s, newspapers felt no inhibitions about the use of phrases like 'yellow snake' or 'black devil',[13] but glanced over carnal matters with genteel vagueness: 'certain relations', 'women of a certain class'. (They were polysyllabic as well as circumlocutory. Those were the days when the *News of the World*, which for years was regarded as the most prurient and vulgar of the papers, could offer its working-class readers a story headlined 'Vicissitudes Of A Prepossessing Girl'.)

This opposition of familiarity and strangeness permeates the material upon which *Dope Girls* is based. It is the polarity which generates the book's current; at an emotional as well as an intellectual level, it has spurred me on through several years of research. At its simplest, there is the delight of surprise: to begin with the familiar collection of received images – music hall and patriotic bunting, soldiers singing 'Tipperary', women handing out white feathers to men in mufti – and to discover its antithesis in a forgotten underworld. There is the unexpected recognition of cultural experiences that people born after the Second World War tend to assume they were the first to enjoy. Fashionable Londoners who were young in the early 1980s might imagine that they invented staying up all night and going to four different clubs, but their forebears beat them to it in the early 1920s. The people of the Aftermath were also the first white generation to feel music in the hips; to begin to swing. Yet even as one recognises a common strand of culture, the gulf between then and now reasserts itself. It was still the age of foxtrots and evening dress.

The styles change; so do the issues. The grand themes may, regrettably, be more durable. Although the undiluted racial venom has been flushed out of the dope discourse, drugs still provide a way to articulate racist themes in code. They act as a discursive alarm bell – halt the debate, declare war, take cover. In such an atmosphere, associations between drugs and a particular ethnic group may become more important than the underlying reasons for those associations. Now that racist themes are largely confined to the subtext of public debate, the payload can be transferred to drugs: the menace implicit in 'black' is shifted to 'crack'.

In its more general lines, the drug problem today retains much of the earlier xenophobic geometry. The theme of foreign criminal conspiracies is accompanied by a profound anxiety about the violation of national boundaries by smugglers; the discourse is dominated by metaphors of war and disease – the 'war on drugs', the 'drug plague'. Drugs remain 'other', and arouse the same passions in the Western subconscious as does the non-European Other. Mrs Thatcher once spoke, notoriously, about British fears of being 'swamped' by an alien culture; the media speak incessantly of being 'swamped' by a 'flood' or a 'tidal wave' of drugs.[14]

The other Other, of course, is Woman. Drugs are no longer a significant ideological vehicle for the rearguard action of patriarchy against female emancipation. In this respect, *Dope Girls* is an account of battles on ground that is no longer being contested. But they retain their relevance as long as the struggle itself continues – which is to say, for the foreseeable future. Women's history in recent years has taught that gains cannot be taken for granted: whatever the surface content of public discourse, there is an implacable resistance movement at work in the subtexts of the media and popular culture. Today the focus of the attack may be the woman at work, and the alleged harm her career does to her psyche or to family life; in the future, who knows? The forces of anti-feminist conservatism may once again identify women at play as the problem; they may turn from *Fatal Attraction* back to *Looking For Mr Goodbar*. The struggle might yet return to the heart of the city at night.

One way to look at a city is to consider it as a text. My own personal copy of the West End is now covered in marginal notes and amendments which have transformed its meaning for me: the street corner on Shaftesbury Avenue, a little way down from Cambridge Circus, where Edgar Manning shot three men one day in 1920, for example; or the building in Gerrard Street that is now a Chinese supermarket and restaurant, but used to be the notorious 43 Club; or the tiny dining room in Lisle Street that today offers 'The Cheapest Chinese Food in Town', but in 1918 was a shady chemist's from which Billie Carleton's circle got their cocaine.

In the actual texts of the dope panic, the combination of resonance and dissonance disrupts the familiar. It makes the present as well as the past look different. Although the characters of *Dope Girls* are drugtakers, prostitutes, playboys and hoodlums, this book is about the cultural ancestry of all of us – even the ones who are without sin.

1

NERVOUS DISPOSITION

*Curriculum vitae: **Edith Yeoland***

Real name: Edith Kate Bowyer
Born: 9 April 1873, Notting Hill

Career: Appeared in *Sweet Nell of Old Drury* at the Globe Theatre, 22 February 1902 – 10 March 1902.

Understudy at Her Majesty's, and at the Haymarket during Mrs Lily Langtry's season.

Appeared on the suburban tour of *Magda*, as a member of Mrs Patrick Campbell's company.

*Curriculum vitae: **Ida Yeoland***

Real name: Ida Florence Bowyer
Born: 6 January 1876, Brixton

Career: Played Mme de Brignolles in Sir Henry Irving's 1897 production of *Madame Sans-Gêne* at the Lyceum.

Took over the role of Lady Gwendoline in *Little Miss Nobody*, at the Lyric Theatre, which ran from 14 September 1898 to 18 March 1899.

Played Victoire Duplay in the Lyceum production of *Robespierre*, led by Sir Henry Irving, from 15 April 1899 to 29 July 1899.

Millicent Farey in *Miss Hobbs*, at the Duke of York's Theatre 18 December 1899 – 13 July 1900.

Fanny in *The Lackey's Carnival*, Duke of York's, 26 September 1900 – 2 November 1900.

Lisette in *The Swashbuckler*, Duke of York's, 17 November 1900 – 15 February 1901.

Mrs Revel in *The Yellow Peril*, Duke of York's, 19 February 1901 –13 April 1901. Understudy, in the accompanying production of *The Adventures of Lady Ursula*, to Miss Evelyn Millard; owing to the latter's indisposition during the last nights of the run, Miss Yeoland undertook the character of the heroine of the piece.

Ida Yeoland's last interview, July 1901

Speaking to the representative of *Woman's Life*, Ida Yeoland reflected on her experience as an understudy. 'I am only afraid it will be a very long time before I shall ever have so glorious a part again,' she said. 'I enjoyed it so much, and for five performances was, indeed, for the first time truly happy.'

Edith and Ida Yeoland's last scene, Tuesday morning, 16 July 1901

A Bloomsbury boarding house.

Mrs Sarah Callaghan, the landlady, is startled by a cry from the speaking-tube: 'Come up at once!'

Hurrying upstairs, Mrs Callaghan finds Ida Yeoland, wearing only her dressing gown, standing in the doorway of the room the young woman shares with her sister. 'We are going,' Ida tells her. 'If you could fetch a cab, we could be taken away at once and save any bother at the house. We have taken poison.' She sinks onto a seat in agony.

Inside the room, Edith is lying on the bed. Mrs Callaghan ignores her plea to be left to die, picks her up and carries her downstairs. Ida is now on the floor of the passage, foaming at the mouth. As her sister is borne past, she calls out, 'Are you gone yet?'

By the time the police arrive, Ida is lying dead in the passageway, and Edith is in convulsions, her arm round Mrs Callaghan's neck. 'I have taken poison; I want to die,' she protests. She is taken, semi-conscious, to the Middlesex Hospital, where she suffers several fits before expiring about an hour later.

Edith Yeoland's last letter

My dear mother,

Ida has at last decided to go under with me. We are heartily sick of this weary struggle and our health is against us. Misery and misfortune seem to be our heritage and surely the best thing we can do is seek peace in nothingness.

Don't worry; we are not worth it, and remember we are far better off. I am sorry to bring this trouble upon you. It is hard for you at the time, but the trouble will blow over soon and we shall be forgotten, I hope.

People will say we are cowards, brutal and mad and countless other things, but that won't matter a bit, will it? We each know our own troubles best, after all, and neither I nor Ida can or wish to endure our existence any longer. We haven't the nerve to push.

It is not the fault of circumstance that has led to this – not a bit; for we should be the same under any condition. It is in ourselves, our temperaments in which our unhappiness dwells, and surely life is not such a glorious thing that we must cling to it for its own sake.

Ida sends her love and begs you will leave the little plain gold-twisted ring on her finger and the long chain round her neck, together with the pearl locket and rope of pearls. All other things of ours keep yourself or give away as you please. If J.B. wants the things he has given me, let him have them.

I am sorry this should happen just now to spoil Harry's holiday, but he will soon get over it and there will be greater happiness to follow. Our love to father and Sydney. They ought to feel happy that the curtain has fallen on our lives – lives that have always spelt tragedy and always would with us.

Good-bye. My best love to you and sorry to give you this extra trouble. Thank Heaven, though, it will not last long. We have instructed Mrs Callaghan to forward all letters to Harry and let them be destroyed.

Your unfortunate daughter,

Edith.

Inquest

The court heard that Edith was excitable, in poor health, and suffered fits of depression. She once told Sarah Callaghan, 'Don't be surprised if you come into our room one day and find us dead.' She had not had any theatrical engagements for a month; Ida had been out of work for two months. The day before the tragedy, they had been told that their applications for places on an American tour had been rejected. In the morning, they sent Mrs Callaghan's servant out to fetch three bottles of cocaine from the chemist's.

Their father, Joseph Bowyer, a silk-merchant of Ladbroke Road, gave evidence of Edith's delicate constitution. 'Was she sensitive?' the coroner asked. 'Most,' Mr Bowyer replied.

The verdict was that Edith committed suicide while of unsound mind, and Ida joined her under her influence.[1]

After lives spent in pursuit of audiences and ended in disappointment, the Yeolands drew a crowd in death. Onlookers gathered in Great Russell Street to watch the removal of the coffins, on open carriages decked with flowers, from the house where the sisters had poisoned themselves. It was a re-enactment, in pathetic miniature, of the cortege which had taken the old Queen and her majestic era to the grave, five months earlier.

The Yeolands resigned in the face of the new century and the new Edwardian age, diagnosing themselves as classically Victorian figures. In Edith's final summing-up, their existence was dominated by illness and a psychological constitution inadequate for the demands life made on them – factors which, in Victorian opinion, dominated the condition of womanhood as a whole. 'We haven't the nerve to push': Edith did not mean they lacked impudence, but nervous strength. Neurasthenia – 'nerve weakness' – was a paradigmatic diagnosis of the period, sufficiently vague and simple to describe a vast range of infirmity, actual and supposed. It was based on the idea that nervous resources were sapped by the artificially accelerated pace of life in industrial society. Those most at risk were those with the most developed and sensitive nervous systems: people who worked by brain rather than hand; people with responsibilities, professionals, businessmen, and 'new' women.

People did not say the Yeolands were 'cowards, brutal and mad'; at any rate, not in the press. The tragedy was reported with decorum and sympathy; the high rates of unemployment in the acting profession were noted, and it was observed that the dead women had been temperamentally unsuited to that precarious occupation.

Melancholy itself is scarcely alien to drama – after all, the commonplace that every actor wants to play Hamlet must have been well worn even by the turn of the century. The grandeur of the role lies in the fact that the tension between being and not being is unresolved. It is explored in a soliloquy, not refuted in a statement. Edith's letter, so bleak in its conviction of the women's worthlessness, could serve as a testament for millions less able to articulate the essence of depression. (Her lucidity becomes the more terrible in the light of her opening sentence, that hints at the power of persuasion she exerted upon her younger, more successful sister to 'go under' with her.) She employs a theatrical flourish – 'the curtain has fallen on our lives' – but she denies the actor's *raison d'être*: she looks forward to being forgotten.

The agent of their deaths attracted comment. It was reported that a large number of cocaine bottles had been found in their rooms, suggesting addiction. 'Guinevere', a commentator for the Referee, described the course of dependency:

The habit grows rapidly; a mild 10 per cent. solution obtained at a chemist's to cure a toothache has given many people a first taste of the joys and horrors of cocaine. The first effect of a dose is extreme exhilaration and mental brilliancy. The imagination becomes aflame. The after-effects – reaction, utter loss of moral responsibility, a blotched complexion, and the lunatic asylum or death.

Yet any chemist will tell you that it has been increasingly in demand by women of late years.

Another reason for thinking they were addicted is that it is difficult to explain why they chose cocaine, other than through force of habit. A number of other poisons were as easily available, and as well or better known. The most popular poison for suicide in the previous decade had been carbolic acid; throughout the century as a whole, opiates topped the list. Morphia or its various relatives would have offered a relatively peaceful end; a cloudy passage, sinking steadily through the depths of unconsciousness, all the way to the place where breath finally ceases.

Cocaine, on the other hand, is anything but merciful. It seizes the organism and galvanises it with an unbearable energy, until the heart or arteries are pushed beyond their endurance. The principal action of cocaine in the body is to emit a neurochemical scream that causes the blood vessels to recoil in shock. They constrict; the space available for the blood to flow is reduced, and so its pressure rockets. The heart is forced to work harder and harder to maintain the circulation; as it loses the struggle, the pressure in the blood vessels forces fluid into the spaces of the lungs, which is coughed up as a pink froth. The victim is also likely to be stricken with a terrible headache, vomiting, convulsions and incontinence. Eventually, the effort of trying to work against the back-pressure may cause the heart to fail. Alternatively, the catastrophe may end with the rupture of a blood vessel in the brain, causing a haemorrhage.[3] Cocaine is not an easy way out.

A couple of weeks after the tragedy, the *Daily Mail* ran a commentary on 'cocaine victims'; familiar figures, it was said, to any West End chemist. The 'cleverest' people took it: doctors, writers, politicians, artists; it had not reached the common people. It was the most dangerous form of inebriety, making the fiend both more refined and more dishonest.[4] Though the connection was not made, the type of person said to be prone to cocainism was precisely the typical neurasthenic. Without stimulation, his refined nervous system was liable to sink into melancholy. In fiction, the most famous example of the type was Sherlock Holmes, who staved off the black dog with injections of cocaine.

Although they were known as fiends, drug addicts were not greatly feared. The only danger they posed was to themselves, not to society at large. They were not criminals; there were no laws against the possession and use of drugs such as cocaine, which could be bought in unrestricted quantities from pharmacists, without a prescription. But the first ingredients of a moral panic were already in the pot.

Drug fiends, as then conceived, were about to pass from neurosis to depravity. A foretaste of the 'drug orgy' was reported the following year by the *British Medical Journal*, though its terminology remained positively genteel. It noted a report in a popular weekly journal of 'Morphine Tea Parties Given By Women':

> The fashion, which is said to have originated in Paris, consists of the formation of what may be termed a morphine club. A number of ladies meet about 4 o'clock every afternoon, tea is served, servants are sent out of the room, the guests bare their arms and the hostess produces a small hypodermic syringe with which she administers an injection to each person in turn.[5]

As in the comment upon the Yeoland case, drug use was specifically associated with women. Here, however, drugtaking was no longer a private weakness, but the reason for a social gathering. The quaintness of the description, with its uncompromised sense of etiquette, indicates the equanimity with which drugs were still regarded. Although the *Journal* commented that there was 'no ruin so utter as a woman's ruin from such causes', there is no sense of a threat to the social order; none of the sense, so strong in later accounts of drugtaking, that the drugs were dissolving boundaries within society. Even the servants were shielded from any glimpses of vice.

The most closely guarded boundaries were those between races. Few dark-skinned imperial subjects or non-white aliens had settled in Britain, but there were tiny colonies, mostly in the major ports. The Chinese had established an enclave in Limehouse, at the gates of the Isle of Dogs docks, providing food, laundry and lodging to their sailor compatriots. In 1901, 120 of them were recorded; their numbers doubled over the following ten years. By 1913, there were about thirty Chinese shops and restaurants in two streets, Limehouse Causeway and Pennyfields.[6]

The Chinese settlement had long been an object of fascination to whites from more prosperous districts. They came in search of the exotic, and they believed that it was concentrated in the Limehouse 'opium dens', the mythology of which had been evolving since the 1870s. In December 1907, the *East London Advertiser* reported that two such places were extensively patronised by Englishmen, many of them well-known figures, who would pay twenty or thirty shillings for a night's pleasure.

> There is a recognised establishment whose premises are unpretentious externally, but furnished within in a lavish style, that caters exclusively for the man of means ... To the visitor here, his first impression on entering is one of surprise at discovering such a display of luxury in so shabby a quarter of London.
>
> Here there is need to give a secret password as in the case of some less reputable resorts. If the personal appearance of the visitor seems above suspicion little other introduction is necessary, and the folding doors, under the supervision of two Chinamen, silently swing open at his approach. The soft light of shaded lamps hanging from the ceiling disclose a spacious hall. The feet sink in the rich, heavy carpet as the visitor passes on to the next floor, where there is an excellent restaurant with weird Chinese decorations and a menu that offers a variety of seductive Chinese dishes. Its patrons sometimes include Society women seeking a new sensation. But only privileged visitors have access to the rooms above, where the opium smoker may surrender himself in retirement to the enjoyment of the pipe for which he has been craving. There are a number of apartments in the upper stories set apart for this purpose. Each contains a couch on which the drug victim reclines. The mattress and the cushions are of silk. An attendant noiselessly enters the room bearing the necessary utensils. To be enjoyed, opium must be prepared by a competent hand, and the number of 'opium masters' in London is limited. They make incomes that, for Chinamen of their class, are reckoned substantial.[7]

White women, in this account, penetrate only as far as the restaurant; aptly, since the account is so strongly reminiscent of a luxurious but fictional brothel. Grafted onto this stem is the idea of an Oriental capacity for sophisticated clandestine organisation. This would subsequently develop into the racist fantasy of the great Oriental conspiracy, headed by Dr Fu Manchu or his supposed real-life counterparts. But the *Advertiser*'s 1907 story, imaginative as it was, posited Oriental organisation as nothing more than a way of profiting from white men's peccadilloes. The containment of opium could be left to a man of the world's discretion.

The prehistory of the drug underground was to last some time longer, until the bedrock of society was shaken by the terrible blows of the Great War. Something of what was to come could be seen in these isolated Edwardian scenes. But it was only when nation and society were felt to be in crisis that the idea of drug use as a social menace emerged. When it did, it took the form of a characteristic arrangement of elements: a cult activity, clandestine locations, a belief that young women were most at risk from the 'drug habit', an association with sexual immorality, and contact between different races. From these arose the view that the worst evil of drugs was that they facilitated the seduction of young white women by 'men of colour'.

Against these threats, however, the forces of conservatism had a great defensive advantage, and the social terrain on which a vogue for drugs could develop was limited. The conditions were most favourable in the entertainment world. Until the 1920s, it remained dominated by the West End, where its population mixed with aristocrats on the one hand and street criminals on the other. Professional entertainers were not limited by conventional hours, or by inhibitions when it came to entertaining themselves. They were also in touch with trans-Atlantic influences. The crime writer Edgar Wallace confidently asserted that cocaine had been introduced to the West End by American chorus girls who were brought over for a musical production in 1911.[8]

The theatres, and later nightclubs, attracted legions of young women willing to take their chances as actresses, singers and dancers. Here they enjoyed a degree of freedom unthinkable for most of their sisters in less glamorous occupations. Elsewhere in the West End, young women who worked in large stores would frequently be obliged to live in dormitories, with strict controls on their movement after hours – such as the directive that a girl seeking permission to visit the theatre had to identify her prospective companions. The stage imposed no such authority, nor offered any security. As ever since, drugtaking was a means of entertainment, an adjunct to performance, and a response to the pressures of the occupation. Many of the 'cocaine girls', like the Yeolands, would be found among the ranks of stage hopefuls.

The women and men who became the first drug criminals were mostly children during the Yeolands' time. One exception, then just beginning to enjoy the life of a young theatrical man about town, was later to become the country's first publicly notorious drug fiend. Raoul Reginald De Veulle, the son of a former British vice-consul at Le Mans, was raised in Jersey; he finished his education, aged seventeen, at the Kensington School of Art, and found a position as a gentleman's secretary afterwards. He then tried his hand as an actor and chorus singer, picking up a couple of engagements in West End shows, but this career soon petered out.[9]

By the end of the 1900s, De Veulle had entered his thirties and realised that he had no future on the British stage: he resolved to go west. A journey to America would be an expensive undertaking, but he was fortunate in having a patron. One day, some time around the turn of the century, while walking in the Haymarket, he had made the acquaintance of a businessman called William Cronshaw. They hit it off, and Cronshaw took him to tea at the Hotel Cecil; they met there regularly afterwards.

Some years later, De Veulle, who was now going by the name of Duvelle, introduced Cronshaw to a young man called Frederick Power. A similar friendship arose; Cronshaw would take Power to the theatre, and then on to supper, generally at the Carlton. His generosity went much further: he lent Power money for various schemes, and invested £2000 to set him up in business. Cronshaw also found about £1500 to clear debts for De Veulle, who did not live modestly.

De Veulle played a murky role in the incident that brought Cronshaw's friendships to public notice. In May 1911, he accompanied Power's parents to Cronshaw's offices, waiting outside while they accused the businessman of sexual relations with their son, and demanded £10,000 to keep silence. The Powers were arrested and appeared at the Old Bailey on blackmail charges. The initial hearings revealed nothing that was more than suggestive about Cronshaw's way of life, but the middle-aged bachelor was vulnerable to innuendo. A deal was struck; the charges were dropped and the allegations withdrawn.

De Veulle was not called to account for his part in the affair. He had set sail for New York shortly after the blackmail attempt, having secured another £500 from Cronshaw to pay for the trip. 'It was on those terms that he consented to leave the country,' was how Cronshaw put it, using a formulation more apt for a deal or a divorce than a straightforward friendship.[10]

From New York De Veulle went to Paris, where he became a ladies' dress designer. It was there that he struck up an acquaintance with a shadowy individual called Don Kimfull, whose friendship he acknowledged with the gift of a book. De Veulle's picture was on the cover, and his adventures as a youth were described inside. One incident took place at the river resort of Maidenhead, where a party he attended was broken up by stone-throwing locals. They were incensed because the male party-goers were all dressed as women.[11]

De Veulle might have remained in Paris had it not been for the outbreak of war. He returned to London and found a job as a 'designer of models' with a Mayfair costumier's which specialised in theatrical work. With him he brought a small quantity of something to which he had been introduced in the United States: like Kimfull, who also made his way to London, he had acquired a taste for cocaine.

2

SNOW ON THEIR BOOTS

David Garnett was a supporting character of inter-war British literature; he was on the fringe of the Bloomsbury Group, and edited T.E. Lawrence's letters. For his first novel, *Dope-Darling*, he used the pseudonym 'Leda Burke' and created a hero of a type not unfamiliar in British popular fiction: the idealistic young Scottish doctor.[1] Roy Gordon's idealism is short-lived, however, succumbing soon after his arrival in London to complete his studies. He is taken to a shady nightclub, favoured by journalists from nearby Fleet Street, where he is entranced by the house singer. A whirlwind affair ensues, tearing him away from his fellow student and childhood sweetheart Beatrice Chase.

His lover, Claire Plowman, is sexually forward; her bitter directness is the result of her experiences in the two years since she came to the city, at the age of sixteen. She arrived from the country, naively trusted the first person who approached her, and was given a sleeping draught in return. She woke up in a room with a black man, and as if one was not enough, several more men came to underline what she had now become. With nothing left to lose, she learned to live by her wits and her body, and she began to take cocaine.

By her own estimation, she has only a few years left to live, but Roy refuses to accept her fatalism. He marries her and tries to cure her; instead, he begins to take the drug himself. The couple abandon themselves to a self-consuming passion, as the great powers prepare, equally deliberately, for conflagration. Summer finds the couple on the Cornish coast:

> Claire had pulled out a gold box which she had hanging on a fine chain round her neck, and, opening it, dipped her finger in it. With extraordinary lightness, like a bird, she lifted her finger to each of Roy's nostrils, standing on tiptoe to do it.
> 'Come darling, come down to the beach.'

On the shore, Claire begins to sing. She is joined by the bass voice of big guns firing out to sea. The war has begun.

As mobilisation begins, Claire and Roy hold a last party. It is a debauch fit for the eve of the end of the world: couples lurch drunkenly off to the bushes, Roy lacerates his feet doing a berserk sword dance, and Claire sets the piano on fire.

Having accepted the imminence of his and Claire's intertwined fate, Roy makes a fearless soldier. He wins the Military Cross and the Distinguished Service Order, but, as his letters to his wife reveal, not through a sense of duty and right:

> Most of the men in my platoon believe in God, and believe in a future life. All of them somewhere believe they won't get killed, and they none of them realise that they will die anyhow, and there's not much point in living till they go blind and deaf and their teeth drop out. I don't find life sweet. When I have been with you I have been so happy that if we can neither of us live again like that it doesn't much matter when we die. When I hear of your death I shan't wait for a German to shoot me. I shall do it myself at once.

In fact, he is wounded, brought back to England and saved by Beatrice Chase; as she does so, Claire is brought into the hospital, dead. Roy has learned forgiveness and is reconciled with Beatrice. His spiritual as well as his physical wounds begin to heal.

The banal redemptive ending distinguishes *Dope-Darling* from the literature of tragic embitterment produced by the Great War. But most of those works – Robert Graves' *Goodbye to All That*, Erich Maria Remarque's *All Quiet on the Western Front*, R.C. Sheriff's *Journey's End*, Richard Aldington's *Death of a Hero*, and Siegfried Sassoon's *Memoirs* among them – appeared in a sudden deluge at the end of the 1920s, releasing an anguish pent up for ten years. Garnett, writing not from experience of combat, but after working on the land as a conscientious objector, published *Dope-Darling* in 1919. Although it endorses the moral conventions of popular fiction in the end, its dominant mood is of faithlessness and nihilism. It is one of the first novels of the Aftermath.

Its promptness entailed back-projection: on the eve of hostilities, its characters are already stricken by the crisis of the spirit that was actually born of the subsequent mass slaughter. The million men who rushed to enlist in 1914 did not do so because they felt themselves to be a doomed generation. As Harold Macmillan explained, 'The general view was that it would be over by Christmas. Our major anxiety was by hook or by crook not to miss it.'[2] The mobilisation demonstrated how a modern mass society worked, calling forth bureaucratic and logistical organisation on an unprecedented scale. This was how the century was going to be shaped, by war organised in an industrial fashion, conducted by immensely powerful and comprehensive state machines.

The call to arms was only the crescendo of a campaign that had been mounted for a number of years by the newly established popular press. A mass medium now circulated the theme of 'King and Country' through a society whose increasing density and coherence gave new weight to public opinion and public mood. With its jingoistic demands for more 'Dreadnought' battleships, to counter German naval strength, the new cultural form promoted the idea of the latest developments in naval technology – and the assumption that all Britain needed to take her into the twentieth century were bigger guns and thicker armour. When war came, it occurred to nobody – least of all the volunteers who blocked streets round recruiting offices, and formed the Pals' Battalions in insurance offices, tram depots or football clubs – that warfare at twentieth-century orders of magnitude would compare with earlier conflicts as a steelworks compares with a sheep farm.

The medievalist rhetoric of chivalry and Crown was as potent as it was illusory. It did not evaporate when its incongruity became apparent. Instead, it formed a heavy miasma of fantasy. Just as the war was a ghastly hybrid of modern technology and archaic values, its popular mythology was the product of modern communications and magical thought. On 29 September 1914, the *Evening News* published a story called 'The Bowmen' by the writer Arthur Machen, who was one of the paper's journalists at the time. It epitomised the medievalist theme, telling the tale of how a British soldier in the trenches has a vision of the archers of Agincourt; 'shining beings' turn the balance of the battle to the British side. Audiences read it as literal truth, and variants began to circulate, such as a version in which Prussian corpses were found pierced with arrows. Soldiers reported that they had been led by St George on a white horse – they knew who he was because he looked like he did on gold sovereigns. The 'shining beings' reached their apotheosis in the legend of the Angels of Mons, who covered the British retreat from that battle.[3]

This was one of the two most famous legends of the war. The other was also a wish-fulfilment fantasy that arose in September 1914 and involved the intervention of mighty forces at a moment of dire peril. They were from the East rather than from the heavens, though. A rumour spread across the country that Russian troops had secretly landed in Scotland 'with snow still on their boots', to assist the Allies in France. They were said to have been transported to the southern ports in sealed trains, but their passage was betrayed by the exhaustion of stocks of coffee and vodka en route. While the Angels of Mons myth originated in the popular press, the Russians were explained as a distortion by the bush telegraph of a message from the electrical telegraph. Somebody had leapt to the wrong conclusion on seeing a commercial cable referring to so many thousand 'Russians', which were, in fact, eggs.[4]

While wish-fulfilment was a striking feature of war fantasy, the traumas of the conflict more often found expression in a virulent xenophobia. The first great outburst occurred after the sinking of the Lusitania in May 1915, with the loss of 1200 lives; by this time, about 75,000 men had been killed at the Front. Robert Blatchford expostulated:

> To every decent Briton, a German is an unclean dangerous and bloody monster ... It is not only that the Germans are enemies and spies. We loathe them. We feel they pollute the air. We see blood on their hands ... We demand that the wretched creatures be removed. The thought that there are 20,000 of them walking in our streets was enough to make all London sick.[5]

'I call for a Vendetta, a vendetta against every German in Britain whether 'naturalised' or not ... you cannot naturalise an unnatural beast – a human abortion – a hellish freak. But you can exterminate him,' thundered Horatio Bottomley, Member of Parliament, leading press demagogue of the day, and, subsequently, the prototype for Mr Toad in Kenneth Grahame's *Wind in the Willows*. Failing his ideal solution, he demanded a programme not unlike one adopted by a future German government in respect of a different ethnic group: German property was to be confiscated, German citizens were to be incarcerated, naturalised Germans would be forced to wear a badge, and their children barred from schools. Looking ahead, he urged that after the war, soup should be thrown in the faces of German waiters.[6]

In the event, organised reaction was confined to the authorisation of internment, imposed on a total of 32 000 German men during the course of the war; women were repatriated without detention. The other immediate consequence of the sinking for Germans in Britain was an outbreak of 'Lusitania riots' in Manchester, Liverpool, London and other cities. The rioters rapidly extended their attentions from German-owned shops and businesses to Jewish, Russian, Swiss and Chinese targets.[7]

Rumour arose to meet the demand for information that wartime press censorship suppressed. The failure of the war to proceed according to expectations created not only the impulse for revenge, but also the need for the manifest shortcomings of Britain's performance to be explained. Inevitably, espionage was blamed. Teams of volunteers unscrewed enamel signs in London after reports that spies left messages behind them; newspaper chess problems were banned except where editors were 'absolutely satisfied that the senders are of British nationality and perfectly reliable'. The enemy within was also suspected of violence: barbers might cut customers' throats, and shopkeepers poison the food. Britain's air defences were for some time unable to counter the Zeppelin incursions; the wife of *The Times* journalist Michael MacDonagh was among those who wondered aloud at the ability of the great craft to fly all the way from Germany and back. 'Don't you believe it,' retorted their charwoman, who rejoiced in the impeccably plebeian name of Annie Bolster. 'We know in Battersea that these 'ere Zeppelins are hidden away in the back-yards of German bakers!'[8]

The raids were the beginning of the definitive mode of twentieth-century warfare; technological, remote, aimed mainly at civilians and – most significantly, in terms of its psychological impact – disrupting the familiar spatial discontinuity between the battlefield and the homeland. For Britons, used to their wars taking place abroad, this was profoundly threatening. (So was the 1916 Easter Rising in Dublin, then still as much a city of the United Kingdom as Edinburgh.) While urban legend was clearly an extremely fertile source of paranoiac-xenophobic lore, the popular media were equally active in its generation and propagation. A book called *German Spies in London*, published in 1915, sold 40,000 copies in one week. The theme flourished despite the fact that by 1917, only twenty-four spies had been convicted.

Its most grandiose manifestation came in 1918, with the 'Black Book' allegations, which linked the themes of moral degeneracy and foreign conspiracy. Noel Pemberton Billing, MP and editor of the *Vigilante* (formerly the *Imperialist*), accused the dancer Maud Allan of perversion. His grounds were her performance in *Salome*, a five-guinea private production of Oscar Wilde's banned play, the accusation being contained in a paragraph headed 'Cult of the Clitoris'. Allan was no stranger to sensation, enjoying a reputation for artistic daring and eroticism, but she sued nonetheless. To support his claims about the menace of moral degeneracy, Pemberton Billing announced the existence of a 'Black Book' containing the names of 47,000 Britons in the upper strata of society, along with details of the vices that put them in the clutches of blackmailing German agents. The failure of Allan's suit against Pemberton Billing stands as a particularly tart snub by a jury to a judge, since Lord Darling was one of those named by the defendant as being listed in the Book.[9]

The fears of an invisible menace were further compounded by the increased presence and visibility of foreigners during the war. There were refugees from Belgium, hundreds of thousands of colonial (and later American) servicemen, and, by the end of the hostilities, about 20,000 black people. Some of these were soldiers; Afro-Caribbean civilians also came to work in munitions factories, ports and shipping. The dockland Chinatowns grew as well.

Michael MacDonagh noted the sloppiness of the soldiery, which was wont to stroll around the West End of London with hands in pockets, cigarettes in mouths, and women on their arms; the Dominion troops were the worst offenders. Meanwhile the remaining civilians were shabbier, there were fewer motor-vehicles, and lights were dimmed or screened as an air raid precaution. 'As I go about I can see the wide spaciousness of London and its vast variety of characteristics slowly but surely contracting to a War Camp,' he wrote in February 1916. The streets were filled with uniformed figures: Tommies, Dominion soldiers, occasional exotic allies such as Serbians; female auxiliaries, nurses, conductors and messengers. Thomas Burke observed that civilians without a uniform to wear sported badges urging 'Intern Them All'.[10]

As the capital went khaki and drab, official initiatives were taken to tighten the discipline of the population as a whole. Inadequate levels of industrial production were causing concern, as was public order. Under pressure from the temperance movement, a drug was identified as a scapegoat: 'We are fighting Germans, Austrians and Drink, and so far as I can see, the greatest of these deadly foes is Drink,' Lloyd George declared in 1915. King George V vowed to abstain for the duration, as an example, and as a gesture to set the moral tone. 'If all trace of modern England were lost except files of the papers; the historian, on examining the evidence a thousand years hence, would be forced to the conclusion that in the year 1914 the population of the country was largely composed of spies and drunken women,' the *New Statesman* observed.[11]

The new regime imposed upon alcohol consumption was characteristic of the Great War's most profound and lasting effect on the structure of the nation – the vast expansion of the reach of the state. Until 1914, A.J.P. Taylor observed, a 'sensible, law-abiding Englishman could pass through life and hardly notice the existence of the state, beyond the post office and the policeman.' Total war required the mobilisation of an entire society, and its detailed regulation from the centre. Some of the changes were hard to swallow: in January 1916, the Home Secretary, Sir John Simon, resigned because he could not accept the introduction of conscription. The state's principal vehicle during the war years was the Defence of the Realm Act, known unaffectionately as DORA. Introduced shortly after the outbreak of hostilities, it was originally intended to control militarily sensitive information and communications. As the war went on, it proved to be a convenient piece of legislation onto which new regulations could be tacked by decree. It gave the police powers to stop and search people, or to imprison them if they refused; it prescribed the death penalty for service personnel (and civilians, until it was amended by the Lords) who assisted the enemy. It permitted press censorship and imposed milk price control; it forbade loitering near bridges and tunnels, and whistling for taxis in London.

DORA's enduring significance was its ability to outlive the threat to the realm; once people had got used to them, regulations justified by exceptional conditions were quietly incorporated into normal peacetime legislation. The most familiar examples are the drinking restrictions, which have never entirely been lifted. The closure of pubs in the afternoon, instigated for the good of wartime production and morale, remained on the English statutes until 1988. Before the war, pub hours had stretched from five in the morning to half past twelve at night; DORA restricted them to two hours at lunchtime and three in the evening. Under the 'Beauty Sleep Order', lights-out time in restaurants and hotels was ten-thirty.

To the indignation of a lobby led by *The Times*, London nightclubs persisted in staging entertainments such as an 'Apache Night' and a 'Bacchanalia Revel'. In November 1915, the Home Secretary responded with the Clubs (Temporary Provisions) Act, which imposed a midnight curfew at weekends. Shortly afterwards, last orders were brought forward to nine-thirty for restaurants, pubs and clubs alike. In response, the clubs went underground; by the end of 1915, there were 150 illegal nightclubs in Soho alone.[12]

Conditions were becoming steadily more conducive to the formation of a drug scene. Nightlife increasingly took place in private, or outside the law. Alcohol was severely restricted. The market for other drugs was seeded by Canadian soldiers, familiar with the well developed North American drug underground, looking for entertainment in the West End. And wartime discipline brought forth its antithesis. London was the logistical hub of the war effort; the South Coast ports that supplied the Front in Belgium and Northern France were not much more than an hour from the martial stations of Victoria and Waterloo. As a 'War Camp', the capital inevitably acquired something of a camp-follower outlook. The bushes of Hyde Park – and the Marlborough Street Police Court Register – bore witness to that.

At the same time, circumstance and psychology combined to give drugs a powerful symbolic potential. The drug habit represented vice and crumbling moral standards, at a time when the established drug, alcohol, was itself arousing fears of public disorder and national inefficiency. Drugs were seen as a foreign phenomenon, at a time of extreme xenophobia. Moreover, opium use was specifically associated with the dockland Chinese communities. In wartime, a nation wants to believe itself ethnically and socially homogeneous; in the face of a military threat to its physical boundaries, it may find the very existence of foreign 'enclaves' threatening. The folklore of the drug fiend offered evocative new stories incorporating the themes of vice, conspiracy and foreign subversion.

Hints of a vogue for drugtaking began to surface in the press late in 1915. At the end of December, the French star Mme Delysia returned from Paris to take a leading role at the Ambassadors Theatre. 'One of the things that made me sad when I was in Paris,' she told Quex, the gossip columnist of the *Evening News*, 'was the number of actresses who have succumbed to the opium craze – one of the results of the war. Girls who three or four years ago were fresh and beautiful, have become lined and haggard and their voices husky. It is terrible.'[13]

The following week, Quex returned to the subject. At this stage, concern came second to a titillating breeziness.

I see that other people are turning their attention to the growing craze for opium smoking, to which I referred last week. West End Bohemia is hearing some dark stories of what is going on. But still more prevalent is the use of that exciting drug cocaine. It is so easy to take – just snuffed up the nose; and no-one seems to know why the girls who suffer from this body and soul racking habit find the drug so easy to obtain.

In the ladies' cloakroom of a certain establishment two bucketfuls of thrown-away small circular cardboard boxes were discovered by the cleaners the other day – discarded cocaine boxes.[14]

Endorsing an idea that was beginning to gain currency, Quex suggested that these drugs should be outlawed, as in America. The police, he assured his readers, had their eye on the situation.

This was true. They were receiving reports that indicated an increase in 'doping', though the intelligence was frequently more of a nuisance than anything else. The YMCA began a campaign to persuade the authorities that prostitutes around the great railway termini were drugging soldiers and robbing them, on the basis of solemn testimonies from men who swore they had drunk no more than a glass of beer and couldn't remember a thing after that. Irritated divisional superintendents dismissed the claims, but the Christian campaigners were undeterred. One urban missionary believed that German agents were stealing the victims' papers, in order to impersonate them at the Front.[15]

In time of war, young men become especially precious. Since the nation's fate may depend on them, their moral and physical condition becomes acutely important. The Great War – the name was adopted almost from the start – was believed to be a conflict between civilisation and barbarity. The YMCA staff were on the moral front line, trying to keep the soldiery from temptation. Their calls for special constables 'to keep the women from molesting soldiers' would have been dismissed out of hand, without the allegations of drugging and robbery to justify them.

The soldier-doping claims reworked elements of the white slavery theme, with the roles reversed. In the archetypal white slave story, an innocent young woman is lured by an agent pretending to befriend her. She is drugged, raped while in a stupor, like Claire Plowman in *Dope-Darling*, and then has to become a prostitute. The drug may be simply a knock-out drop, or a narcotic, the craving for which forces the hapless victim to submit to sex. 'Her slavery lasts some five or six years as a rule, and then she is flung out upon the streets, her character gone, her hope dead, her body diseased, to die before long either in a workhouse or a Lock Hospital.'[16] An important variation is the theme of an international traffic – Buenos Aires was a popular destination – controlled by a criminal conspiracy. This clearly provided a prototype for the idea of international drug trafficking conspiracies.

Despite police scorn and lack of evidence, the scare persisted until the end of the war. By that time, when the public thought of drugs or 'dope', they thought immediately of drugs of pleasure. Instead of an unspecified stupefacient, the prostitutes were now said to be using cigarettes laced with cocaine to knock their victims out.[17] (The name of the drug was widely known; its stimulant properties apparently were not.)

Other reports reaching the police during the second winter of the war were more personally motivated. Captain Ernest Schiff, a man about town in his mid-forties, sent a letter to Sir John Simon in December 1915. 'A very bad fellow, Jack May, is the proprietor of 'Murray's Club' in Beak Street – a quite amusing place,' he wrote. 'But for vice or money or both he induces girls to smoke opium in some foul place. He is an American, and does a good deal of harm.'[18]

Murray's was one of the leading clubs of the day, managing to be regarded as both racy and reputable. As well as its Soho premises, it maintained an outstation at Maidenhead which drew revellers to the Thames resort throughout the war, and for years afterwards. If the proprietor of Murray's was involved with opium, then clandestine drug use was present from top to bottom of the club scene. In the event, the police found no evidence to suggest May was corrupting young women with opium, nor that he was the same May who had been named as a supplier by a Chinese man, caught smuggling two trunks of the drug from London to Hong Kong. A couple of years later, however, May would be publicly named as the man who introduced one particular young woman to the opium pipe. Her other smoking-partner was identified as Schiff.

Clandestine opiate use certainly had a place at the very top of society, as another letter written in December 1915 illustrated. Lady Diana Manners, the leading socialite of the day, described to Raymond Asquith, the son of the Prime Minister, how she and Raymond's wife Katharine had lain

in ecstatic stillness through too short a night, drugged in very deed by my hand with morphia. O, the grave difficulty of the actual injection, the sterilizing in the dark and silence and the conflict of my hand and wish when it came to piercing our flesh. It was a grand night, and strange to feel so utterly self-sufficient – more like a Chinaman, or God before he made the world or his son and was content with, or callous to, the chaos.[19]

Lady Diana's closing observation is remarkable. At one level, she has simply transferred the familiar Chinese associations of opium to its active principle, morphine. But the appearance of God and a Chinaman as alternative similes is intriguing. It suggests an ingenious resolution of an apparent paradox in British views of China. The antiquity of its civilisation was acknowledged, and the Chinese were frequently ascribed an elevated level of spiritual consciousness. At the same time, they were seen as unemotional, to the point of amorality – although spiritual refinement should have brought them closer to the moral truth of the Christian deity. Lady Diana's reflections link the Chinaman with God before he created his son, and thereby acquired humanity. The Chinaman is thus more spiritually advanced, but less human. It is a disturbing combination, and one that lends itself to the construction of a race enemy: his advancement may inspire fear, while his inhumanity debars him from compassion.

Far more disturbing, however, is the idea of a God 'content with, or callous to, the chaos'. For many, this was precisely the implication of the carnage in Flanders. Lady Diana's hint of identification with such a deity suggests a way in which what couldn't be beaten, could be joined.

Another source of solace was chloroform – 'jolly old chlorers'. Her biographer Philip Ziegler observed that her preferences were shaped as much by class as chemistry: 'to reduce oneself to a stupor with morphia was risky, perhaps immoral, but to drink a whisky and soda would have been common – a far worse offence.'

In her autobiography, Lady Diana affirmed how she came to treat morphine 'as a friend and then as a staunch partner in times of stress'. She also pointed out what an everyday commodity it still was at that time: 'a tube of quarter-grains was always sent in our war parcels of brandy, handkerchiefs, pencils and pocket classics.'[21] Such practices were encouraged by the Mayfair chemists Savory & Moore, who put an advertisement in *The Times* for cases containing gelatine sheets impregnated with morphine and cocaine, a 'useful present for friends at the front'. In February 1916, both Savory & Moore and Harrods received token fines for infringing the regulations governing the sale of these preparations. 'It was an exceedingly dangerous thing for a drug like morphine to be in the hands of men on active service,' the prosecuting counsel in the Harrods case observed. 'It might have the effect of making them sleep on duty or other very serious results.'[22]

Along with concern about the effect on military efficiency of drugs supplied with the best of intentions, and missionary fears about soldiers being drugged by thieves, anxieties began to arise about servicemen's use of drugs for pleasure. The day after reporting the Savory & Moore case, *The Times* ran an article headlined 'The Cocaine Habit – A Soldier's Temptation', which deemed the drug 'more deadly than bullets'. It asserted that the habit had reached India a few years previously, and was calculated to kill the natives there within three months. Uncharacteristic for its time, in omitting any reference to women or sex, the piece instead gave cocaine an aura of violence: 'Most cocainomaniacs carry revolvers to protect themselves from imaginary enemies.' It added a patriotic flourish, claiming that the drug was mostly smuggled on Austrian steamers.[23]

The article appeared in the wake of the first case to provide hard evidence of cocaine use by soldiers; part of the Canadian contingent, which had a reputation for ferocity in battle and unruliness off duty. The commander of a unit stationed near Folkestone estimated that forty of his men were addicted to cocaine; he deployed a corporal to find and trap the supplier. The NCO succeeded in buying two shillings' worth of 'snow' from a man in a pub. Horace Kingsley, aged forty, was arrested, along with a woman called Rose Edwards, who also obliged Corporal Price's request to buy the drug.

He was a petty criminal; she was a London prostitute, who claimed to buy her cocaine from a man in a West End pub – 'He sells it to all of us girls.' Kingsley himself got his supplies by simply walking into a Dover chemist's and buying them. The early cocaine trade had no need of supplies smuggled on enemy steamers, only of a few chemists prepared to sell the drug without seeing a prescription or recording the purchaser's name. The legal sanctions were scanty, though the prosecution came up with charges of 'selling a powder to members of His Majesty's Forces, with intent to make them less capable of performing their duties'.

In his defence, Kingsley claimed he gave the cocaine away to his soldier friends. 'It makes you most keen on what you are doing,' he said, which is as pithy a description of cocaine's subjective effects as any formulation before or since. The magistrates were unpersuaded that cocaine sent the men more enthusiastically about their duties, however, and sentenced both the defendants to six months' hard labour.[24]

That same month, a Canadian lieutenant named Georges Codere was convicted of bludgeoning a canteen sergeant to death at a camp in Surrey. Testimony revealed that Codere had a history of violent and bizarre behaviour; one witness said that it was as if he had been doping himself.[25] This was apparently taken literally, because the murderer was subsequently described in the press as a cocaine addict. Together, the Codere and Folkestone cases encouraged a widespread belief that Canadians were responsible for bringing the cocaine habit to Britain.[26]

Although laying the blame for cocaine at the Canadians' door had the appeal of simplicity, it was an inadequate explanation, and in any case lacked supporting evidence. But the idea that the Canadians had a significant hand in popularising cocaine around the streets and pubs of the West End is plausible. South of the Canadian border, a train ride away, was the world's most developed drug underworld. In the New York area, the combination of a pharmaceutical industry and a streetgang subculture had already produced a familiar pattern of delinquent drug use. Heroin, a drug virtually unknown in Britain at this time, was an established feature of gang rituals. As in Britain, however, the drug scene was dominated by cocaine.[27]

North America offered the hustler and the drifter a vast terrain over which to roam, moving on to a new town when unsettled debts and scores became too pressing. The way of life is described in Francis Chester's *Shot Full: The Autobiography of a Drug Addict* (Methuen, London 1938). Though much of it is plainly fictional, it has the underlying credibility of a narrative made up by somebody who knew what he was talking about. Its earlier chapters illustrate just how Canadians might have picked up the drug habit and brought it across the Atlantic. Though the details may be invented, the broad pattern of the story must have been duplicated a significant number of times in real life.

Chester's story begins in 1912, at the age of sixteen, when he leaves the ailing family farm in Canada in search of better prospects. Getting a job as a messenger boy in New York, he finds he is delivering packages of 'Joy Dust' – cocaine. He joins the circle of dopers, and starts selling 'decks' – paper packets – of heroin for a dollar a time. He falls into an itinerant life of jail, hopping freight trains, and fleecing the gullible through a variety of street-corner tricks and fairground scams.

Heading back to Canada, he takes a morphine habit with him. Eventually, finding it difficult to afford drugs and a comfortable life on what he makes from casual work, he joins the army.

In October 1915, his unit arrives in England, and is posted to Folkestone. He spends much of his time malingering or absent without leave, heading first for Leicester Square to look for drugs. Drawing a blank in two favourite haunts of overseas soldiers, the Leicester Lounge and the Province Lounge (correctly, the Hotel Provence), he has to go to Limehouse, where he is able to gamble and smoke opium to his heart's content. He hears, however, that 'junk' is sold around Shaftesbury Avenue,

> secreted in the packets of postcards of 'Views from London' which were so popular with Dominion visitors. One packet cost only 5s. A woman pedlar told me that she sold ten times more 'snow' than she did morphine, and it was only the Colonials who used it, except some of the ladies of pleasure.[28]

Chester and his friend Snuffy get caught and shipped back to Canada, but not before holding up a Folkestone chemist's while in uniform. Though he gives the date as January 1916, he does not mention the existence of any other drug users in the camp.

If he had looked a bit harder, he might have found what he was looking for in the Hotel Provence. In April 1916, Inspector Kerry of the Marbour Street police station in Soho received a letter in a mixture of French and bad English. The police translation read:

> There is more than ten boys who sell cocaine to the girls, you can get them and here are their names: (1) Willy Johnson, ex-porter from the Ambassadors Café de Paris, No. 3, West Street, with his friend Paul told boy that his Swiss Man sold it there every night till 12 night and afterwards you can see them go to Shaftesbury Avenue, (No.89) a sandwich shop.
> (3) Motty is a Jewish boy.
> (4) Alfy Benjamin, always in the Palace Tavern, Charing Cross Road.
> (5) Jew Cook.
> (6) Bernard, always wears a mackintosh.
> (7, 8, 9, and 10) Four Jewish boys, always in the sandwich shop at 89 Shaftesbury Avenue.
> Willy's woman named Phyllis also sells it in the public house, the Provence, Leicester Square, Voilet [sic] Gordon always in the public bar, The Scots and Jimigrim and mother in the Square. We beg of you in the

name of humanity and goodness to put a stop to this dirty band of scamps, who are nothing more than robbers.[29]

The letter was signed by 'Charles Dupond, Louis Vernaud, Ex Agent of the Detective Service, Brussels; Committee of the Belgian Refugees'. Another letter was sent to an inspector at Paddington, purporting this time to come from 'Henry Lenkerk, Charles Leroi; Liège detectives, living at the Belgian Refugees' Home, Berwick Street'. It named the gang members as Willy Johnson, Alfy Benjamin, and the present porter at the Ambassadors Café. 'Willie, the former porter, has a wooden leg, and promenades from one end of West Street to the other,' it said, adding that he 'puts full boxes of cocaine in a black glove, which he has in his pocket'.

Alfy Benjamin was said to procure the drugs for Johnson, obtaining them from a Lisle Street chemist. There was only one chemist's in Lisle Street at the time: Wooldridge & Co, at No.26. The shop was at the back of the Empire, which fronted onto Leicester Square, and Thomas Wooldridge was proud of the theatrical celebrities among his clientele. He would have opportunities to boast about them publicly in the future, when he found his name linked on subsequent occasions with the underworld drug traffic.

This first time, the police seem to have left him alone. They checked the sandwich shop at 89 Shaftesbury Avenue, however, and found it to be 'patronised chiefly by prostitutes and Continental undesirables'. The Ambassadors Café, over the road from the Ambassadors Theatre, was likewise 'the resort of Continental prostitutes and thieves of the lowest type'. Its proprietor was convicted of allowing prostitutes to gather and remain on the premises, and it was closed down – to the chagrin of the police, who had found it convenient for the undesirables to be collected in one place, where an eye could be kept on them.

As the informants had claimed, Willy Johnson had taken a pitch by the café, on the corner of West Street and Litchfield Street. Around ten o'clock one night, Police Sergeants Hedges and Venner watched him accost a woman passer-by. A few minutes later, he did the same thing again, and the policemen moved in. Failing to escape – the police report did not mention whether or not he was hampered by an artificial leg – he dropped a woollen bag containing eleven boxes of cocaine. He had become the object of London's first drug bust.

Willy Johnson was a representative specimen of the country's first drug-pedlars. Aged twenty-six, he had a string of convictions for theft; he lived with a prostitute who was thought to be a cocaine user, in a

room in nearby New Compton Street. This was close to the centre of
the West End underworld heartland, which filled the side-streets off
Charing Cross Road and Shaftesbury Avenue, and concentrated
around Seven Dials and Leicester Square. The westward drift that
made Soho synonymous with vice was, by and large, a later
development. Significantly, the underworld shared the same terrain as
the West End's theatreland. The Leicester Square hotel lounges were
notorious for getting away with allowing prostitutes to gather and
remain on the premises. Theatreland's two main thoroughfares were
also the principal prostitutes' beat; they were known as 'the Front'.

The mark-up from Benjamin to Johnson to the customers was steep,
but the amounts were petty. Johnson sold his boxes, each containing
about a penny's worth of cocaine, for two-and-sixpence each, making
ninepence for himself. (Possibly when Francis Chester was told of
packets on sale in Shaftesbury Avenue at five shillings apiece, he was
being quoted the tourist price.) Drugs were not going to make him a
rich man.

Nor did he appear to be catering to dyed-in-the-wool drug fiends.
The police found that the boxes contained about two and a half grains
of cocaine each, though they did not specify whether or not it had been
adulterated. Press reports around this time said that half-crown boxes
generally contained one and a half grains. This suggests that cocaine
was sold in units of between a tenth and a sixth of a gramme. By
comparison, a survey of New York cocaine sniffers in 1983 recorded
an average weekly consumption of four and a half grammes. Some
users get through five grammes a day. A trade based on the pill-box
units would have been geared to casual or light users only.

After the Folkestone case, the Army Council acted to tighten its
regulations concerning drugs. Kingsley and Edwards had faced
vaguely-worded charges which might not prove adequate in future
prosecutions. It issued an order banning the unauthorised supply to
soldiers of a wide range of drugs with the potential for non-medical
use, including cocaine, morphine, opium, heroin, barbiturates and
cannabis. The only sanction against selling such substances to civilians,
however, remained the Poisons and Pharmacy Act of 1868. Intended
to regulate shopkeepers rather than street hustlers, it provided for a
maximum fine of just £5.

This penalty, moreover, applied only in cases of sale. Hedges and
Venner had not seen Willy Johnson actually sell any cocaine; they had
merely observed him trying to do so. Johnson was acquitted. In his

report, Sergeant Hedges wrote that he and his colleagues 'have spared no energy in our efforts to detect the persons responsible for the sale of this insidious drug to prostitutes etc., but unless the existing regulations are supplemented, it is useless for Police to devote further time and attention to these persons.'

The Assistant Commissioner of Police, who favoured making the unauthorised sale of drugs illegal (he made no comment on whether to criminalise their possession), recognised that the police had lost the battle but might thereby win the war: 'The prominence given in the Press to the failure of the prosecution in this case would probably make it easy to pass a Bill to amend the law: it will – unless there is legislation – embolden traffickers in this dangerous drug. There is evidently more money to be made out of it than most people wld [sic] have supposed.'

His assessment was shrewd. Although the police failed to secure a conviction, the hearing had given them a platform from which to set out a case for strengthening the law, a measure endorsed by the magistrate. The police counsel suggested this could be achieved by an addition to the Defence of the Realm Act.

The comments of the police surgeon were reported: he spoke of the damage the drug did to willpower and the moral sense. Most of the users he had encountered were women; he had also seen one or two Canadian soldiers under the influence. He made no connection between the two; the Folkestone case, in providing solid evidence of a prostitute selling cocaine to soldiers, was exceptional.

The papers continued to push the story, backed up by a clutch of sensationalist films with drug themes imported from the United States: *The Curse of a Nation*, *The Curse of the Poppy*, *Black Fear*. Quite suddenly, the drug panic had arrived. 'From a habit much more vicious but fortunately much more rare even than that of veronal, the use of cocaine has become in six months a veritable mania, an obsession only too terribly common among the women who haunt the West-end at night,' the *Daily Chronicle* announced.[30] It described the pitiful sight of soldiers, desperate for the drug, crawling on their hands and knees into chemist's shops. In the *Evening News*, the insouciant gossip of the New Year had been replaced by the classic hyperbole of drug journalism: 'Practically unknown a few years ago, cocaine-taking has spread like wildfire in all classes of the community until, next to alcoholism, it is far and away the commonest form of drug-taking.'[31]

In fact, the drug was quite restricted in its social distribution. It certainly had adherents of both high and low social standing, but only among those who occupied marginal zones where ordinary conventions of morality and behaviour did not operate. The point was implicitly endorsed in the *Evening News* article which appeared on 14 June, headlined 'The Cocaine Curse – Evil Habit Spread By Night Clubs': 'Social workers, mental experts and police officials all bear testimony to the ravages of the drug habit among young women, especially of the leisured class that regards itself as Bohemian.'

The piece claimed, plausibly, that cocaine had become popular in nightclubs to dispel fatigue: this was also its appeal to weary soldiers. It suggested that the traffickers were individuals who had been run out of Paris and Belgium by police action and the war.

The following day's paper resumed the theme, highlighting the role of women in retailing the drug. It also described the inroads cocaine had made into the theatre: 'Stage Stars With "Fluffy Memories" ' were one consequence. Elderly actors encouraged young actresses into the habit, at the cost of the women's careers and looks. As a footnote, it added: 'It is suggested in some quarters that the desire for drugs is implanted in many young girls by the fashion for buying sweetmeats packed with highly flavoured chemicals.' A woman had written to the Queen about this; Her Majesty and the Prince of Wales had bought toffee to encourage the revival of the traditional British industry.

The police campaign against the trade intensified, resulting in several cases that boosted the campaign for increased powers. In July, a gang of dealers was entrapped by Gilbert Smith, a Canadian military police sergeant, who bought half-crown boxes posing as an ordinary soldier. The list of defendants evokes the working-class immigrant culture that was such an intimate part of London society in the early decades of the century, and has now all but vanished: William Brown, aged twenty-one, a tailor, of Church Street, Soho; Georges Wagniere, eighteen, Swiss, a porter of Manette Street, Soho; Harry List, eighteen, a tailor of George Street, Euston Road; Frederich Freemuller, nineteen, a butcher, of Wells Street, Aldgate; Ivan Benjamin, twenty, Russian, a tailor, of Little Tongue Yard, Whitechapel; Mark Cohen, forty-six, Russian, a dealer, of Tottenham Street; and Samuel Heller, twenty-three, a cabinet-maker, of Hanbury Street, Spitalfields. They were jailed for two or three months, and the aliens among them were deported.

'Foreigners Convicted', a newspaper report pointed out.[32] The self-described 'Belgian detectives' had referred in their letter to a 'Swiss

Man' and various 'Jewish boys': it is conceivable that their 'dirty band of scamps' had been brought to book. But the fit is not at all close, and there may well have been a number of cocaine gangs at work in the area. Interestingly, despite a number of instances in which convicted drug traders had Jewish-sounding names, the xenophobia associated with drugs did not take a specifically anti-semitic form.[33] That the pedlars were foreign was enough.

In the view of the *Umpire*, Americans and Canadians were to blame. One of the most sensationalist publications of the day, it adopted the histrionic language in which popular accounts of illegal drug use have been articulated ever since: 'Vicious Drug Powder – Cocaine Driving Hundreds Mad – Women And Aliens Prey On Soldiers ... London In The Grip Of The Drug Craze ... Secret "Coke" Parties Of "Snow Snifters".' Having been introduced by the Canadians, the paper explained, the drug habit had been spread by Americans in night clubs. Possibly it had Jack May in mind. The Americans had also established 'hop joints' – opium dens – around Charing Cross Road, Leicester Square and Seven Dials; these were patronised by visiting Americans (not servicemen: the United States did not enter the war until the following year), women of the demi-monde, underworld types, theatre people; and journalists.

According to the *Umpire*, an entire clandestine drug scene was flourishing; it featured 'needle dancers' who injected morphine and 'herowin'. Another intoxicant was ether, which was also occasionally alleged to be supplied to German troops; either to dull their terror under bombardment, or, in the case of *Sturm-Truppen*, to send them into berserk frenzy.[34] Drugs were also linked with violence and a foreign breed in America, where 'cocaine has been a cause of a great deal of the bloodshed between the black and white races. It has demoralised the negroes of Alabama, and caused outrages of the most terrible description.' Cocaine, 'carried by women of the better class in silver bonbonnieres', was acknowledged as the drug of choice in London. The latest craze was for cocaine parties; these, however, were

> usually made up of men, as there is an element of danger which makes the exclusion of women a necessity. Under its influence they become wild-eyed and feverishly excited, and babble out their innermost secrets to each other. Cigarettes are consumed, and so it continues from midnight to six o'clock in the morning, when quantities of brandy are served as an antidote to dull the effect of the cocaine and induce sleep, for sleep is impossible to the cocaine fiend.

This description, at least, has a ring of truth about it. All-nighters, loquacity and the disclosure of confidences are a familiar feature of stimulant drug use – cocaine then; cocaine, amphetamine or ecstasy now – as are crammed ashtrays and downers at dawn. It also underlines the development of a social scene centred on drug use, as distinct from the incidental use of drugs in the course of a night out. One might surmise that the exclusion of women had more to do with the desire for man's talk than the 'element of danger'.

In Whitehall, the cocaine flap revived a pre-war project which had all but succumbed to administrative inertia. Britain had been a reluctant participant in a series of international drug conferences instigated by the United States. The British government was cool on the idea of international collaborations of this sort, and considered that the longstanding embarrassment of the British-sponsored opium traffic from India to China was well on the way to being terminated without American interference. Agreement was reached in principle, at the Hague in 1912, to limit the use of opium, morphine and cocaine to 'legitimate medical purposes', but in practice it was stymied by the commercial interests of Germany, the world's leading cocaine manufacturer, and Britain, which dominated the world's morphine industry.

In Britain, there was little moral pressure acting to oppose these worldly considerations. The long-established movement opposing the British opium traffic to China still had some influence, but it was a campaign whose course had largely run. In the United States, the rise of the moral campaign against colonial opium use had coincided with the start of domestic moral panic around narcotics. For the past thirty years, British morality campaigners had been pressing, with some success, for the extended use of the criminal law to improve the moral character of the nation. But drugs had yet to become associated with the dangerous classes, and there was little interest in banning them. The proposals knocked about in committee before the war went no further than a tightening of the regulations governing retail sales and prescriptions.

There was also little official interest in doing anything at all about them, as Virginia Berridge emphasises.[35] The Foreign and Colonial Office didn't want to take on the job; nor did the Board of Trade or the Home Office. Up to the outbreak of war, it looked as though the implementation of the Hague agreements would be largely the province of the medical and pharmaceutical professions.

As well as the street trade, Britain's involvement in the international drug traffic also required the government's attention. Despite a wartime ban on the export of opium, Chinese seamen smuggled the drug to their native country on British merchant vessels; morphine was also sent illicitly to the Far East, mainly via Japan, and cocaine to India. Alfred Holt & Co., operators of the Blue Funnel Line, sent a memorandum to the Colonial Office outlining their concern at the use of their ships as vehicles for the traffic to the Far East.

The man who emerged to seize the opportunity offered by the transformations of war was an energetic Home Office under-secretary called Sir Malcolm Delevingne. At the inter-departmental conference called to discuss the Holt memorandum, on 19 June 1916, Delevingne argued that the 'most convenient' way of dealing with the problem was to add another regulation to the Defence of the Realm Act. He acknowledged 'that its bearing on the "Defence of the Realm" is neither very direct nor important', but added that 'the only alternative method would be legislation which may be difficult to get and would possibly not be regarded as uncontroversial.'[36]

Strong support for Delevingne's proposal was forthcoming from the police and army. 'At present there is believed to be an extensive sale to all and sundry by retailers of Malthusian appliances, quack medicines and that class of offensive literature which we have long and vainly sought powers to deal with,' the Commissioner of the Metropolitan Police, Sir Edward Henry, complained to the Home Office. He reported that among the known dealers caught in possession of cocaine were a pair of thieves and a man charged with soliciting males for immoral purposes. He favoured criminalisation, and jail for some of those convicted of possessing cocaine. 'It might then be possible to deal severely with the unauthorised persons who, using as their tools burglars, thieves, prostitutes, sodomites, men living upon the earnings of women and other nefarious persons, are at present with impunity doing such infinite harm.'

Despite Henry's vehemence, the controls he favoured fell far short of the comprehensive prohibition regime installed around most of the world today. His animus was specifically directed against cocaine, 'the most baneful drug in the whole Pharmacopoeia'; on the other hand, he opposed sanctions against opium, 'which in most of its forms is a more or less beneficent drug'. The police and army also felt that morphine should be left out of the proposed order – as, more predictably, did medical and pharmaceutical interests. Even without the legislation that he considered might have been controversial, Delevingne's bold move thus faced opposition from institutions of power, let alone from the dope underworld.

He got his way on opium, but had to back down on morphine. Nor, unlike the earlier Army Council order, did the final draft of the edict cover drugs such as cannabis or heroin. The significance of Defence of the Realm Regulation 40B was not its range, however, but the fact that it established the fundamental principle of prohibition: it forbade certain substances. From 28 July 1916, the possession of cocaine or opium – other than by authorised professionals; doctors, vets and chemists – was a criminal offence. The drug underworld, thereby placed outside the law, had gone through its decisive rite of passage.

3

THE DAUGHTERS' INHERITANCE

'Have you any women-folk worth defending?' In view of the failure of the recruiting campaign to meet the war's manpower demands, the answer collectively given by the men of Britain might seem to have been 'not enough'. The adroitness of the slogan is undeniable, though. It suggested that the defence of the realm and the defence of the women were one and the same; that women were the repository of all that the nation held dear. In his mother, sister or wife, the humblest Tommy had his own Britannia. And what kind of a man, the question implied, was he who did not have womenfolk of quality to defend? At root, this was the monkey-troop calculus of maleness as a function of the ability to have and hang on to females. Patriotism was equated with virility.

At a less primitive level, the slogan invoked a traditional schema of men at the front and women at home. Posters showed women waving from safe indoors as the soldiers marched off. But after exhortation was replaced by conscription, posters showed women in factory overalls and nurses' uniforms. In campaigning for 'the right to serve', the women's movement also identified womanhood with the realm. The *Suffragette*, newspaper of the Women's Social & Political Union, was renamed *Britannia*.

The strategy of the women's movement was a simple and honest one: to show that women's contribution merited full citizenship; to earn the franchise. But their opportunity was men's bloodshed: women were included among those whom many fighting men believed to be doing well out of their misery.

A soldier desires the home he has left behind him to be stable. The very idea of a home front is disturbing. Modern warfare not only made this oxymoron a reality, but also threatened a far more profound revolution in the social order. Sandra M. Gilbert recognises what seemed to be at stake, in her observation that with the sacrifice of the sons, the daughters appeared to stand to gain the inheritance. Without patrilineal succession, where would patriarchy itself be?[1]

Gilbert also notes the contrast between the exuberance of the women and the corresponding resentment of the men. In a sense, the spirit of 1914 lived on among the women. They continued marching – most notably on 17 July 1915, 30,000 strong, behind Mrs Pankhurst and the slogan 'Women's Battle Cry is Work, Work, Work' – while the men were bogged down in the mud of Flanders. Robert Graves recalled that by 1916, 'The civilians talked a foreign language; and it was newspaper language.' He quoted a 'typical document of this time' by way of illustration. The Little Mother's Letter is notable not just as an example of civilian and press language, but in its chillingly ambivalent representation of womanhood.

The 'Little Mother' wrote to the *Morning Post*, upbraiding another correspondent, who had styled himself 'A Common Soldier'. The Little Mother claimed to speak for 'the mothers of the British race ... It is a voice which demands to be heard, seeing that we play the most important part in the history of the world.' She insisted that women would tolerate no talk of peace before victory.

> There is only one temperature for the women of the British race and that is white heat. With those who disgrace their sacred trust of motherhood we have nothing in common ... We women pass on the human ammunition of 'only sons' to fill up the gaps, so that when the 'common soldier' looks back before going 'over the top' he may see the women of the British race on his heels, reliable, dependent, uncomplaining.

She went on to speak of women as the 'gentle-nurtured, timid sex' – and in the next breath to warn, 'If the men fail, Tommy Atkins, the women won't.' In her matter-of-fact words, the human condition was reduced to a zero-sum equation: 'Women are created for the purpose of giving life, and men to take it.'

Thanks to popular demand, her letter was reprinted as a pamphlet; the publishers boasted that 75,000 copies were sold in less than a week. The Queen was said to be deeply touched; appended testimonials called it 'a masterpiece', 'exquisite', 'beautiful'. 'My God! she makes us die happy,' exclaimed 'One who has Fought and Bled'.[2]

Others found such mother-Britannias terrifying. To claim the capacity for motherly grief, but nonetheless to insist that their own offspring was expendable ammunition: this was a paradoxical, chimerical kind of woman. She loudly asserted her gentleness and dependence in the same breath as she warned the men she would be on their heels if they wavered. Perhaps the Little Mother was an invention, but the demand for her 'Letter' confirms that she was true in spirit.

The image of the Victorian woman, with her constitutional lassitude, had been replaced by that of the war-woman, an electric energy coursing through her. While the Little Mother spoke of a pure 'white heat', those who railed against the change in womanhood often depicted the energy as libidinal in nature. In Richard Aldington's *Death of a Hero*, the dead hero's mother is depicted as a harpy, incapable of feeling anything deeply but lust and narcissism.

Mrs Winterbourne uses up men callously and copiously, like ammunition. She is with one of her twenty-two lovers when she learns that her son is dead: '... the effect of George's death on her temperament was, strangely enough, almost wholly erotic. The war did that to lots of women. All the dying and wounds and mud and bloodiness – at a safe distance – gave them a great kick, and excited them to an almost unbearable pitch of amorousness.'[3]

This theme was expounded in psychological theory as well as in literature. Citing an anecdote about a 'young lady of Rheims' whose lusts were inflamed by a bombardment to the point where her partner 'had to use all his power to free himself from this woman and fled to a cellar', Professor Magnus Hirschfeld observed:

> The odd fact that the nature of war atrocities and bloody deeds have an erotic effect upon women was made long before the war and was merely confirmed during it. Throughout the war there were many parallels to the execution of Damiens reported by Casanova, which the ladies of Paris observed from their windows in a veritable paroxysm of erotic delight and amused themselves throughout the day with the most terrific suffering of the poor tortured creature.[4]

On hearing that her son is dead, Mrs Winterbourne is impelled to couple with her lover, whose death she also causes: she is 'not only a sadist, but a necrophilous one'. Freud's theoretical emphasis on sadism and masochism provided an underpinning for this vision of women. The Freudian repertoire was also a boon to vulgarisers like H.C. Fischer and E.X. Dubois, who produced a more sensational, Anglicised version of Hirschfeld's *Sexual History of the World War*. War, they argued, was the result of primeval urges bursting through repression; women subconsciously desired it, masochistically longing to be dominated by battle-hardened warriors, and sadistically excited by the men's suffering. A chapter resumé gives the flavour: 'Women's Clubs Hiring Soldiers – Erotic Effect of Wounds ... Women Turn to Old Men – Sexual Perversions – Women and Child Lovers – Story of Boy Seduced by Woman – Woman Seduces Entire Class of Boys – Lad Raped by Women – Vogue of Foreign Soldiers ... Ashantis, Bedouins and Senegalese ... Case of English Lady and Arab Boy – Sexual Capacity of Negroes'.[5]

The machinery of war, with its insatiable appetite for manhood, threatened to pitch the entire erotic order into polymorphous chaos. Yet at the same time, it offered men the possibility of men reaching their apotheosis. Aldington's hero George Winterbourne is transfixed by his first sight of the 'lean and hard and tireless' men – 'not boudoir rabbits and lounge lizards' – that war produces. 'There was something intensely masculine about them, something very pure and immensely friendly and stimulating. They had been where no woman or half-man had ever been, could endure to be.'

The fighting men had a common bond and understanding, as Robert Graves attests in a different way, that separated them from the people at home. Men attained their destiny in combat – and were then destroyed wholesale. Society was divided into these true men on one side, and women and inferior men on the other. 'I do know you're the first real men I've looked upon. I swear you're better than the women and the half-men, and by God! I swear I'll die with you rather than live in a world without you,' George Winterbourne vows.[6]

The examples given by Fischer and Dubois depict the catastrophic results of separating the women from the real men. Instead of coupling with the fittest, women take the sexual initiative with boys and old men – which necessitates perverted practices – or each other, or become frighteningly masculinised themselves. When the natural order of sexual selection is thrown into crisis, with the strongest males of the race unable to take possession of the females, all manner of lusts become possible – and desirable.

Implicit also in this is the prospect of racial degeneration, as inferior specimens and aliens usurp the place of 'the young and the strong and the healthy, the physical pick of the race', in Aldington's words. He suggested another consequence of segregation. 'All men, too, and no women. That'll set up a pretty nice resentment between the sexes – more sodomy and Lesbianism.'[7]

According to Hirschfeld and his interpreters, even women's fashions were influenced by the enforced redirection of the female libido.

> While on the one hand skirts became shorter and shorter, and more and
> more of the feminine body was revealed by the discarding of superfluous
> clothes, there was a surprising vogue for high boots reaching almost to the
> knees, which gave women an almost boyish gait. A military cap perched
> saucily on one side of the head added a suggestion of swaggering virility to
> the feminine face.[8]

The explanation for this apparent paradox was not lesbianism, but
women's need to appeal to the 'sexual inverts' common among those
males, 'inferior in virility', who had been rejected for military service –
Aldington's 'half-men'. It suggests the extent – reaching even into
perversity – of the opportunism that many men believed the war had
revealed in womankind. Fischer and Dubois seem almost to suggest
that Victorian woman had been shamming; waiting for the moment.

> Where were the timid young ladies of yesterday, who would faint at the
> sight of a mouse, and the perpetually anxious wives and mothers who,
> only shortly before, when the first motor-buses appeared in the streets of
> London, spent their days in an agony of fear in case their husbands or
> sons were travelling by one of those 'dangerous' vehicles while out at
> work? They had all disappeared, and instead of them, England, like the
> rest of the world, was full of bright-eyed women, slightly hysterical
> perhaps, but certainly neither timid nor anxious. They suddenly
> developed an unusual avidity for enjoyment, and although many of the
> women who filled the fashionable restaurants in London and other
> capitals, must have inwardly trembled, for all their outward gaiety, for
> one or more loved ones who were exposed to the worst sufferings and
> dangers at the war fronts, when the catastrophe did occur they showed,
> after the first paroxysm of grief, a most remarkable resignation.[9]

The suggestion of hypocrisy, and the pursuit of a selfish agenda
behind a rhetoric of high-minded idealism, is the basis of Richard
Aldington's description of the women in George Winterbourne's life.
George's two sexual partners, Fanny and Elizabeth, wrap themselves
in the progressive rather than the patriotic flag. They preach free love;
when George takes them at their word, he is the one who gets hurt,
while they coolly pass on to new liaisons. In fact, the narrator suggests
that they actually cause his death. Even in the hell of trench warfare,
George's emotions are hung on the wire of the modern love-tangle in

which he finds himself. A few days before the Armistice, in battle, he leaps up into the line of enemy machine-gun fire. Like his mother, his wife Elizabeth is with a lover when she is brought the news. The younger Mrs Winterbourne finds consolation the same way as the older. Whatever her professed ideals, Aldington says, Eve is eternal, malign, and dissimulating.

> Elizabeth and Fanny were not grotesques. They adjusted to the war with marvellous precision and speed, just as they afterwards adapted themselves to the post-war. They both had that rather hard efficiency of the war and post-war female, veiling the ancient predatory and possessive instincts of the sex under a skilful smoke-barrage of Freudian and Havelock Ellis theories. To hear them talk theoretically was most impressive. They were terribly at ease upon the Zion of sex, abounding in inhibitions, dream symbolism, complexes, sadism, repressions, masochism, Lesbianism, sodomy, etcetera.[10]

From the feminist camp, Vera Brittain affirmed educated women's new sexual awareness in piquantly similar terms: 'Amongst our friends we discussed sodomy and lesbianism with as little hesitation as we compared the merits of different contraceptives, and were theoretically familiar with varieties of homosexuality and venereal disease of which the very existence was unknown to our grandparents.'[11] For Aldington, women's possession of such sexual knowledge, articulated through a modernist ideology, was a homicidal force. Woman's nature, unleashed by modern war, led inexorably to the death of men.

The horror of reversion into a primitive femininity is the theme of D.H. Lawrence's short story 'Tickets, Please'.[12] In a wartime Midlands town, the trams are driven by reckless 'cripples and hunchbacks', and conducted by young women, 'fearless young hussies'. A group of them spring revenge on the philandering inspector who has trifled with their affections, demanding that he choose one of them. 'At that moment they were rather horrifying to him, as they stood in their short uniforms.' They set upon him, tearing his clothes – 'The sight of his white, bare arm maddened the girls' – and pin him to the ground. One kneels on John Thomas (for he has been named with Lawrentian pointedness): "You ought to be killed." And there was a terrifying lust in her voice.'

They ought, if they had been bold enough to let their atavistic passion run its course, to have pulled his head off. The tram-conductresses are acting the part of Maenads, the wild women who followed Daphoene, or Daphne, 'the bloody one', and Dionysus.

The Maenads epitomised orgiastic excess; a ferment of eroticism, savagery, and intoxication. In their festivals, the women would tear a boy apart with their bare hands and eat him. Dionysus invented wine; the Maenads also fed their frenzy with the leaves of ivy and laurel. (Robert Graves believed that they used hallucinogenic mushrooms too.)[13]

The erotic Dionysus became the Roman Mars, god of war. The Romans maintained an older tradition of colouring male fertility figures red, by reddening the faces of the victorious generals who represented Mars. This might explain the claims made by Fischer and Dubois that Romanian officers of all ranks wore make-up: they describe a general, reviewing his troops, with scarlet lips and powdered face. One of the most striking aspects of the changes in women's fashions during the war was that women of all classes, not just the unfortunate one, now appeared in public wearing their 'war-paint'.

While one facet of the paradigmatic Maenad orgy formed the dénouement of 'Tickets, Please', the orgy motif frequently appeared in other forms. The word had a broader meaning then than now, being applicable to more or less any bout of sensual indulgence involving more than one person. It had a specific connection with drugs: Lady Diana Manners, for example, described her morphine-injecting sessions with Katharine Asquith as 'orgies'. Where there was a sexual element, the corsets of decorum left the precise extent of the depravity to the reader's imagination.

> Men and women who led sober lives in 1914 have abandoned themselves in many cases to orgies which are incredible. But a few weeks ago at a great London music hall two women arrived in a Rolls-Royce car, sent for the commissionaire, and said they would like to entertain a couple of guardsmen if such were in the house. They gave the man a sovereign. The soldiers were brought in, entertained afterwards to a champagne supper, and remained with the women until morning. The incident is characteristic of what is being done every day in the West End. The air is electric with this current of abnormal sexuality.[14]

The element of intoxication, fundamental to the orgy, is present in the ingredient of champagne. According to those sober scholars Fischer and Dubois, there were also some who got a kick from cocaine.

> The numerical discrepancy between the representatives of the two sexes on the 'home front' produced the logical consequence that in a great many cases a number of women would expect sexual satisfaction from one man. Frequently parties were organised, consisting of a number of women and

only one or two men, and, generally after prolonged bouts of drinking combined with drug-taking the worst sexual orgies took place. Cocaine addicts, losing all self-control and all moral sense, would practise every variant of 'group love' which sometimes took such disgusting forms that it would be impossible to describe them even in a scientific work.[15]

From a group of women tearing a lone male apart and eating him, to a group of women gratifying their sexual desires upon a single man, the orgy was a terrible vision of women simultaneously out of control and in control. It was a carnival of female uncontainability and dominance. But such a singular event, floating free of the normal calendar, was an occasional symbol of disorder rather than a source of quotidian anxiety. Among the most significant of the latter were the ever-multiplying signs of female autonomy and control in public space.

The most basic terms referring to women's public presence are sexually loaded. A 'public woman' was a prostitute; so, still, is a woman who 'walks the streets'. As Elizabeth Wilson notes, the issue in the nineteenth century was whether all women in public did not become public women; whether it was possible for female respectability to survive the promiscuous turmoil of the city.[16] During the Great War, the boundary between public women and respectable women in public, already unstable, was felt to be undergoing further deterioration.

In some instances, women's occupation of new territory met with neutral or approving comment. In the autumn of 1915, the *Daily Mail* reported on 'Dining Out Girls': 'The war-time business girl is to be seen any night dining out alone or with a friend in the moderate-price restaurants in London. Formerly she would never have had her evening meal in town unless in the company of a man friend. But now, with money and without men, she is more and more beginning to dine out.'[17] The significance of this was a feminine move into the nocturnal city. From the 1870s, an increasing number of establishments, such as the Criterion in Piccadilly Circus, had begun to cater to women at lunchtime. Now women at night were not necessarily women of the night.

Their incidental behaviour in these places was also noted. Women began to smoke in public, and, as the ever-dependable Fischer and Dubois remark, they 'began to make up not only in the presence of company in the most exclusive drawing rooms, but also in restaurants, cafés, and anywhere else in public'.[18] On the surface, these activities seem dissimilar except in the fact that they had previously been regarded as socially unacceptable. Perhaps, however, the offensiveness of each lay in its narcissism. A woman's gaze is an issue in public, where the male gaze is supposed to rule; a woman making herself up in public is not only gazing, but gazing at herself. Smoking is a sensual, self-gratifying pleasure.[19] Born to the assumption that women exist for others, male reactionaries (in the strict sense of the term) were unable to stomach the idea of women pleasing themselves.

Just as the euphemisms imply that prostitution is the fundamental condition of women in public, the complementary expression 'working girl' suggests the same of women earning money. Women might be forced to work by poverty, or might do so electively before getting married: the 'working girl' marks the extreme end of a schema that considers various forms of female employment as failures to attain, or temporary exceptions from, the ideal of containment within marriage and the home. Thanks to wartime exigencies, women challenged this paradigm on all fronts. While the bizarre new fauna of sexual possibilities for women may have been largely confined to the imaginations of conservative commentators, the war certainly gave women's work a new polymorphousness.

In doing so, it did irreparable damage to the mode of employment most consistent with the patriarchal ideal. Domestic service kept women in the home – not their own home, but one in which they were kept under strict bourgeois discipline. Nearly half a million women left domestic service and sweated trades, like dressmaking, to go into war production work or jobs left vacant by the military demand for manpower. In the home, women also enjoyed a new autonomy, earning and disposing of their own wages. The state substituted itself for husbands, paying wives a 'separation allowance' to compensate for the men's absence on military service. Some changes, like this one, were temporary; the rest would have happened in due course anyway. But taken as a whole, in their context and in the rapidity of their occurrence, their impact appeared revolutionary.

The greatest freedom, naturally, was enjoyed by young unmarried women. The 'munitionettes' enjoyed both high wages and the rude camaraderie of industrial labour. Inevitably, this was a cause for moral concern. 'Girls who, in peace-time, would have thought themselves lucky to earn a pound a week, often earned five pounds, and munition workers often became as extravagant as the miners of South Wales, who at one time could earn £15 or £20 a week ... The moral effect of this new kind of life ... can easily be imagined.'[20]

D.H. Lawrence's choice of tram-conductresses to illustrate his own vision of such moral effects was not untypical. The 100,000 women who went into transport industries attracted more than their share of curious attention. Here were young women in uniform, directing the public, channelling the flows within the impure turbulence of urban space. 'With a tram packed with howling colliers, roaring hymns downstairs and a sort of antiphony of obscenities upstairs, the lasses are perfectly at their ease. They pounce on the youths who try to evade their ticket-machine. They push off the men at the end of their distance.'[21] 'Conductorettes' posed the old question about women in public anew: was their virtue and respectability the price they had to pay for this new power? Lawrence's affirmative answer could hardly be more emphatic.

Meanwhile, the traditional female economy of low wages, casual work and sweatshops persisted. Women in this sector would not necessarily stick to a single occupation, but would combine more than one meagre source of income. Among the options was prostitution. A small survey, taken in 1921, of the occupations given by women who appeared in two West End police courts (now known as magistrates' courts), suggests something of the demographics of the unfortunate class. There were ten who said they were domestic servants, seventeen dressmakers, eight 'chorus girls, etc.', three clerical workers and two waitresses.[22]

Even allowing for sample size, euphemism and the legal reasons for not admitting prostitution as a trade – though one woman did – there is no reason to discount the general impression it leaves, and it is broadly consistent with other surveys.[23] The ranking of domestic service and dressmaking in the first two places is unsurprising: those were the twin pillars of the low-wage female economy. The presence of chorus girls immediately after them emphasises the marginality of theatrical employment, and the particularly colourful character of the West End underworld.

It also recalls the traditional equivalence, dating back to ancient Rome, of the prostitute and the actress. Across the Channel, the most celebrated *grandes horizontales* were stars of the stage as well, drawing crowds to the theatre on the strength of their reputations as stars of the boudoir.[24] The archaic opprobrium attaching to actresses derived to a large extent from the idea that their public display was close in nature to prostitution; just as, for women, being in public was dangerously close to being public women. The relationship between the occupations was also seen as having an economic logic: 'The chorus, ballet, or cabaret girl can usually afford "the stage" because she is already immoral and the glamor of the footlights increases her earning capacity; the same conditions of course tend to force into immorality a girl who has hitherto been honest.'[25]

The celebrity courtesans of Paris affirmed that prostitution and stage performance could be complementary occupations, capable of taking a woman to a position of great wealth and influence. British social mores were not as elastic. But the performer-courtesans illustrated the way that, on both sides of the Channel, the stage permitted vertical movement through a society dominated by the rigidity of its horizontal stratifications, without demanding radical moral and social transformation. It allowed the demi-monde to rise to the level of the monde, if not to become part of it. Despite the impeccable respectability of most stage performance, and performers, the theatre continued its time-honoured role as a haven for the louche.

As a vertical section through a horizontal society, the world of theatre and entertainment seems an obvious conduit for the movement of drugs from the street classes to the servant-keeping ones, from Soho to Mayfair. Underemployed actresses and chorus girls would rub shoulders with prostitutes in the bars and restaurants around Leicester Square or Shaftesbury Avenue; some would work as prostitutes themselves. It is highly plausible that the social connections formed this way might funnel the street drug traffic up into the more outwardly respectable levels of the entertainment industry.

The nocturnal world of the West End also provided an easy target for the patriarchal backlash against women's new self-assertion. Drug use in this milieu was a case of a modern phenomenon occurring in an old-fashioned social formation, whose nature and weaknesses were well understood. Other symbols of independence were legitimised by patriotic duty. Shorter skirts and looser clothing – the brassiere replaced the camisole – were more practical for working women; economising on material was also consistent with the austerity drive. It made intuitive sense that female office workers, employed in the war bureaucracy or substituting for men on active service, should use their wages to stay in town after work and dine out unaccompanied. After all, if women were doing men's work, why should they not enjoy some of the rewards men took for granted? And even if women war-workers wanted to express their independence in mildly shocking ways, like wearing cosmetics, it seemed at least that they had earned it.

The women of the drugtaking class were not only practising a far less acceptable form of behaviour, but lacked this sanction of merit. Drug use could, in some cases, be understood as a side-effect of duty. It was not unknown among nurses, used to administering drugs professionally, under arduous discipline, and having to cope with a procession of terrible wounds and death. Battlefield exhaustion and shell-shock were diagnosed in the case of Mary Boshell, who died in a St John's Wood nursing home at the age of twenty-two, with a box of drugs under her pillow and her arm covered in needle marks. Boshell, a former Voluntary Aid Detachment nurse who had undergone bombardment while serving in Belgium, used morphine and the barbiturate veronal.[26] The extent of less catastrophic drug use among nursing and medical personnel can only be a matter for speculation.

War nurses were the subject of a variety of accusations, ranging from pseudo-Freudian claims of sadism and voyeurism (the objects of their gaze being both wounds and men's private parts) to the allegation that many were former prostitutes.[27] In the end, however, the respectable professional woman won the recognition that was her due. The conclusion of David Garnett's *Dope-Darling* can be seen as an expression of that triumph. Here the separation of the professional woman from the prostitute is absolute. Beatrice Chase, the medical practitioner, is the virtuous restorer of life: she saves Roy Plowman from his battlefield injuries. Claire Plowman, the marginal prostitute and nightclub singer, is doomed as a result of her sexual downfall and her cocaine addiction; 'a renegade, a traitor; she valued life at nothing.' Claire dies; Beatrice is left with Roy – and, by doing her duty, she has earned him.

The women of the drugtaking class did not earn anything, in that sense. Nor did they have unions, associations, causes, leaders or any of the other new resources of women's solidarity. They were old-fashioned women who were at the front of the latest fashions, whether in dances or drugs. That combination of marginality and modernity made them the ideal raw material for an awful warning to women as a whole.

4

THE FASCINATION
OF THE ORIENTAL

It did not especially perturb the British that the Chinese among them liked to gamble, or that they smoked opium. What they feared was the ability of the Chinese to attract white women; the dangers of the other vices were seen to lie mainly in their capacity to aid seduction across the racial divide. Nor did it matter whether, as individuals, the Chinese themselves were good, bad, or indifferent. The principal theme of the British discourse upon its Chinese communities in the first quarter of the twentieth century was the intrinsic evil of sexual contact between the races, and its issue.

Such contact was the inevitable result of the nature of the Chinese population. The Chinatowns – the word was first used by a journalist in 1902 – were shoreline communities, fed by the sea. As merchant shipping brought Chinese sailors to the major British ports, a few of them began to settle near the docks of the major ports. Some spotted the demand for services from their compatriots, and set to providing accommodation, laundry and food. The communities arose in the Edwardian period, as boarding houses, cafés and restaurants became social centres; opium and gambling answered the demand for relaxation and recreation. A wealth of social organisations provided the enclaves with sinews and a voice.

Gradually the proportion of sailors among the Chinese population fell, and that of those engaged in providing services rose. But there remained an overwhelming imbalance between the numbers of men and of women. In 1911, 220 Chinese men and just twenty-seven women were recorded in London; there were only sixty more women in the entire country, compared to a total male population of 1232. Ten years later, the men still outnumbered the women by nearly ten to one.[1] There would also have been several hundred seamen temporarily present at any given time.

Nowadays, these elementary demographics would be accepted as sufficient explanation for attempts by Chinese settlers to find partners in the indigenous population. At the time, commentary upon the problem scarcely ever acknowledged that the reason Chinese men were drawn to white women might have something to do with the almost total absence of Chinese women. Instead, it harped on the theme of a perverse fascination, posing the twin questions of what drew Chinese men to white women, and what some white women saw in them.

The Chinese man's impermissible lust for white flesh could be considered as one instance of a generally transgressive sexuality. In 1907, a Commission of Inquiry established by Liverpool City Council reported: 'The evidence shows that the Chinese appear to much prefer having intercourse with young girls, more especially those of undue precocity.'[2] A spiritualised version of such a predilection animated Thomas Burke's story 'The Chink and the Child', upon which D.W. Griffith's film *Broken Blossoms* was based.[3]

Another Burke story, 'Tai Fu and Pansy Greers', told of how a young white woman had to submit to a dreadful degradation at the hands of a loathsome Chinese man, 'a dreadful doper', in order to pay for her mother's funeral. 'What he did to her in the blackness of that curtained room of his had best not be imagined ... She came away with bruised limbs and body, with torn hair, and a face paled to death.' (After losing her job as a result of Tai Fu's sexual boasts, she descends into promiscuity, but eventually achieves her goal of murdering him.)[4]

On a lighter note, a running joke in Sax Rohmer's *Dope* is the 'empty and decadent' Molly Gretna's thrilled contemplation of what she imagines Chinese practices to be. She is told that a white woman acquaintance is married to a Chinese man: ' "Oh!" Mollie's eyes opened widely. "I almost envy her! I have read that Chinamen tie their wives to beams in the roof and lash them with leather thongs until they swoon. I could die for a man who lashed me with leather thongs. Englishmen are so ridiculously gentle to women." '[5] The 'past-mistress of the smartest vices' is similarly excited by the prospect of being arrested, or more specifically, of being handcuffed. It all must have seemed so innocent in those days.

The theme of indescribable perversity would eventually play a significant role in the greatest of the London Chinese drug legends, but for the most part it was marginal. A more pressing need was to account for the Chinese men's ability to attract white women.

Some commentators were happy to accept the explanation that the Chinese simply made good husbands. 'He makes no great demands upon his womenkind, and is always ready to help in the tasks around the house. The white wives of Chinese have plenty of money to spend on amusements and dress, are able to employ other women to do the rough work of their homes, and have an easy time generally.'[6] The vicar of Limehouse described the Chinese husband as 'usually kind, generous, and, making allowance for his Oriental upbringing, faithful to her. He is extremely fond of his children (especially if they are boys) and bestows upon them every care.'[7] With worldly equanimity, the Chief Constable of Liverpool told the Home Office, in 1906, that '... they treat their women well, they are sober, they do not beat their wives and they pay liberally for prostitution.'[8]

Down in London some years later, a book about the East End that referred to Whitechapel's Jews as 'malignant bacilli' nonetheless allowed the Chinese a few generous words:

> The Chinese make very good husbands, kind and industrious; and if anything goes wrong with the marriage it is generally the English wife who is to blame. They are not usually Poplar women, however, who marry them, but girls from less fastidious Hoxton: Poplarites have a healthy prejudice against mixed marriages.[9]

It was not the conduct of Chinese husbands that was at issue, however, but the fact of them. 'To the ordinary decent Briton there is something repulsive about inter-marriage or its equivalent between white and coloured races,' an editorial in the *Evening News* confidently asserted.[10] As a Northern correspondent of the *Empire News* put it, 'The fascination of the Oriental for many young girls owing to his industry, sobriety, courtesy and good nature has long been regarded here and in Leeds as a moral yellow peril.'[11]

Even with the underpinning of a belief in fundamental differences between the races, such a proposition teetered on the brink of absurdity. To resolve the dissonance between the supposed intrinsic evil of interracial marriages and the benign character of the husbands, many commentators denied the latter. One of the obstacles they had to overcome was the absence of complaints from the wives themselves. H.L. Cancellor, an East London magistrate, suggested that these women existed in a form of slavery, brutalised and corrupted:

> Distasteful as these unions seem to our Western minds, the magistrates seldom receive complaints against husbands from the white wives. On the other hand, the women often give evidence to screen their yellow spouses, and show in court that they have taken lessons in the art of lying from their lords and masters. When these women appear in court they are

always well dressed and wearing jewellery. It is to be feared that these outward signs of prosperity are a cloak to many stories of hidden cruelty. If the testimony of students of the life of the Chinese colony is true, a Chinaman treats a white wife well so long as she is faithful to him, but is terribly cruel if she looks at another man with affection. The women are so conscious of having sold their souls and bodies to their yellow masters that they are afraid to publish the tragedies of their lives.[12]

Inevitably, there were those who considered it was the women's own fault, for throwing themselves at the Chinamen.[13] The Reverend J. Degen believed that such perverse behaviour arose from psychological abnormality:

Many girls have a latent pathological infatuation for coloured men, who very often are in a position to give them a lavish supply of furs and jewellery, and introduce them into opium dens and bogus night clubs.

This colour fascination constitutes a danger in regard to which girls should be warned. The morals and civilisation of the Yellow man and the European are fundamentally different.[14]

According to others, though, the main cause of the trouble was the Chinese use of subterfuge to lure the young women. The means – gambling or opium – aroused less anxiety on their own account than the end that they were said to serve. Nor was the one necessarily regarded as worse than the other.

Gambling and opium have plenty of connotations in common: clandestine sessions, exclusivity, the adherence of the especially depraved, dens, the night. The focus of agitation was not upon red-eyed circles of rakes, huddled round tables in some midnight 'gambling hell', however, but on the Chinese cousin of bingo. Pai-ke-p'iao, or pak-a-pu, did not even draw players to any particular venue. All they had to do was buy a small square of paper, on which were printed eighty Chinese characters; such as the dragon, the sea, the sun, flowers or gold. These might form statements, such as 'cold comes, and heat departs'. Either the player or the pai-ke-p'iao bank's agent would then mark a number of these, usually five to ten, using a brush dipped in ink. The agent would then make a copy, stamp the paper with the date, and take it to the bank, where the winning combination was marked up. On a stake of sixpence, punters might win a shilling if five of their ten characters matched, ten shillings for six, four pounds ten shillings for seven out of ten, and twenty pounds for eight. In the exceptionally rare event that all ten of a gambler's choices matched the bank's, the prize might be eighty pounds; or in one account, £170 for a shilling. Much of the demand for this cheap and simple – though illegal – form of gambling came from white East Enders.[15]

The alleged perils of this pastime were identical with those claimed for drug use. It was said to be compulsive, to reduce its devotees to poverty, and to lead to other vices; its worst aspect was that its victims were female, and that it was 'the bland Celestials' way of gaining influence' over them. The Chinese, it was said, allowed young women to win in order to snare them – in the same way that drug dealers are perennially alleged to hook new customers with free samples.[16] Soon they were dragged into utter degradation. A mother was said to have been seen taking the shoes from her baby's feet to pay for the game. 'Their moral sense has gone. They behave as though hypnotised by the Celestials and seem helpless to break the spell.'[17]

Pai-ke-p'iao was generally seen as a ghetto menace, to be contained in Limehouse. When three men were caught at it in Poplar High Street (along with a boy of thirteen and a girl of eleven), the police described it as a very serious case, because of its location on the edge of Chinatown, threatening to spread through the indigenous population.[18] In this respect, the pak-a-pu subgenre of the Yellow Peril theme differed from the opium scare, which turned upon the idea of a channel of vice linking the East End and the West End. Drugs injected moral infection directly into the heart of the metropolis; pai-ke-p'iao acted by local diffusion. Francis Chester stood outside the mainstream with his claim that Pak-a-Poo utilised the same network of vice as drugs and prostitution; in the latter lay the danger for young women who bought tickets for a 'little flutter' in West End clubs.[19]

In certain accounts, pai-ke-p'iao was actually regarded as worse than opium. Under the headlines 'Yellow Peril In London – Vast Syndicate Of Vice With Its Criminal Master – Women And Child Victims', the *Daily Express* alleged that this vice syndicate 'promotes the pernicious opium trade, operates gambling houses, and more important still from the national standpoint, is corrupting women and children by the fascinations of the Chinese lottery game known as puck-a-boo.'[20]

One of the influences on this order of priorities may have been the survival of a strain of tolerance towards opium, despite the prevailing climate of opinion about drugs. This was partly the result of first-hand observation, and partly the legacy of British colonial policy. Britain founded its Indian administration upon revenues from sales of opium to China in the eighteenth century, and even in the late nineteenth century, eighteen per cent of the Indian government's income still came from the state opium monopolies.[21] The British establishment was bound to resist the anti-opiumists' claims that the drug was a social evil. Sir George Birdwood wrote to *The Times* in 1881, maintaining that, from his personal experience in India, opium smoking was 'absolutely harmless'.[22] In 1895, the Royal Commission on Opium countered anti-opiumist pressure with a report that endorsed the use of opium in India as a medicine, and compared its use for pleasure with the consumption of alcohol in moderation.[23]

Favourable comparisons with alcohol were a recurrent feature of those reports from Limehouse which did not embrace the imaginative repertoire of the modern drug genre. Even Sir William Collins, the leading anti-opiumist of the day, returned from a tour of inspection in 1911 with the feeling that opium smoking was less objectionable than gin palaces.[24] 'I saw two or three men coming out of a house a day or two ago looking stupid, but their appearance was nothing so disgusting as that of a drunken man,' a *Daily Telegraph* correspondent observed in 1916.[25] Some local magistrates recognised opium as a Chinese cultural equivalent of alcohol. Told that two Chinese men who faced him on opium charges had been arrested at the Chinese New Year, one magistrate let them off with modest fines, observing that 'It does mitigate it to some extent – like Scotsmen, on our New Year's Eve, having a scotch and soda. Only the Chinese don't go to St. Paul's.'[26]

Opium was also considered mild in comparison to other drugs. Dr Arthur Shadwell, a 'well-known sociologist', declared:

> The fact is that a little opium-smoking is quite harmless, and a regular debauch can be indulged in only by persons who have nothing to do.
> Of all forms of intoxication this is the weakest and least dangerous. Eating or drinking opium is another matter, and even that is incomparably less dangerous than the modern practice of injecting or inhaling narcotic alkaloids.[27]

Broadly, then, there were two accounts of the Chinese competing with each other. The benign view saw the Chinese as essentially untroublesome characters who practised their social customs and pursued their grievances in private, rarely disturbing public order. They were understood to belong to a fundamentally different civilisation, with a different moral architecture, but their day-to-day behaviour was compatible with British society, and indeed had much to commend it. They were alien but basically respectable. In the malign view, they were considered to be an alien menace, concealing their evil behind a placid facade; vectors of vice, infecting a strategically and symbolically important part of the capital – the docks, barely any distance from the City itself – with gambling and drugs, and threatening to spread these to the heart of the metropolis. The premier evil of miscegenation was frequently acknowledged even by those who spoke up in favour of the Chinese.

In general, the supporters and opponents of the Chinese divided along lines of attitude, rather than class or occupation. Those who were most heavily influenced by the dogma of racial incompatibility, like Rev. Degen, tended to see the worst in the Chinamen; while those who gave more weight to their empirical observation of Chinese behaviour, like Rev. James, were more tolerant. One magistrate might see opium as the Chinaman's version of scotch; another might see 'dens of Asiatic vice' as a 'frantic problem', as did Mr Cairns of Thames Police Court, whose remarks prompted the *Evening News* 'Yellow Perils' leader – and a riposte from the eminent lawyer Sir Ernest Wild, who later became the Recorder of London.[28] Wild appeared for Doe Foon, a Limehouse restaurateur, who successfully appealed against a deportation order imposed after conviction for keeping a disorderly house – Chinese men and young white women were said to have kissed and cuddled on his premises. Wild claimed, quite inaccurately, that the Cairns and the press between them had cut the Chinese population of Limehouse from 4800 to 300. 'The remedy is worse than the disease, for in the place of these Chinamen, who were perfectly well-conducted citizens, the houses have been taken over by people of another nationality, who are very much worse than the people they replace,' he commented.

There was, however, one occupational group with a particular axe to grind against the Chinese. Although a mere 480 of the 15,000 foreign seamen registered in Britain in 1911 were Chinese, this small band incurred the special displeasure of the National Seamen's and Firemen's Union, who campaigned against it for many years. NSFU agitation did much to keep the pot of anti-Chinese prejudice bubbling in the port cities – and in Parliament, where the seamen's leader James Havelock Wilson sat as M.P. for Middlesbrough.

The British seamen resented what they saw as a lack of solidarity, accusing the Chinese sailors of strikebreaking and undercutting wages. During disputes, the Chinese may have allowed themselves to become exposed: other foreign seamen joined in the Cardiff strike of 1911, but the Chinese continued to work. Foreigners as well as Britons took part in retaliatory attacks on the Chinese; all thirty Chinese laundries in the city were destroyed.[29] Less seriously, friction and scuffles were a perennial feature at shipping offices where sailors went to be hired.[30] The outbreak of the War brought a temporary reduction of hostilities, when the NSFU called off its campaign, but by 1916, old habits had reasserted themselves, and Havelock Wilson was claiming Chinese seamen were used as spies.[31] It was a topical variation on the usual theme of clandestine, conspiratorial activity, that of the opium traffic.

Besides wages and blacklegging, another reason for the singling out of the Chinese may have been that they were more mobile, and therefore more competitive, in the labour market than the much more numerous Indians, known as Lascars, who tended to be tied to particular employers.[32] The net result was a spiteful contempt. 'You know, we know and they know, that the Chinaman isn't worth a toss as a seaman ... his only claim to indulgence is that he is cheap.'[33]

While the British seamen's resentment was founded on the belief that the Chinese were taking 'their' jobs, using unfair means, their accusations were by no means confined to the domain of labour. During the war, after criticism from the local Trades Congress, Chinese men connected with the Chinese Seamen's and Firemen's Association hotly rebutted the whole range of claims made against them, in a letter to the *Liverpool Courier*. Their sense of injustice was pricked in particular by allegations that they were involved in the dissemination of opium.

> Who began the opium traffic? we ask. Who first forced opium into our country against our wish and will, and made us poor as a nation, yet we do not complain; we only want the truth, and the truth is opium smoking is entirely stopped as our critics ought to know ...
>
> Let it be said that it is neither opium, gambling, Fan Tan, or Chinese dwelling houses that annoy and exasperate our assailants; their grievance lies deeper, it is that British shipowners employ Chinese firemen on their ships for a trifle less money than that paid to Britishers. For this reason meetings are held for the purpose of digging down deep into the slutch in order to rake up something nasty and untruthful that will help to blacken our people's characters (how Christian like), but in order to end all strife and controversy, if such be possible, we challenge our assailants to deny what shipowners have said regarding us, *viz;*- That the reason they employ us is we are steady, reliable, and stick to our ships, and that to get Britishers to work on board ships is almost impossible unless it is they cannot work on land. The most flagrant lie ever invented is that in order to raise money to come to England we sell our wives and children.[34]

The Chinese seamen's claim that opium smoking was 'entirely

stopped' would not have borne scrutiny, although the practice had certainly been restricted by the passing of DORA 40B a few months before. The implication of their larger question, 'who began the opium traffic?', was, however, irrefutable. In fact, they might have asked who was continuing it by other means. The trade's death knell had sounded with the election of a Liberal government in 1906, and it had finally come to an official end in 1913. That same year, British morphine production began a steep rise that continued until 1916, after which it plummeted. If the increase in production had been caused by the demand from the battlefield, it should not have begun as early as 1913, nor reached its lowest point for the decade in 1918, during which heavy fighting continued until the Armistice in November. Terry M. Parssinen has argued that after 1913, the Chinese demand for opium was largely met by its active principle, morphine, produced in Britain.[35]

Pointing to the fact that in the late 1920s, with strict drug controls in place, Britain's legitimate requirement for morphine was a tenth of what it had appeared to be between 1911 and 1920, Parssinen estimates that 175,000 ounces of the drug had been diverted from the medical market during each of these years; some remaining in Britain, and some being exported. But the bulk of the export traffic was legal, proceeding to China via Japan. In 1917, Japan imported 700,000 ounces of morphine, almost all British-made; before 1913, its annual imports had never exceeded 30 000 ounces. Japan's strategic war aim was the extension of its influence in Manchuria; one of the more squalid manifestations of this influence was an addict population supplied with morphine by Japanese dealers. Untroubled by the kind of domestic agitation that had led to the enactment of DORA 40B, the Foreign Office could review the situation with a cynicism of Cowardian standard: 'The prohibition of morphia exports would preclude a considerable number of Japanese from earning their living by poisoning the inhabitants of Manchuria and would therefore add fuel to the fire of Japanese irritation. In fact it seems essentially a question to be postponed to the end of the war.'

In public, however, the government was embarrassed by anti-opiumist pressure, including questions in the House from Sir William Collins. In 1917, the granting of export licences was made contingent upon the presentation of certificates from the Japanese government, confirming that the morphine was for medicinal purposes. Legal morphine exports to Japan promptly ceased, though an illicit traffic arose to fill the gap within a couple of years.

At home, the effect of DORA 40B upon the Chinese community

was to criminalise a large portion of it. Opium smoking was already confined to private houses in Limehouse, since a London County Council regulation had prohibited it in Chinese seamen's lodging houses in 1909. Now the opium ban gave the authorities throughout the country a pretext to invade Chinese domestic privacy, to stage exemplary deportations, and thereby to intimidate the entire community. If that assessment smacks of leftish hyperbole, consider the verdict of a Home Office civil servant, written on the cover of a file dealing with opium prosecutions:

> This is a very comprehensive and encouraging report. The 12 Chinamen against whom deportation orders were made have been successfully packed off to China and their passages paid for out of the sale of their opium without any surplus to speak of to H.O. The prompt execution of the orders has spread a holy panic throughout Liverpool and cast a feeling of terrible insecurity among the Chinese population. Chinese societies have held meetings and voted moneys to appeal to the Chinese ambassador, who appears wise enough to turn a deaf ear.[36]

If a civil servant could gloat unashamedly over the 'encouraging' news of 'terrible insecurity among the Chinese population', the popular press could sink to whatever depths it chose. Perhaps the deepest dive was that made by the *Empire News* (formerly the *Umpire*) in 1921, by which time black men had been deemed part of the drug race-enemy. Contrary to the prevalent opinion, the paper claimed that it was 'not the nature of the Celestial to mate with the women of the West'. The 'Celestial scum' only did so in order to 'use the beauty and knowledge of their wives' to distribute the drugs that made them wealthy.

Extending its condemnation to the black men who, it claimed, also preyed on 'shopgirls, mill-girls, and many of the higher-grade domestics' – this was a report from the North – it stopped only a little way short of advocating genocide. 'If the habit were confined to the foreigners who introduced it to our shores, the law might make a provision for an unlimited and free supply. The end would justify the means.'[37]

For all the attraction the Chinese and other men of colour held as extras in the popular melodrama of 'dope', the narrative demanded leading characters in order to get a firm purchase on the nation's attention. Two such figures – one Chinese, one Jamaican – would eventually emerge as the most notorious dope villains of the 1920s. The first great dope drama, however, was enacted in the immediate Aftermath of the War. Among its characters were a Limehouse couple: a Chinese man and his Scottish wife.

5

FEMALE LEAD

Billie Carleton came into being sometime between 1911 and 1916. She began simply as a stage alias, equipping a young chorus girl with a jaunty, fashionable forename, and a surname that, somewhat obviously, said 'class'. She became a persona too: vivacious, charming, accomplished at the piano and in languages, an ornament of chic theatrical circles; all in all, 'the very essence of English girlhood'.[1] Strangely, she remained all these things in memory – indeed, became more so – after her death precipitated Britain's first great drug scandal.

Though it did her no good, that was no small achievement for an individual who had begun where she did. The girl who became Billie Carleton was born on 4 September 1896 in Bernard Street, off Russell Square in Bloomsbury, and was christened Florence Leonora Stewart. On her birth certificate, her mother is given as Margaret Stewart, a chorus singer. The space for the father's name has a damning stroke ruled across it.

The record of her early life is similarly blank, protected by shame and the proprieties of the time. Florence Stewart was raised by her aunt, Catherine Jolliffe, who in 1919 said that her niece's parents were both dead.[2] One acquaintance cryptically observed that Billie Carleton was a 'victim of heredity', whose childhood experiences had given her a fear of alcohol. Yet it was he who affirmed that, despite this ominous shadow, she had become well read, fluent in French and German, and an excellent pianist.[3] (The French may have derived from family rather than schooling; she was said to be also of Irish descent.)[4] On the one hand, she could boast a portfolio of aptitudes eminently suitable for a well-bred Victorian woman; on the other, she left home at fifteen and went on the stage.

In later years, many a memoirist and reminiscer were keen to claim her acquaintance, but most seemed to have been better acquainted with press cuttings, or their own imaginations. The earliest recollection that seems genuine came from Charles B. Cochran, the celebrated theatrical

Billie Carleton. (Mander & Mitchenson)

impresario.[5] He first encountered her in 1913, at an exhibition in Ghent. She had found her way there in the company of a man called John Darlington Marsh, under whose wing she remained for the rest of her days. Over twenty years her senior, Marsh was an Edwardian playboy with private means and a colossal insouciance about spending it, a combination essential to the way of life Carleton sought to pursue.

At that stage, as far as Cochran seems to have been concerned, she was just a sixteen year-old girl in tow: he found Marsh the more remarkable character. Marsh was asked for a loan of £1500 for the catering and lavatory concession; finding the notion amusing, he bought the franchise himself. After entertaining lavishly and advancing cash to subcontractors, he found himself £100,000 down. Cochran travelled to Ghent after being asked by a mutual friend to invest the debacle; when he told Marsh that the money would not be coming back, Marsh laughed and ordered a champagne lunch. Marsh pursued his financial affairs further in Paris, where he startled his bank manager by cracking a bottle of champagne at half-past nine in the morning.

At home it was more lavish entertainments, a flat in Savile Row, champagne, and trips to Ascot in a Rolls: luxury beyond the dreams of avarice for the vast majority of the population, and certainly for a girl with little more than stigma for a birthright. How much of it she shared in is unclear, but he always said she could have any sum she wanted, within reason – and within reason, to Marsh, might mean four figures. There was a period when her bank balance reached £5000, although the highest wage she ever earned was £25 a week.[6] The exact nature of their relationship never emerged – though Cochran's Ghent anecdote suggests that Marsh did not require intimacy in order to throw money at people. The polite way of putting it was that Carleton was under Marsh's protection; an inapt term to denote cash on demand.

Men of a certain age loomed large in Billie Carleton's life. Marsh was one of an ill-assorted trio who, in different ways, did as much as any of those around her to shape her fate. Without making too glib an equation between the absence of a father in girlhood and the notable presence of men a generation older in her early adulthood, there is an unmistakably paternal theme in these relationships. And just like her real father, they all failed to live up to the role.

Marsh, the sugar-daddy, gave her money; her doctor managed it for her. Frederick Stuart, a Knightsbridge physician, first met Carleton in 1915. Not only did the friend become a patient, but she eventually

Carleton wears De Veulle. This creation was called 'The Laughing
Cavalier'. (Mansell Collection)

began to make her income over to the doctor, who then settled the bills that she, despite their magnitude, was apt to forget.[7] As the guardian of her purse, Stuart stood *in loco parentis*; the position was guaranteed by his professional standing – but that standing itself made such a role professionally and ethically questionable. For Billie Carleton, Dr Stuart was an inherently flawed support.

She met the third of the trio around the same time that she met Stuart, on the eve of her theatrical arrival. Billie Carleton was an attractive young chorus girl who needed to be noticed among all the other attractive young chorus girls if she was to graduate to name roles. And at Hockley's, a Bond Street theatrical costumier, Reggie De Veulle was creating flamboyant designs that needed a model to show them off. He also had contacts in the press. The alliance between Billie Carleton and Reggie De Veulle was a natural one, and friendship also developed. Unfortunately, costume was not their only common interest. Reggie used to say that he took cocaine because his work was creative, and he needed the drug for inspiration.[8]

It was Charles B. Cochran who gave Carleton her first big break. When Ethel Levey left the leading role in *Watch Your Step*, at the Empire in Leicester Square, Cochran lifted Billie Carleton from the chorus to the top of the bill. It was a big production at a prestige venue: there were Irving Berlin songs, ballet interludes, corny gags; and to close the evening, the Bioscope, a film show. Despite the pageant of frivolity, the war was permitted to intrude. Theatres showed newsreels, and the programme promised that 'The Latest War Telegrams Will Be Announced As They Arrive'. Also included was a lingerie advertisement that admitted the possibility of more direct intrusion: 'Every common-sense Eve' – the *Tatler*'s fictional commentator on society and the times – 'wears pyjamas nowadays, for if the "Zepps" come and one had to flee from the sanctity of the house one wouldn't feel quite so – so – much of a refugee as in a nighty.'

In nostalgia, Cochran recalled the debut of 'a young girl of flower-like beauty, delicate charm, and great intelligence'. But during her successful run at the Empire, he was told that Carleton was going to opium parties. Throughout the short course of her career, Billie Carleton's public success was accompanied by gossip within theatrical society about her drug use. The better the circles she moved in, the more influential were the people who heard about her doping. 'It was rather public property,' a friend observed later.[9]

To have started on opium in 1915 put Billie Carleton in the

vanguard of the drug underground. According to Frederick Stuart, she named the man who taught her to smoke the heavy pipe as Jack May, the club proprietor of whom (as recounted in Chapter 2) it was alleged that 'for vice or money or both he induces girls to smoke opium in some foul place.'[10] May engaged Sir Edward Marshall Hall, the most histrionic of legal thespians, to deny the allegation in court.[11] Photos of Carleton and May together show they were friendly – and that May was another of those men of a certain age. So too was his accuser, Captain Ernest Schiff, who was the other man Stuart believed to have induced Carleton to smoke opium. Schiff was a man of private means with a reputation for bold play on the stock market: cut, therefore, from a similar cloth to John Marsh.

Although her employment with Cochran was ended by the drug rumours, and a disappointing performance when he gave her a second chance, Carleton found an engagement with the other leading revue producer of the time, André Charlot. The two men had between them established the 'intimate' style of revue, which relied on wit and charm rather than spectacle. It was the form to which Billie Carleton was best suited, with her delicate image and tiny voice. And it was enjoying its heyday, just before the onrush of the cinema.

For a stage apprenticeship, Charlot productions could not be bettered. The sets were cheap, as was the wage-bill; the pace exhausting, and the discipline strict. Larking about was punished with fines, posted on the noticeboard. Nonetheless, 'Uncle André' was sometimes defeated by the irrepressible high spirits of young actresses. During the production of *Some*, at the Vaudeville Theatre in 1916, he was 'driven nearly frantic at the rehearsals by the everlasting gagging by Billie Carleton and Beatrice Lillie. They were always at some sort of mischief, and often the only way I could get them under control was to lose my temper terribly.' The pair paid no attention.[12]

Beatrice Lillie later recalled that the cast would sometimes run into the Strand to watch the Zeppelins. Inside, the audience would be largely in khaki; the bill of fare offered them the lightest of relief from the war. There were sketches on Modern Mothers, and the inadequacies of the telephone system, and much self-deprecating comedy: backstage spats, 'cursing the manager', the ricketiness of the production. For a couple of scenes, Miss Carleton's dress was designed by Reggie De Veulle.

In one scene, 'The Nursery', the Kids were appropriately played by a trio of young actresses; Carleton, Lillie, and Gertie Lawrence. The

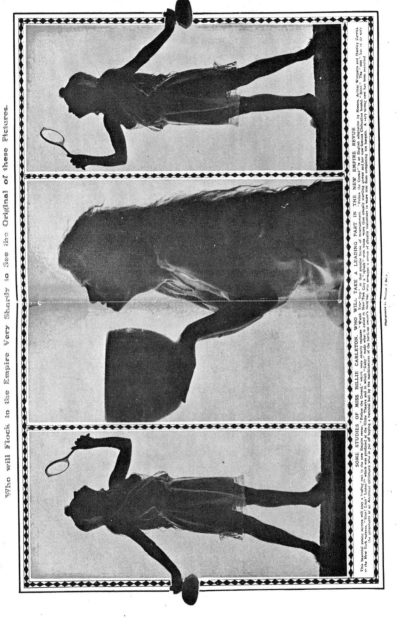

Classical studies. (By permission of the British Library and the *Illustrated London News* Picture Library.)

show was the latter's first West End appearance; she had been spotted in the provinces and hired to understudy Billie Carleton. All three became famous in due course; all were remembered after their deaths. Gertie Lawrence died in middle age, but her name survives, intertwined with Noel Coward's. Beatrice Lillie earned admiration over many years for her distinctive talents as a comedienne, and lived to the age of ninety-four. Billie Carleton's fame arrived earlier and faded quicker; the consequence of her death, not her work.

Her brief series of appearances shed only limited light on the question of whether she could have achieved fame, rather than having it thrust catastrophically upon her. The common thread in the roles she played was how little they demanded of the performer. What they did display was strength in personality and weakness in execution. 'If only her singing and speaking voice were a little stronger I could see a very brilliant future for Miss Carleton in musical comedy,' the *Tatler*'s critic observed. 'She has cleverness, temperament and charm.'[13] In life, as on stage, she had her wits and her looks to see her through.

She became a photo-portrait starlet, a 'beautiful young actress' gracing the *Tatler* and other pictorial publications. Sometimes she appeared in De Veulle creations; once, by contrast, she appeared in nothing but a diaphanous slip and a classical pose.[14] (Nudity in the *Tatler* is by no means a modern development.) The peg was a forthcoming production called *Follow the Crowd*. The show caught the popular mood. 'I loved the scene when two Anglo-German-Jewish travellers on board a liner tell each other how, with members of their family in nearly every capital in Europe, they will make pots of money whichever side wins the war,' chortled 'Arkay', the *Tatler*'s critic, his enthusiasm apparently undampened by the fact that the music was by the American-Russian-Jewish Irving Berlin.[15] Despite the *Tatler*'s advance claim of a leading role, Billie Carleton was not in the cast when the show opened.

Carleton's theatrical progress was not meteoric, but certainly rapid. In *The Boy*, based on a Pinero farce, she played a nightclub 'flapper', a type that predated the war, though it came into its own in the 1920s. Flappers were, in their own way, as significant as young women in uniform or at suffrage meetings. The idea of a particular sort of young male identity, revolving around adornment, display, flirtation and pleasure, had long been recognised in a succession of terms – 'swells', 'knuts', or 'blades'. The emergence of the flapper asserted the possibility of an equivalent identity for young women. It also contributed to a sense of young women as a particularly distinctive group in society, whose profile was to become most sharply defined in the years of the Aftermath.

The point about flappers was that, albeit frivolously, they were an active sort of species. Their wartime role was satirised in one of *The Boy*'s songs:

> There are certain daughters of Eve known as Flappers
> They flirt with all officers home on leave, even sappers
> They take them to dinner and teach them to dance
> The poor blighters wish they were 'Somewhere in France'

The laughter must have been hollow for many of the soldiers sitting in the stalls, a few days or hours from crouching in the trenches. Siegfried Sassoon's poem 'Blighters' damned such attempts to link the theatre of inconsequence with the theatre of war:

> The House is crammed: tier beyond tier they grin
> And cackle at the Show, while prancing ranks
> Of harlots shrill the chorus, drunk with din;
> 'We're sure the Kaiser loves our dear old Tanks!'

> I'd like to see a Tank come down the stalls,
> Lurching to rag-time tunes, or 'Home, Sweet Home',
> And there'd be no more jokes in music-halls
> To mock the riddled corpses around Bapaume.

In her next engagement, Billie Carleton made speeches from the stage appealing for money, or auctionable gifts, for war charities. After their total failure, she was told by colleagues at another theatre that the trick was to invite the audience to throw money. She withstood being pelted with coins and jewellery uncomplainingly, according to Fay Compton, her partner in the enterprise.[16] Like Beatrice Lillie, Compton stayed friends with Carleton after they ceased working together; like Lillie, also, her success was to endure: she played the part of Aunt Ann in the 1960s television adaptation of *The Forsyte Saga*.

Carleton and Compton appeared together in a Broadway farce called *Fair and Warmer*, at the Prince of Wales' Theatre. Compton played a young woman who drank a strong cocktail and got herself into a situation which, though innocent, looked otherwise. Carleton played the 'extremely alluring maid'. By this stage, in the summer of 1918, she was earning £15 a week. In September she left for the Haymarket, to appear in a comic adventure called *Freedom of the Seas*. Lightweight as the part was, it took her income up to £25 a week, and made her the youngest leading lady in the West End.

Between *The Boy* and *Freedom of the Seas*, the photographs seem to show her changing from one woman into another. The flapper of 1917 looks buxom and happy; the romantic lead of 1918 looks drawn and uneasy. A quirk of costume and photography, possibly; or perhaps portraits of the actress rather than her characters. Billie Carleton's professional advances in 1918 were accompanied by growing chaos in her private life.

The qualities of temperament and charm noted by the *Tatler* critic governed her life as well as her art. She was stubborn, and good at getting her own way. The gossip did little to deter her from using drugs; nor did the warnings and pleas of those around her. Legally, she smoked cigarettes heavily, but scarcely drank at all; illegally, she smoked opium and sniffed cocaine. On one occasion in May 1918, Dr Stuart confiscated some cocaine from her. She petulantly complained that he was very mean: now she would have to go to Notting Hill Gate for some more, and would be late for the theatre.[17] Stuart wrote to her:

> I'll do anything to save you from the bottomless pit of darkness, despair and depression. Some of your acts are disappointing and a great shock to me. Get over these lapses. Get over the influence and existence of this damned stuff. Leave it to do its useful work as a local anaesthetic and kill pain, not people.[18]

Despite its unequivocal tone, Stuart's message was mixed. He wrote as a doctor in asserting that the proper use of cocaine was medical, but as a friend in his passionate pledge of commitment. He had allowed his professional relationship with her to become muddled still further by taking on the responsibility of managing her finances. And he was urging her to do as he said, not as he did. While warning her about cocaine, he was giving her morphine injections to relieve pain from wisdom teeth. Even by the liberal standards then applied to medical narcotics, this was lax prescription. He also supplied her with sleeping drugs.[19]

On the one side stood Stuart, a figure of authority but flawed in his judgment, who supplied her with drugs legally; on the other was the dubious Reggie De Veulle, who supplied her with drugs from the underground channels of supply. As her dress designer, he could receive sums of money from her without suspicion, though not authorised by his employers to collect accounts. He was no trafficker in the popular sense of the term, however. His sole requirement was to get hold of supplies for himself, and for Carleton, his partner in doping. She knew the same dealers as he did, but he was willing to make the arrangements, just as Stuart was willing to make sure her bills were paid. De Veulle would incur grave legal consequences as the result of his readiness to take care of such matters for his friend.

Reggie De Veulle had been married in July 1916, to Pauline Gay, a Frenchwoman. In several respects, it looks like a marriage of convenience. She was a family friend, a forty year-old spinster (five years his senior) who worked as a dressmaker and lived a few doors away from him in Half Moon Street, in Mayfair. After their marriage, they were employed together by Hockley's as dress designers, on a combined salary of £1200 a year.[20] Pauline De Veulle came to be fond of Billie Carleton, but resented the influence Carleton had over her husband, complaining that the actress 'was always sending him here, there and everywhere'.[21] Reggie was the first to agree: 'I practically did all her shopping for her all the time.'[22]

He also claimed he had to borrow money from Billie because of Pauline's grip on the purse-strings. 'She often lent me a fiver, because my wife keeps all the money. I am so frightfully extravagant.'[23] Just like Billie, in tone as well as habit. They were birds of a feather, also, in another financial respect. Billie had a rich patron in John Marsh; in his own youth, Reggie had enjoyed the largesse of the middle-aged businessman William Cronshaw – a relationship which would come back to haunt him.

Billie Carleton was both a new woman and an old-fashioned girl. She was ambitious in her career, and lived to a standard that far surpassed her sisters' aspirations, remarkable as these were at the time. But she had chosen a traditional means by which women could rise from poverty to celebrity; one which had very little to do with labour solidarity or feminist campaigning, and very much to do with the relationships between young women and older men in positions of power. She had placed herself at the centre of a triangle of such men: Marsh with his money; De Veulle with his publicity contacts; Stuart with his status as a physician.

It was an arrangement she was adept at manipulating. One way or another, Billie had all three of them wrapped around her finger. She behaved as a girl was expected to behave, tending to the infantile; she asked for presents and got them; she persuaded others to take on her chores or her adult responsibilities. But none of these relationships had the emotional depth to save her 'from the bottomless pit of darkness, despair and depression' to which Stuart had so dramatically referred.

She does not seem to have been close to anybody else, either; or not for long, at any rate. Her friendship with a cinema actress called Malvina Longfellow deteriorated into recrimination over drugs and De Veulle. One evening, tired of Longfellow's strictures about dope, Reggie De Veulle took a manicure instrument from Billie's dressing-table and sniffed some cocaine off it, Billie following suit. Despite her anger, Longfellow continued to urge him not to give Billie cocaine. Carleton herself ended up calling Longfellow a 'snake in the grass', believing that Malvina was spreading malicious stories about her and Reggie.[24]

Malvina Longfellow also tried to snatch a packet of cocaine from Carleton over tea at the Carlton Hotel one day, but it was retrieved by Billie's escort, an American lieutenant named Boyle.[25] He was most likely the officer who, in September 1918, kicked down the door of Billie's flat in Long Acre after she rejected his proposal of marriage. When he threatened to kill her, Carleton fled from Covent Garden to the De Veulles' flat in Mayfair.[26]

The officer followed, trying to kick down the De Veulles' door as well. Reggie called the authorities, and in due course the man was sent back to the United States. Billie's stay continued to disrupt the De Veulles' domestic life: she was hardly a model guest.

A clique of drugtakers had now coalesced around her and Reggie. De Veulle had originally bought cocaine from a couple in Limehouse, Lau Ping You and his Scottish wife Ada. Dissatisfied with its quality, however, he turned to Lionel Belcher, a cinema actor. Reggie and Billie had met Belcher and his girlfriend Olive Richardson earlier in the summer at a flat in Notting Hill Gate. Dining at the Savoy and discussing the eternal question of where to obtain cocaine, Billie had told Reggie she knew somewhere where it was to be had. They arrived at the Pembridge Road flat around one in the morning: Reggie's old acquaintance Don Kimfull was not very pleased to see them. Belcher, semi-conscious on heroin, mustered the courtesy of pulling himself to his feet to shake Carleton's hand. Kimfull laughed at Carleton's request for cocaine, but gave De Veulle a brandy and soda to send him on his way.[27]

Belcher knew that Don Kimfull bought drugs from Wooldridge's, the Lisle Street chemist's shop patronised by the West End street dealers before the passage of DORA 40B. He called at the shop and did the same, selling some of the cocaine to De Veulle at double the price. The new connection was a boon to De Veulle's servant, nicknamed by him McGinty, who now found herself hanging round the side of the Café Royal or calling at the flat Belcher shared with Richardson in Great Portland Street; a great improvement on 'water up to your knees and dirty black rooms' in Limehouse.[28]

Carleton also got Belcher to take her down to Limehouse himself; she returned early the next morning suffering from the after-effects of opium again. Pauline De Veulle cannot have been pleased: she was a reluctant doper, being persuaded to smoke for the first time at one of a series of opium parties held by her husband, Carleton, Belcher, Richardson and a couple of other friends. Despite Pauline's objection, Carleton hosted one of these parties during her stay at the Dover Street flat. Late one Saturday night in September the clique assembled after dinner to recline in a circle on their cushions, where they remained until three o'clock the following afternoon.[29]

In the centre of the group, Ada Lau Ping 'cooked' the opium. A pellet of the drug is stuck on the end of an instrument resembling a knitting needle, and heated in the flame of a lamp. When it starts to bubble, it is scraped into the bowl of the pipe. Keeping the tarry resin alight is difficult, the movie Chinamen with their churchwardens and billows of smoke notwithstanding.

The advent of peace, on 11 November, set in train Billie Carleton's final drama. After four years, Reggie De Veulle had almost ended up serving the country himself. The manpower shortage was so acute that even De Veulle, in his late thirties, had been called up. In the eventful month of September, Dr Stuart had testified at the draft tribunal that, as a cocaine addict, De Veulle was unfit to be a soldier. In the taxi after the hearing, Stuart warned De Veulle not to give Billie Carleton any cocaine.[30] And as De Veulle danced with Malvina Longfellow at the Criterion on Armistice Night, in evening dress instead of a khaki uniform, she pressed the same message upon him.[31] A week later, Scotland Yard had learned about De Veulle's involvement with the drug traffic.[32] But events were to move too quickly for tragedy to be averted by police action.

Carleton was now installed in her own flat at the prestigious Savoy Court, a block of self-contained apartments built before the war at the back of the Savoy Hotel. The address suited her aspirations but not her means. Her impressive savings had gone – unsurprisingly, given that she was capable of running up bills for flowers alone of over twenty pounds; a week's wages for her, and a month's for a relatively well-paid factory worker. Drugs were expensive too, now they were illegal. Carleton spent five or ten pounds a time on her cocaine and opium.[33]

Savoy Court was a fine base from which to seize the opportunities of peace. Foreign travel would be easier, and thanks to her agent, engagements abroad were in prospect. She was to appear on the Paris stage, for £40 a week, and was in line for her first film role, at £50 a week.[34] And pleasure would no longer be restrained by patriotism. The blinds had been lifted briefly on Armistice Night, when the carnival of the day was permitted to carry on and light the darkness which had been imposed on the capital for the past four years. Though DORA remained irksomely in force, its restraints were loosened. Within days, preparations were under way for a great Victory Ball, to be held at the Albert Hall (despite threats of a blackout by electricians, in protest against a ban on the use of the venue for a Labour rally). Billie Carleton wanted to look 'wonderfully brilliant'; she commanded Reggie De Veulle to create her a 'wonderful frock' for the occasion.[35]

The Ball was sponsored by the *Daily Sketch* and its proceeds were to go to the Nation's Fund for Nurses. It was a celebration of women's achievement as well the Allied triumph. 'To-day women of the Allied nations take part in the festival of victory as a right,' the *Daily Sketch* observed. 'They have earned that right in hospitals at home and abroad; in the fields as labourers ploughing and garnering the grain; in the workshops turning out shells; in the towns doing men's work; in the homes suffering in silence.'[36] The *Daily Telegraph* recalled that the last fancy dress ball to be held at the Albert Hall, celebrating the centenary of peace between Britain and the United States in June 1914, had been interrupted by a suffragette who harangued the crowd until removed 'amid angry thrusts from the palm branches of those grouped around'.[37] A couple of weeks after the Victory Ball, women – those of them over thirty, at any rate – were able to exercise their newly won right to vote for the first time.

Whatever Reggie De Veulle may have thought about the historic symbolism of the event, his immediate concern was that he 'knew perfectly well you could not get a single drink there'.[38] The solution, naturally, was cocaine. There was a complication, however. The Saturday before the Ball, he and Billie went round to Belcher's for a doping session, staying out until four in the morning. Pauline De Veulle was furious, objecting both to the drugs and to the indiscretion. Billie and Reggie had to keep their arrangements to buy cocaine secret from Pauline. In the next few days, Reggie sent McGinty to collect 'coke' from Belcher twice.[39]

On Wednesday, the day of the Ball, Billie's first call was at noon. She met John Marsh and went with him to the pawnbroker's where her jewellery was in hock; that night, luxury would not only be permissible, but obligatory. Marsh paid £1050 – not much less than the De Veulles' combined annual income – to redeem jewellery worth twice that, most of which he had given her himself.[40] By this point she had precisely £9 13s left in the bank, and owed £175; most of it to Hockley's.

To expedite a busy schedule, she hired a taxi for the day. She went on to Hockley's, where she encountered Pauline. Mrs De Veulle was still incensed about the previous Saturday, and gave Billie a piece of her mind. Pauline did not suspect a dalliance herself – or said she didn't – but did not want the entire West End suspecting one either. To her, Billie and her husband seemed set on a course of self-absorbed folly. Incidents like the flaunting of cocaine in front of Malvina Longfellow, pricelessly amusing to Billie and Reggie, looked childish and foolhardy to Pauline. Having a drug fiend for a husband would be bad enough in itself; it was intolerable that he should carry on with a young actress in a way that risked his wife's public humiliation.

Both women ended up in tears, and Billie stormed out in a fury. Reggie, meanwhile, had slipped over the road for a drink. Later in the day, Billie went to tea with John Marsh, and then it was time for the theatre.[41]

Freedom of the Seas consisted of featherweight comedy resting on stilted adventure, twice nightly. The male lead, trapped in morning-coat and top hat at the high Victorian desk of a solicitor's office, is spurned as a weakling by Billie Carleton's character. Her emotional evolution turns her towards older men of substance, one of whom is conveniently available. 'I fancied somehow that a woman could only find happiness in the love of a strong man who dominated her,' she reflects. 'Well, I've changed my mind. I want to marry an old slow-coach.'

The action transfers to a steamer, where the male lead becomes a hero by defeating the smuggler who plans to rendezvous with a U-boat. The submarine is sunk, with loud reports, by a seaplane; the hero and Billie are together, the smuggler's prone body to one side. The hero sweeps Billie into his arms and they kiss. The curtain falls.

That night of 27 November, the curtain fell on Billie Carleton for the last time. She left her public and got ready to go among her peers. She summoned two visitors to her dressing-room. One was an Italian officer (yet another gentlemen in middle life) who had been recently paying her court, whom she wanted to admire her Ball costume. The other was her maid, May Booker, whom she had instructed to bring a little gold box – borrowed from Pauline De Veulle and not returned – from her dressing-table at home.[42]

She ate dinner with Fay Compton before they went to the Ball, Compton escorted by a lieutenant and Carleton by Dr Stuart. It was a night, overwhelmingly, of colour, ceremonially replacing the drab and mourning of wartime. Blue and white dominated the decorations, to honour the nurses, who mingled on the floor with Guardsmen in their scarlet dress uniforms. Out of their boxes at last, after the sobriety of the martial period, the ladies' jewels glittered conspicuously. Revellers in mufti wore evening dress or fancy dress. Pauline De Veulle's costume represented France, while Reggie went as Harlequin, in ruff and hose.

The greater glory was that of the pageant, which swept in to the sound of 'Pomp and Circumstance' just before midnight. The cohort of society women was led by Lady Diana Manners, as Britannia. Behind her the gamut of symbolic figures ran from Britain's constituent nations, through the Dominions to the Allies; the United States, France, Belgium, Portugal, Japan, Egypt, Serbia, Montenegro, Siam, Romania, and China; and onwards. There were the Sun, the Stars, the Arts, Cleopatra, a Beardsley Drawing, and the Spirit of 1919, in a white gown and a silver-lined cloak of cherry velvet. Last of all came Peace, riding on a chariot drawn by six ancient British shepherds, and followed by six tall maids, carrying wheatsheaves and lilies.[43]

All grouped themselves around a living Union Flag, while the Brigade of Guards band played 'Rule Britannia'. Then they dispersed and the dancing resumed until the small hours. Billie Carleton danced with Frederick Stuart for a while, then made for a box. She avoided the De Veulles; Belcher, however, bumped into Reggie in the sanctuary of

THE CURTAIN.

More final than they knew. (Mander & Mitchenson)

the gentlemen's lavatory, where Reggie was about to sniff some of his cocaine. Pauline had thrown one packet of it away before they set out, but left the silver box he said was for Billie. Elsewhere in the Hall, Duff Cooper asked Lady Diana Manners' mother for her daughter's hand in marriage.

At two or three in the morning, Billie departed with a taxi-full of friends. Fay Compton and her lieutenant were dropped off in Kensington, Dr Stuart got out in Knightsbridge; Lionel Belcher and Olive Richardson accompanied Billie back to Savoy Court. Another visitor called; the dance star Irene Castle, internationally renowned for the partnership with her husband Vernon that had ended with his death in a military flying accident earlier that year. Billie donned her jewels again, so expensively ransomed, and popped out to show her costume to Mrs Castle.[44]

When Billie returned, the three of them breakfasted on the bacon and eggs she had ordered, and she talked; about Pauline De Veulle, heatedly, and about her own bright prospects. Eventually she changed into a kimono and got into bed, continuing the conversation. She spoke excitedly of her coming engagement in Paris, and of going to America to get into the movies. At five or six o'clock, her guests left. Belcher turned the lights out as he went, leaving one burning by the side of the bed. Billie was sitting up; happy, awake, and expectant.

At around ten, she telephoned a friend, Violet Chown, to postpone the previous night's tea arrangement from the afternoon to the early evening. May Booker arrived to begin work at eleven-thirty. Hearing loud snores from the bedroom, she assumed her mistress would sleep till about noon. At about half past three, Booker realised that the snoring had stopped. She went in and tried to wake Carleton, unsuccessfully; she called the doctor. Stuart gave her artificial respiration, and injected her with brandy and strychnine. Those treatments proving unsuccessful, nothing remained but to pronounce her dead.

6

UNHOLY RITES

Soon attendants began to bustle and hover around the body. The police surgeon arrived, and the hotel manager, and Gianni Bettini. The surgeon, Dr Hamerton, recorded the appearance of the corpse: she lay on her side, her pupils dilated, a blueness under her fingernails, a stain at the corner of her mouth. She looked peaceful among the blankets and discarded clothes.

The little gold box was on the dressing table, half full of cocaine. Bettini also told Hamerton that he had seen a box of veronal cachets – barbiturates – the day before. But when he took the doctor to the corner of the bedroom where it had been, he found it gone. (Under the circumstances, the question of how he had been in a position to see it was overlooked.) Hamerton declared that it had to be found. Dr Stuart, who had been in the sitting room, terminated the search by producing a box of cachets from his pocket. At Bettini's suggestion, he handed it over to the police surgeon.[1]

Stuart knew that Carleton's death would raise awkward questions, particularly concerning the sources of the various drugs she took. Other friends of the deceased shared his reflexive impulse to cover their traces. The following day, Inspector John Curry called on De Veulle, ostensibly to check his nationality papers. Surprising him in bed, Curry took him in to Scotland Yard. On the way, De Veulle told the officer he had been upset because he thought the visit was about Carleton's death. She had lunched at his flat on Wednesday, he said, and afterwards they went to the Ball together.[2]

This was a pointless and easily disproved lie: De Veulle was panicky. He told Mary Hicks, 'McGinty', that detectives were following him. His nerves were further tested by a visit from Lionel Belcher, who had read of the death in the paper late on the Friday morning. Belcher arrived with his solicitor, George Rose Cran, whom he had extracted from a Mayfair establishment called the Nimrod Club, reputedly a gambling den. The actor asked De Veulle directly whether he had given Billie Carleton any cocaine. 'Nobody has seen me give it to Billie, except Miss Longfellow,' De Veulle replied. He knew nothing about the affair, was not going to know anything about it, and advised Belcher not to know anything either. The solicitor thought Belcher should listen to that advice.[3]

Belcher also went to see Alfred Angelo Toose, a bohemian dilettante – variously described as an actor, drama critic, playwright, art critic and journalist – who had also been part of the drug network that was now threatened with exposure. He gave Toose a bottle of cocaine and told him to destroy it. Instead, Toose kept it, and later sent it over by messenger to Cran, for use as evidence; the idea was to shield Belcher from accusations of supplying cocaine by showing that the bottle was full.[4]

For a few days, the scandal brewed. Carleton's *Times* obituary, which noted her 'considerable reputation as an actress of charm and intelligence', referred to poor health following a bout of influenza.[5] This was the time of the great influenza pandemic; over the past six weeks, the disease had killed 32,000 people in Britain, many of them young and previously healthy.[6] But rumours rapidly began to circulate that this particular death had been caused by dope.

They were confirmed when the inquest opened the following week. After the first session, De Veulle's tension exploded into fury, directed against his hapless servant. 'If you give me away, I will get your separation allowance stopped, and see your baby starved,' he threatened.[7] Hicks decided she respected the court's authority more than her master's, and became a key witness against him.

Belcher began his testimony by perjuring himself, then took Cran's advice to make a clean breast of it. If prosecutions were to follow, he would be better off as a Crown witness. He turned up at Scotland Yard one day, where he was seen by Sir Henry Curtis-Bennett, later an eminent barrister, but then on attachment to the police from the Secret Service. Curtis-Bennett took Belcher to see the coroner, Samuel Ingleby Oddie, who was discussing the case with Sir Basil Thomson at the time; the actor made a full confession.[8]

That did not prevent the inquest dragging on through December and January, keeping the fire of scandal fuelled. Outside the court, the crowds began to gather from seven in the morning, even though Oddie did not sit until two-thirty in the afternoon.

Ada Lau Ping was the first judicial casualty, arrested in the 'dirty black rooms' recalled by Mary Hicks. The dilapidated house stood at the eastern end of Limehouse Causeway, huddled under the railway bridge, still in use today, that leads to the Isle of Dogs. After a lengthy search, a squad led by Inspector Curry unearthed opium utensils and a phial of the drug, as well as two revolvers. When the phial was found, Lau Ping You tried to get his hands on the small quantity inside. He told the police he had been smoking since he was eleven, and needed his daily dose to stave off the withdrawal sickness.[9]

Ada was charged with possession and supply offences arising out of the Dover Street opium party. At Marlborough Street Police Court, she was unlucky enough to find herself in front of Frederick Mead. This septuagenarian beak knew himself to be a Victorian anachronism; it seemed to strengthen his resolve to brandish the stick of patriarchy to the last. He made his stand under the banner of a conservatism preoccupied with vice, indecency and the containment of women within a domain where they would not be exposed to such evils. As such, he was the bane not just of defendants, but of the new women police. He had a horror of discussing vice cases in the presence of women, and was appalled that women should be policing such matters. When a 'Woman Patrol' described 'backwards and forwards' movements made by a couple accused of having sexual intercourse in Hyde Park, an incident observed by two other eye-witnesses, Mead dismissed the charge and called the patrolwoman one of those 'abnormal women who seem to suffer from some sort of moral obliquity'.[10]

As late as 1927, Mead fined a man for sunbathing in the Park without a shirt on. In 1919, the prosecution case against Ada Lau Ping must have brought him close to apoplexy. The court heard how the 'circle of degenerates' at the opium party had undressed and changed into nightclothes; pyjamas for the men, and chiffon nightdresses for the women.[11] Pauline De Veulle later insisted, with professional precision, that the women wore chiffon dresses trimmed with lace and *crêpe de chine* tea gowns.[12] But pyjamas and nightdresses were *de rigueur* for American opium parties, which were particularly popular in entertainment industry circles.[13] Though the British public was ignorant of such debauches, which were to flourish in the 1920s, both Billie Carleton and Reggie De Veulle had American connections. Perhaps Jack May had told Billie about the practice, or Reggie had indulged in it while in the States.

The prosecution called the case 'disgraceful to modern civilisation', and Frederick Mead heartily concurred. 'That this orgy, as it has been described, had gone on for a number of hours, from 9 o'clock to 3 o'clock in the afternoon, is disgraceful,' he commented, describing Ada Lau Ping as 'the high priestess at these unholy rites'. He gave her an exemplary sentence of five months' hard labour.

Her husband, charged with possessing opium, fared very differently. His case was heard at Thames Police Court, by a magistrate with local knowledge. 'I have a difficulty here to contend with,' said Mr Rooth, who refused to take the background to the arrest into account. 'A man comes before me who is suffering from what I must call a national vice. It is one which is almost universally practised, as I understand, in his own country, but it is an offence if committed in this country.' Lau Ping You could have been sentenced to six months' hard labour, fined £100, and given a deportation order, but Rooth let him off with a £10 fine.[14] Not long afterwards, Rooth refused to issue a deportation order on a Chinese cook caught with a whole pound of opium, fining the man £22 for the 'national vice'.[15]

Between them, the two magistrates demonstrated the range of opinion within the realms of power concerning drugs. Mead readily lent his authority to the moral panic that had ensued from Carleton's death, using imaginative terms as rich as anything dreamed up by the popular papers. For a man so intransigently opposed to allowing women even an approximation of the authority of a constable, criminal vice presided over by a woman was akin to blasphemy, or witchcraft.

For Rooth, on the other hand, opium charges were no more than an unfortunate contradiction between the law of one country and the culture of another. He might have seen it differently from the bench at Marlborough Street, however. The tradition of tolerance towards opium rested on the assumption that the introverted Chinese community would not transmit its vice to the indigenous population. A Chinaman might enjoy his pipe in Limehouse without posing a threat to society, but a woman crossing the East-West divide to bring the foreign drug to Mayfair was a different story. As Mary Douglas has observed, pollution is matter in the wrong place.[16]

A second summary case arising from the inquest shed further light on Mead's attitudes. Alfred Toose was arrested by Detective-Sergeant Burmby and charged with possession of the cocaine bottle that Belcher gave him to destroy, but which he passed to Belcher's solicitor. Despite the prosecution's claim that Toose was a dealer who bought cocaine from Don Kimfull and sold it to De Veulle, Mead acquitted him, saying that nobody could blame him for putting his friend before

THE OPIUM SMOKER'S OUTFIT.

OPIUM JAR

THE LAMP

PIPE

NEEDLE

AN EAST-END OPIUM DEN.

A WEST-END OPIUM DEN.

OUR ARTIST'S VISIT TO OPIUM DENS.

Effect of opium on the artistic imagination. (2 January 1919. By permission of the British Library.)

his duty to the state. In other words, the codes of male friendship were above the law. The decision was greeted with applause.[17]

As the inquest itself progressed, it dwelt increasingly on character. Lionel Belcher had begun badly by lying and then admitting it. His credibility as a witness was undermined by his nonchalant admissions of drug use. He was 'more addicted to heroin than anything else', he said, probably indicating a preference rather than a dependency.[18] Both addiction and heroin were relatively new terms; the exact meaning of the former may have been unclear to Belcher, and that of the latter would have previously been unknown to most of his listeners.

Taken to task over his admission that he sold the cocaine from Wooldridge's to De Veulle for twice what he paid for it, he revealed an equally casual attitude. 'I don't look upon it as any more despicable than selling a bottle of whisky at an over-charged rate, after time,' he replied. A couple of women in the court gave a muffled 'hear, hear', quickly suppressed.[19]

Not all the publicity Belcher received was bad. Reviewing a new film in which he starred, entitled *Bonnie Mary*, the *Kinematograph & Lantern Weekly* praised 'Leon' Belcher's 'remarkable powers as an emotional. His acting in certain scenes has yet to be beaten by any screen actor we have seen.'[20] Less happily, the magazine subsequently advertised another five-reel drama entitled *Love's Legacy*, 'featuring Lionel Belcher (so prominently before the public of the present day). A great story – showing how the unselfish love of a woman saves a young boy from the dangers of London life.' The principal danger was the 'Drug Curse'.[21]

Belcher's real-life relationships with women presented a less edifying spectacle. On cross-examination, he admitted that he was married, that he was living with Olive Richardson, and had been sleeping with another woman while she was in a nursing home the previous summer.[22] Mrs Gladys Belcher was most interested to read about all this in the papers, and filed for divorce.

When the plea was heard some months later, Mrs Belcher described how he seduced her when she was sixteen and he about twenty, then married her two years later, in 1915. Once, at her mother's, he threw a vase at her, after getting into a jealous rage because soldiers billeted at the house were recounting stories from the front. Another time he went into a fury because he found the signatures of 'men of colour' – music-hall artists – in her autograph album. He dragged her across the

MISS OLIVE RICHARDSON.
(Foulsham and Banfield.)

MR. LIONEL BELCHER.
(Foulsham and Banfield.)

Daily Graphic, 3 January 1919. (By permission of the British Library.)

floor by her hair, and hit her in the face. Later he said she was silly to make a fuss, and could go with any man he liked. Next day he brought a man back to their Hammersmith home and suggested she did; when she refused, he hit her in the face again. Sick of his cruelty and boasts of sexual conquests, she left him and settled down with someone else. Her divorce petition was dismissed, on the grounds that she was at liberty to live a chaste life if she wanted.[23]

All that came out some time after the Carleton proceedings had been concluded, however. At the inquest, it was Reggie De Veulle who faced the most determined attempts at character assassination. The press were quick to note that he did not present the figure of an upstanding Englishman, describing his 'somewhat foreign appearance and accent', or, more boldly, his 'effeminate face and mincing little smile'.[24] Keen to divert opprobrium away from their own clients, the lawyers representing Belcher and Kimfull worked this vein gratefully.

The more devastating assault was mounted by Cecil Hayes, Belcher's counsel. 'How long have you been engaged in the gentle art of designing ladies' dresses?' he began, leading De Veulle to reply that

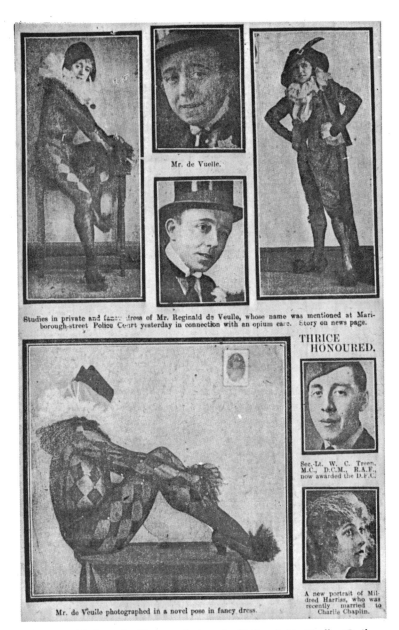

'The one with the arched instep, nicely poised': Reggie De Veulle. (*Daily Sketch*, 21 December 1918. By permission of the British Library.)

he had previously been on the stage. 'You were what we may call, without being offensive, in the chorus?' Hayes inquired. 'How were you dressed – as a girl, or a boy?' De Veulle indignantly denied ever appearing as a girl. The lawyer handed him a copy of the *Daily Sketch* containing pictures of Reggie in his Victory Ball costume. 'Did you supply this photo to the paper – the one with the arched instep, nicely poised?' Reggie's vanity had rebounded on him. The newspaper had not run the shots of him at the time of the Ball, but pulled them out when the scandal broke.[25]

By this stage, Reggie was anything but nicely poised. Having softened him up with innuendo, Hayes moved in for the kill. 'I put it to you that while your youth lasted you often made curious friendships with older men?' he said. De Veulle knew what was coming. 'Has that anything to do with this case at all?' he demanded. 'You have put yourself forward as a man of honour,' Hayes pointed out. 'More than that, you attack Belcher's character,' the coroner added.

Hayes closed in. 'I believe these curious friendships that you made with older men that you made in your youth were sometimes very paying, were they not?' De Veulle fenced, claiming not to understand the question. 'Were some friendships with men much older than you very remunerative for you? Don't answer in a hurry,' Hayes sarcastically advised. De Veulle conceded that he had been given money by William Cronshaw, and was forced to listen as Hayes gave details of the 1911 blackmail case.[26]

Don Kimfull evaded his subpoena by sending a message that he had pleurisy. He managed, in fact, to avoid appearing at any of the hearings in the entire affair. His counsel, Mr Myers, began by referring to Hayes' line of inquiry about theatrical cross-dressing. He succeeded in getting De Veulle to deny any suggestions that Kimfull was involved with drugs, before producing his own skeleton from De Veulle's closet. This was the book he had given Kimfull, describing his adventures, and including the account of the drag party at Maidenhead that had been broken up by outraged locals. At this point, the coroner upheld the objection of De Veulle's counsel and ruled the book inadmissible – frustratingly, before Myers had given enough information to make it traceable.

Persisting on a different tack, Myers was able to needle De Veulle into a gaffe that did nothing to allay the doubts raised about his character. 'What was it that attracted Miss Carleton to you so much?'

DAILY SKETCH, FRIDAY, JANUARY 24, 1919.

BILLIE CARLETON AND DE VEULLE: THE JURY'S VERDICT

DAILY SKETCH.

No. 3,680. Telephones: { London—Holborn 4412. Manchester—City 4361. } LONDON, FRIDAY, JANUARY 24, 1919. [Registered as a Newspaper.] ONE PENNY.

DE VEULLE CHARGED WITH MANSLAUGHTER.

One of the latest portraits of Billie Carleton, the dead actress.

De Veulle in the witness-box at the Coroner's Court yesterday, answering questions put by Mr. Ingleby Oddie, the coroner.

Another studio portrait of Billie Carleton. She was one of the most beautiful women on the stage.

De Veulle reading an account of the previous hearing.—(Daily Sketch.)

De Veulle in fancy-dress costume. He was a regular patron of fancy-dress balls.—(Exclusive Photograph.)

De Veulle in the attire of a man about town. He was always well dressed, and latterly was a familiar figure in theatre-land.

Lionel Belcher, a witness, who, said the coroner, had been guilty of an unlawful act.

Mrs. de Veulle in a fancy dress costume she wore at a recent ball.

Another snapshot of De Veulle in the witness-box.—(Daily Sketch.)

Mrs. "McGinty," whom the coroner described as "more simple than wicked."

At the conclusion of the inquest yesterday on Billie Carleton the jury returned a verdict that the actress died from an overdose of cocaine self-administered, but that she had no intention of committing suicide. "We are of opinion," added the foreman, "that the drug was supplied by De Veulle." This being a verdict of manslaughter against De Veulle he was taken into custody, the Coroner refusing to grant bail. Full story on news pages.

By permission of the British Library.

94

Myers demanded. 'Really, that is an extraordinary question,' De Veulle protested. Myers repeated it. 'My beauty, I suppose,' returned De Veulle. Apt as that sort of brittle repartee might be in a theatrical green room, in court it hit ice. Irony was not only unseemly, as Myers was swift to point out, but unmanly.

These exchanges brought the cross-examination of witnesses almost to a close, leaving De Veulle to await the verdict covered in odium. The coroner's direction to the jury was clear, his final observations recalling the appeals made by Dr Stuart and Malvina Longfellow for De Veulle not to give Billie Carleton any cocaine. The jury took fifteen minutes to find that Carleton died of an inadvertent cocaine overdose, 'supplied to her by De Veulle in a culpable and negligent manner'.[27] It had found him guilty of manslaughter. After letting him give Pauline a farewell embrace, Inspector Curry took him into custody.[28]

Brixton Prison and the winter months took their toll on De Veulle's health. He collapsed in the witness box at one point during the committal hearings; the drama was subsequently lowered, however, when his lawyer revealed that his complaint was haemorrhoids. The magistrate refused bail, so as not to give him the opportunity to take drugs.[29]

The case eventually reached the Old Bailey in March. Raoul Reginald De Veulle faced two charges; manslaughter, and conspiracy (with Ada Lau Ping) to supply cocaine. He was defended by Huntly Jenkins and prosecuted by Sir Richard Muir. The notorious murderer Crippen had quailed when told that Muir was to prosecute him: the Scottish advocate was renowned for his ruthlessness and attention to detail. The judge was Mr Justice Salter, known as Drysalter on account of his temperament.

The trial went over the same ground as the inquest and committal proceedings. Like Ingleby Oddie, Salter gave the jury a clear direction to find De Veulle guilty of manslaughter. This time, however, there was a surprise ending. After retiring for fifty minutes, the jury returned to announce his acquittal. For once, Muir had failed to get his man. The courtroom was pierced by a shrill scream from Pauline De Veulle, followed by muted applause from the public benches.[30]

De Veulle did not escape jail, though. He pleaded guilty to the conspiracy charge, for which there was more than ample evidence. Taking into account De Veulle's clean record and poor health, Salter sentenced him to eight months without hard labour. Despite the mitigation, and despite the fact that, unlike the street dealers who had been the principal targets of drug policing after the passage of DORA 40B, De Veulle had not supplied drugs for gain, he received the heaviest drug sentence so far. Times had changed, irreversibly. Before sending De Veulle off to Wormwood Scrubs, Judge Salter observed that it was 'a strange thing to reflect that until quite lately these drugs could be bought by all and sundry like so much grocery'.[31]

The jury had taken remarkably little time to reject Judge Salter's encouragement to convict Reggie De Veulle of manslaughter. Whatever its reasons, it had terminated a train of legal error that had begun when Ingleby Oddie dismissed the uncertainties of the forensic evidence in his summing-up at the inquest. The manslaughter charge should never have been brought in the first place.

The principle was unarguable; that a person doing an unlawful act, which led to the death of another, was guilty of constructive manslaughter. There was no reasonable doubt that Reggie De Veulle had supplied Billie Carleton with cocaine, and had done so shortly before the Victory Ball; nor that Carleton had sniffed cocaine in the hours preceding her death. There was no reason to doubt that her death was drug-induced. But the question of manslaughter hangs on whether the drug in question was cocaine.

To put it at its simplest, what happened to Billie Carleton just doesn't smell like a cocaine death. She did not meet her end as the Yeoland sisters had, back in 1901; convulsively, in a sudden crisis, her head a cauldron of pain, her heart forced precipitately beyond its endurance. There is a certain horrible glory – or drama, at least – to a classical death by cocaine. The theatrical overtones that accompanied the last hours of Billie Carleton's life, by contrast, were those of tragedy disguised as farce: the loud snores that, had her maid but known it, were the last attempts of a failing respiratory system to keep the breath in her body.

The manner of Carleton's death suggests she was killed by an agency that depressed her vital bodily functions to the point where they ceased, or failed to overcome any modest challenge with which they were presented, rather than by something that stimulated her organism past its limits. In other words, candidates for the lethal agent would be narcotics or sedatives – opiates or barbiturates – rather than a stimulant such as cocaine.[32]

This immediately suggests a scenario; one that has been repeated, with tragic results, countless times since. On the morning of the day she died, Carleton had been awake since at least noon the day before. She had begun with a busy round of encounters that ran an emotional gamut, from a bitter row with Pauline De Veulle at Hockley's, to spending over a thousand pounds of John Marsh's money at the pawnbroker's where her jewellery had been in hock. Then she appeared in two performances at the Haymarket, went to supper, and then spent several hours at the Ball, before entertaining Lionel Belcher and Olive Richardson over an early breakfast. She showed off her jewellery to Irene Castle, boasted of her glittering prospects to Belcher and Richardson, and complained of Pauline De Veulle's jealousy. When Belcher and Richardson left, she was sitting up in bed.

It is not difficult to imagine how she felt then. She was exhausted, overexcited; she had been chattering and holding court for hours. There was nothing to do except get some rest, but the static from the cocaine frustrated the demands of a fatigued body. She took some sort of depressant, which reached a stalemate with the residue of the cocaine and smoothed the rough edges off the stimulant hangover. She dozed for an hour or two, then found herself awake; phoned Mrs Chown while she remembered to do so, and took some more depressant to get back to sleep, making a further debit from a nervous system now overdrawn after its cocaine spending spree. Sleeping under this burden of toxic substances was like sleeping on a precipice. She entered a profound coma, and eventually choked; on some fluid secretion, or perhaps on her tongue.

Although this scenario is unverifiable, it is consistent with forensic evidence and the testimony of witnesses. It also provides a simple and plausible suggestion to fill in the gap of witness testimony between the departure of Belcher and Richardson and the arrival of May Booker, the maid. And above all, it has the ring of drugtaking truth about it. Billie Carleton was what is now called a multiple drug abuser. She used cocaine regularly, smoked opium, and had tried heroin; she also took hypnotics – sleeping drugs – on prescription. In that mode, depressants follow stimulants as night follows day.

Of the depressant candidates, opium can be ruled out immediately. Although police procedures at scenes of death left much to be desired in those days, investigators could hardly have missed the paraphernalia needed to smoke opium. Heroin, on the other hand, could simply be sniffed, like cocaine. According to Dr Stuart, Carleton had not liked heroin when she tried it, because it had no effect on her.[33] Lionel Belcher, one of the last two people to see her alive, admitted taking some heroin with him to the Ball.[34] He and Carleton had a track record of taking drugs together; he was not averse to making a few pounds selling drugs to fellow users. It is not beyond the bounds of possibility that he sold Carleton a quantity which she took in its entirety; whether because her judgment was scrambled by cocaine and fatigue, or because her previous experience led her to believe she was resistant to its effects; or because, inexperienced, she made the disastrous assumption that heroin required as big a sniff as cocaine.

Heroin would not potentiate the action of cocaine; in other words, Carleton would have suffered a heroin overdose, rather than a combined overdose of cocaine and heroin. De Veulle's action in supplying her with cocaine would not have led directly to her death, and he would therefore have been innocent of manslaughter. And so would Belcher, since heroin was not covered by DORA 40B.

It is unlikely that Belcher bore even moral guilt for Carleton's death, however. Not only is the heroin hypothesis entirely speculative, but it does not fit the observations well. Heroin has a relatively short duration of action, producing its maximum effects within minutes. In fatal overdose, it tends to slow the breathing rate, to three or four breaths a minute, and then halt it altogether. Barbiturates, on the other hand, are likely to act over a longer period; a more regular breathing rate, and snoring, are characteristic of their effects. Billie Carleton's death has the typical aroma of a barbiturate overdose.

Dr Stuart confirmed that Carleton had used a hypnotic to relieve the sleeplessness induced by cocaine. It was not a barbiturate, however, but trional, a relative of a compound called sulphonal that had been in use since the 1880s. Contemporary pharmacopoeias do not list acute overdose among its possible hazards. The box Stuart admitted giving her had contained just four twenty-grain cachets, one of which she had given to a friend.[35]

Not, then, an item to be terribly concerned about; of negligible value, and less than a toxic quantity. Indeed, Stuart's testimony, that he had lent the cachets to Carleton, rather than prescribing them to her, implied that he regarded trional with insouciance. Yet, with his friend and patient lying dead nearby, he was concerned enough about that little box to pocket it – a quite improper action for a medical man to take at the scene of a death that would require an inquest. His subsequent explanation, that it was his property and might be lost in the commotion, was no more convincing than Reggie De Veulle's claim that what he had sniffed in front of Malvina Longfellow was face-powder, not cocaine.

The disappearance of the box was noted by Gianni Bettini, the Italian officer, who believed that it had been labelled 'veronal'. Stuart testified that the officer had been mistaken; a reasonable possibility, in the shocking presence of a corpse. But even if that were the case, the question remains: why remove it, in breach of the proper procedure? Perhaps Stuart was worried that its discovery would lead to more searching inquiries about the drugs he supplied to Billie Carleton. Both veronal and trional came in cachets. May Booker reported having seen black pills not long before: possibly other drugs lay unnoticed among Carleton's untidy belongings. These observations were not followed up, and the matter of the box escaped close scrutiny in court. In his summing-up, Judge Salter observed that he could not see what bearing it had on the case.[36]

Veronal was the trade name of barbitone, the first member of the barbiturate group to be introduced into medical practice, in 1903. Its toxic effects were well known by 1918, although it was widely prescribed, and its possession not controlled under DORA 40B. Stuart denied prescribing it to Carleton, but said she had received it – in cachet form – on the instructions of a Harley Street practitioner the previous June, when she had influenza and a temperature of 105 degrees. The contemporary pharmacopoeias do not shed any light on why a powerful hypnotic should have been thought beneficial for a patient in such a condition. A year before Billie Carleton's death, it had been the poison chosen by Topsy and Primrose Compton-Burnett, younger sisters of Ivy. The women were found dead in their locked bedroom, lying together in their dressing gowns – a tableau pitifully reminiscent of the Yeoland tragedy. Topsy had become dependent on veronal after being prescribed it for toothache.[37] It could be argued that the doctors of the day were as great a menace to young women as the drug dealers.

Doctors, however, were not considered quarry. The Carleton case demanded punishment to fit the scandal. Having exposed an underground network of 'degenerates', engaged in criminal activities, it was scarcely apt for the court proceedings to dwell on the possibility of an error of professional judgment. Nor would an inconclusive inquest verdict have been satisfactory. This was not only the first major drug scandal, but the first drug incident to reach national prominence since the passage of DORA 40B. Samuel Ingleby Oddie wanted a manslaughter verdict against Reggie De Veulle, and the jury followed his direction.[38]

As Judge Salter later acknowledged, the first condition of a such a verdict was that cocaine caused Billie Carleton's death. Salter devoted a substantial portion of his summing-up to this question. For Ingleby Oddie, though, it sufficed that the pathologist, Dr Jewesbury, was of the opinion that death was due to cocaine. According to one account, the coroner actually said that there was no doubt in the matter.[39]

It was one thing for a coroner's jury to find that De Veulle was criminally responsible for Carleton's death, but another to convict him of manslaughter. The expert witnesses did not furnish the prosecution with a watertight case. They differed among themselves. George Hamerton, the police divisional surgeon, thought that Carleton had been in a very poor state of health; Jewesbury maintained her state of health had been very good. Percy Richards, the public analyst, said that though his tests for veronal had given negative results, that did not necessarily mean Carleton had not taken any. Jewesbury insisted that if she had, it would have been detected.[40]

Given the state of the pathological and toxicological sciences around the time of the Great War, most experts today would probably go along with Richards' caution rather than Jewesbury's certainty. But Jewesbury's pronouncements were the ones that counted in both the inquest and the trial. If the jury accepted Dr Jewesbury as a competent authority, Judge Salter observed in his summing-up, he disposed completely of the possibility that veronal was the cause of death. Salter's 'if' was rhetorical, but from a modern perspective, it looks like rather a big 'if'.

Besides the question of whether any veronal would be detectable, on which he differed from his colleague, Jewesbury based his rejection of the veronal hypothesis upon the claim that the barbiturate would have taken about twenty-four hours to cause death. That might be the case where the victim was under medical supervision, with airways maintained, but Billie Carleton died of asphyxia after having been in an unattended coma for several hours at least. More bizarre was Jewesbury's assertion that cocaine could induce sleep. And most egregious of all was his claim that a person who had died of an overdose of cocaine would suffer no pain.[41]

Such unsound remarks helped tip the balance of evidence in a case where the experts admitted that the signs were consistent with both cocaine or veronal poisoning. It remains possible that cocaine was the cause, but unlikely. Cocaine overdoses may sometimes induce coma – but first they are liable to cause convulsions, agitation and terror, not to mention vomiting and incontinence. There was no sign that Billie Carleton's demise had been anything other than peaceful.

Apart from their effects on the judicial process, the pathologist's remarks gave the public a misleading impression of the dangers of cocaine. This was compounded by the coroner and the judge, both of whom drew attention to the alleged ease of overdose. 'Do you mean to say you got through nine grains in one day?' Ingleby Oddie asked De Veulle, incredulously, holding up a tiny phial of powder. 'Look at that. You can hardly see it. That is a fatal dose.' De Veulle replied, 'Then I ought to be dead a long time, if that is a fatal dose.'[42]

In a sense, they were both right. Most cocaine *aficionados* probably regard a quarter of a gramme as the minimum for a night's entertainment; heavy users can easily consume a gramme a day. (Nine grains is rather more than half a gramme.) Very occasionally, however, low doses of cocaine – even as little as thirty milligrammes – can prove fatal.[43] The coroner took the exception as the rule. He reiterated the point in his summing-up: 'You have seen the minute dose which is fatal ... and you will readily understand that people going about in that casual way with cocaine, sniffing it up their noses, were very likely, sooner or later, to overdose themselves.' Clearly failing to grasp that cocaine had a stimulant effect, Ingleby Oddie went on to suggest that Carleton had taken a dose when her visitors left, and then again on going to bed.[44]

At the end of the trial, Judge Salter also held up the illustrative phial. 'I thought some mistake had been made,' he commented, 'when it was stated this was a fatal dose of cocaine. But it was not a mistake, and to take the drug in such a casual manner between the finger and thumb makes it amazing to me that accidents do not happen much more frequently.'[45] In the course of the hearings, the public had been assured by the press that cocaine use led inexorably to mental and moral degeneration. The full weight of judicial authority, backed up by science and medicine, further assured the public that the young women who flirted with the drug were at risk of their lives from just a single sniff of it.

The Carleton court proceedings were a transitional episode in the process of criminalising drugs. The scandal established cocaine and the drug underworld as a moral menace, but the foundation of criminality was still shaky. Ingleby Oddie acknowledged that the jury might 'not feel quite inclined to press hardly' in a case where the illegality arose solely from emergency war regulations, or might feel that such

regulations ought not to be the basis of a constructive manslaughter charge. In 1916, Sir Malcolm Delevingne had suspected that permanent drug legislation might have proved controversial; the Carleton case both shaped public opinion and highlighted the inadequacies of the laws then in force.

Other aspects of the judicial apparatus were found wanting in their first test. As Judge Salter pointed out, the first condition of a manslaughter conviction was that cocaine was the cause of death. The technical capacities of the forensic investigation were sufficient to identify a drug overdose, but fell short of the resolution needed to confirm the cause, requiring the assistance of circumstantial evidence. This inadequacy was compounded by a general lack of understanding of the drugs in question, and the patterns of their use. The shortcomings of the experts were already apparent at the inquest: there may well have been something in Huntly Jenkins' suggestion that the prosecution later added the conspiracy charge to the manslaughter count because the experts had 'let them down'.[46]

More profoundly, the case revealed the inability of the criminal law to address questions of responsibility arising from non-medical drug use. Huntly Jenkins' defence employed two tactics. One was to stir up the jury's sense of reasonable doubt: lots of people committed suicide without apparent reason; Billie Carleton must have been troubled to have taken drugs in the first place; the forensic evidence was not strong enough; Belcher was an unreliable witness; the drug Stuart concealed might have been veronal, which was a drug more likely to be taken by somebody going to bed. And so on; the conclusion was that De Veulle might be guilty, but on the other hand he might well be innocent, and the jury should not risk a conviction.

That finale also rested on a challenge to the principle of constructive manslaughter itself. The second thrust of Jenkins' strategy was to argue that even if De Veulle had done something illegal, his action might not constitute criminal negligence. When 'another mind came into play', the distribution of responsibility was altered. To punish De Veulle for Carleton's death would be to deem him responsible for another person's acts. What Billie Carleton did with her cocaine was up to her; as Jenkins pointed out, she was an experienced drug user who knew as much about drugs as De Veulle or any of the other witnesses.

Judge Salter rejected this argument. 'Nothing much more dangerous than this drug could be imagined'; if De Veulle had given a 'formidable' quantity of it to a young woman addict, 'knowing she was likely to take it in this loose and dangerous way without any skilled supervision', then that was ample grounds for determining his action to be criminally negligent.

Salter's remarks depend more than is immediately apparent on his description of Billie Carleton: young, female, and, in her addiction, dependent. She was immature and needed supervision; she was irresponsible, and De Veulle responsible. This was an instance where an older man had failed in his duty to protect a young woman. Its structural configuration was of a piece with other scenarios involving older men and young women; leading astray, taking advantage, seduction. It was also related to the conventional model of drug traffic, in which a dealer corrupts or imperils his victims, who are more sinned against than sinning.

Huntly Jenkins had made the opposite case: Carleton and De Veulle were peers, equally responsible for their own actions. Billie Carleton was a subject with the same freedoms and the same responsibilities as anybody else, unimpaired by her sex. That would imply reversibility: if he had died and she had been suspected of supplying the fatal dose, she should have been charged. At that point in history, such a prosecution would have been as radical a prospect as a woman judge.

The fact that the trial jury took less than an hour to reject the judge's clear direction is striking. They had heard endless testimony of doubtful relevance, they were uneasy about the shortage of conclusive evidence ... and in the secondary charge, they had a way out. Reggie De Veulle was obviously guilty of something, but did this murky and sordid affair amount to an instance of manslaughter? The conspiracy charge allowed them to punish him without ruling that it did. Nonetheless, the speed with which they reached their first verdict scarcely suggests agonised deliberation. While the general uncertainty surrounding the affair must have been a factor in the decision, a fifty-minute retirement looks like a pretty unambiguous rebuff to His Lordship. Perhaps the jury, forced to look in detail at the lives and behaviour of drug users, rejected the idea of the enslaved victim in favour of the view that this was a conspiracy of equals.

Even now, the idea of drug users as individuals capable of exercising free choices appears eccentric, despite the inadequacy of the dealer-victim schema as a model of the complexities of social drug use. The question of responsibility for drug-induced death also continues to defy resolution. In 1983, a teenager called John Williams was killed by a drug injection that he had asked a friend to give him. His mother,

Pauline Williams, campaigned for three years to get the friend convicted, combatting reluctance from the Director of Public Prosecutions and spending £16,000 of her own money. She was outraged at the fifteen-month sentence eventually imposed, by a judge who noted that the injection had been her son's choice and request. The law was ill at ease with the case; she was unhappy with the outcome; and the sentence was not in itself a deterrent, since those engaging in similar activities could face similar sentences simply for possessing drugs. It affirmed what the very first such prosecution had shown, nearly seventy years before; that drugtaking cannot be fitted into the conventional criminal duality of perpetrators and victims.[47] Indeed, it sits uneasily in the criminal domain altogether.

7

BROKEN BUTTERFLY

In the wake of the exposure of a 'circle of degenerates' after Billie Carleton's death, the public was treated to a stream of similar spectacles; some explicitly fictional, others presented as fact. But although Billie Carleton herself had been part of the circle, she was posthumously removed from it. Having filled the leading role in the dope drama, she was given immunity.

Exploitation of the theme began within a fortnight of her death, with a short *Daily Express* series on the drug menace. Recapitulating wartime themes, it described cocaine cigarettes and a German conspiracy, *à la* Pemberton Billing, to subvert the nation by means of the drug habit. Cannabis was also mentioned, with a broadly accurate description of its effects, but those of cocaine were confused with those of opiates.[1]

The drug habit was claimed to be largely the result of wartime restrictions on alcohol and legitimate entertainment (specifically, according to one account, of the non-availability of bottled stout, the chorus girls' favourite tipple). Now the traffic was controlled by a great 'Vice Trust', which also had interests in prostitution, gambling and nightclubs. The trust's drug profits came from women, who were both its agents and its victims: 'The woman drug fiend is almost invariably a missionary of her vice.'[2]

The specific object of concern in this piece was the well-educated, independent-minded young woman who might aspire to be an actress or an artist. She was apt to be drawn to a bohemian fringe that now included dope fiends.

> You will find the woman dope fiend in Chelsea, in Mayfair, and Maida Vale. An obscure traffic is pursued in certain doubtful teashops. The sale of certain beauty specifics is only a mask for the illicit traffic in certain drugs.
>
> A young and attractive girl deeply interested in social conditions and political economy made the acquaintance of another woman through a

mutual friend. Within three months she had become a confirmed haunter of a certain notorious café. She had lost her looks and health. Before she closed her miserable existence a bare nine months later she had introduced at least four other decent girls to her practice of vice; and for the last two months of her existence she was acting as a decoy for a notorious gambling hell ...

The queer, bizarre, rather brilliant bachelor girl is a frequent victim to the insidious advances of the female dope fiend.

This was a thoroughly feminised version of the clandestine conspiracy myth, with teashops and beauty parlours under suspicion instead of German bakeries. But it played on a sense of instability in female identity. The young woman's interest in economics and politics indicated an interest in the way the world worked, a concern asserted by a politicised generation of educated women; but it combined fatally with her innocence, a quality ascribed to such women by their paternalist critics. The elliptical suggestion that an interest in politics did women no good gained piquancy from the timing of its publication, a few days before the election.

More than this, however, the piece hints that a disordering of femininity underlies the young woman's downfall. She is the highly-strung, neurasthenic type believed to be vulnerable to artificial stimulants. Her neurosis has also destabilised her sexual identity: her bizarreness and brilliance make her neither a maiden nor a spinster, but a bachelor girl – a young woman with masculine attributes. She is thus vulnerable to the 'advances' of another woman. It does not require the modern meaning of 'queer' to read this as a warning of homosexual seduction.

Suggestions of sexual ambiguity also coloured a subsequent account, purportedly first-hand, of a dopers' party at a flat in the Piccadilly area. The 'Special Correspondent' is invited by the host, who 'lisped like a woman, had a nervous, jerky motion of the hands, and reeked overpoweringly of perfume'. He is introduced to a guest: 'The hand he offered me was limp and clammy to the touch.' The man has 'dull, heavy eyes, a languorous manner, and a silent, almost cat-like, gait'; at home among the 'sensual-coloured carpets, curtains and hangings, low-shaded purple lights and uncanny atmosphere of lassitude'.[3]

The mood of the account is decadence in the 1890s mould, but the world-weariness is induced by drugs rather than aesthetics. Like David Garnett's *Dope-Darling*, it also stands for the exhausted despair of the Aftermath, yet to be overtly acknowledged. Another of the guests is a soldier, outwardly healthy, who subsequently blows his brains out. The man with the cat-like gait is prey to vertiginous swings between elation and depression, and is watched over constantly by a 'confidential male servant'. The guests are apathetic and silent; conversations and piano tunes fade away almost as soon as they start.

These dope fiends are the living dead; their nervous systems irreversibly ravaged and their sanity in tatters. The party's closest equivalents in real life were probably to be found in the nursing homes where victims of 'shell-shock' were sent. A less sensitive connotation is suggested in the account, which describes the host coughing blood into his handkerchief. As well as its mood of decadence, the narrative is coloured with images of tuberculosis, the archetypal disease of melancholy souls with delicate nervous constitutions.

Cocaine was increasingly represented as a drug of femininity or effeminacy. The *Daily Mail* called it 'a fashionable habit, an artificial war product, which will disappear with the return of more normal conditions. It is a vice of the neurotic, not a habit of the normal. "Men," said a specialist, "do not as a rule take to drugs unless there is a hereditary influence, but women are more temperamentally attracted." '[4]

Although the hereditary influence was not identified, the general drift was that it was a feminine sort of weakness. At the time of Billie Carleton's death, a former military flier named John Hall remarked to friends that the man who becomes a cocaine taker must be an effeminate sort of person. He was a morphine addict himself, and later died of an overdose after four years' unemployment.[5]

John Hall's prejudices were confirmed by Reggie De Veulle; between them, Billie and Reggie epitomised the femininity and effeminacy of cocaine users. In those days, of course, deviations from the masculine ideal were named with the greatest reluctance, if at all. Effeminacy, transvestism and homosexuality were neither discussed nor differentiated. Only the most vulgar papers ever drew attention to homosexuality, and then only rarely: a report from the 'far end of Bohemia', for instance, of men dressed as women 'nigger-dancing' at a party in Chelsea. This was ascribed to the regrettable influence of regimental shows at the Front, where men had to masquerade as women out of necessity – not, as was alleged of De Veulle, out of perversity.[6]

Reggie De Veulle was also a former art student, gentleman's secretary, actor, alleged accessory to homosexual blackmail, financial beneficiary of a relationship with an older man, and was now a dress designer. In his studio photographs, whether in costume or a suit, he appeared 'nicely poised', as Belcher's counsel nastily put it. At the trial, Sir Richard Muir alluded to De Veulle's friendship with 'a person of extremely debased character ... associated with persons of perverted sexual practices' (possibly a reference to Don Kimfull).[7] Jury and public were left in no doubt as to what sort of man Reggie De Veulle was.

Ironically, that might have helped save him from conviction on the manslaughter charge. Since the case against him appealed to a conventional model of male-female relationships – the man in control and responsible for the woman – it was actually weakened by the innuendos with which he was smeared at the inquest. Though Muir avoided this tactic in the trial itself, the mud had stuck. De Veulle appeared not as a manipulative seducer, luring Carleton into the drug habit for gain or worse, but as an equally weak, neurotic, feminine partner in folly. It would have looked a lot worse if they had been having an affair.

The deeper effect was to strengthen the sense of drugs as other – the province of women, effeminate men, inferior men, men of colour. In the wake of the war, which seemed to distil the ideal of manhood from the combatant nation, the contrast was all the more marked between the men who did their duty and the degenerates who sat at home and doped. Servicemen who became addicts were one thing (and, at this stage, had yet to be widely recognised); a man like De Veulle, excused conscription because of his cocaine use, was quite another. The nearest approach to the virile ideal in Carleton's set was Belcher, a bogus man who escaped military service, presumably on grounds of infirmity, and then found lucrative employment as a dashing film hero while others died as heroes on the other side of the Channel. Here were people doing the supposed German agents' work for them, voluntarily sapping their own moral fibre; they demonstrated the polymorphousness of vice, mixing together currents of dope, sexual perversion, fornication and miscegenation. The sense of outrage to civilised values was captured in Frederick Mead's memorable phrase about 'the high priestess at these unholy rites' – an inversion of the sexual and spiritual order.

These themes were further explored in explicitly fictional forms, enthusiastically highlighting their relationship to events in the news. The dope genre had existed in the movies almost since the beginning of cinema: a short, entitled *Chinese Opium Den*, was made for Thomas Edison in 1894. During the war, the medium mushroomed in popularity, with weekly attendance figures of twenty million – the equivalent of half the population. The craze included a vogue for drug films, both American imports and British productions such as *London's Yellow Peril*.

Moral purity campaigners subjected the cinema to close scrutiny – not just what was on the screen, but what might be going on among an audience unfortunately consigned to the dark – and the drug theme naturally aroused a degree of concern. In 1915, the *Bioscope* concluded that '... there being no reason to suppose that this habit was prevalent in this country to any serious extent, the evils of arousing curiosity in the minds of those to whom it was a novel idea, far outweighed the possible good that might accrue by warning the small minority who indulged in the practice.'[8]

While this line of argument has persisted down the years, it was never as strong as before the Carleton scandal brought the novel idea of dope to the British public as a whole. With the cat out of the bag, the film industry could trade on topicality. A bid to revive a film called *The Curse of the Poppy*, for example, used an advertisement featuring a montage of sensational newspaper headlines.[9]

A number of drug films were announced at the time of the scandal, as well as theatrical ventures ('Drug Fiends ... The Brilliant Detective Dope Drama ... Scene 1: "A mother's last chance to save her daughter" ... "Secret vice lurks below silken gowns" ... Scene 6: The orgy den, the Devil's circle – "The depths to which drugs drag their victims" ').[10] While most of these probably foundered a considerable distance short of their intended audiences, the drug theme was incorporated that year into a milestone of early cinema, D.W. Griffith's *Broken Blossoms*.

The director's attention had been drawn to Thomas Burke's *The Chink and the Child* by Mary Pickford and Douglas Fairbanks Sr (who was not a man to be fazed by a drug scene: he had played Detective Coke Ennyday in the 1916 comedy *The Mystery of the Leaping Fish*). Griffith ignored warnings that the public would not stand for a theme of miscegenation, and enhanced the hostile depiction of the white man already developed by Burke.[11]

Broken Blossoms is the tragic story of Cheng Huan (played by Richard Barthelmess), a pacific Chinese poet who comes to England; his purpose to bring Oriental spiritual enlightenment to a continent that has plunged itself into the barbarity of war. Its brutalisation is underlined at one point by a casual reference to 'only 40,000 dead this week' – a remarkably sharp directorial sally, especially since a state of war still technically obtained during the period in which the film was made. Western brutality is personified in the figure of Battling Burrows, an East End prizefighter who terrorises and beats his daughter Lucy, played by Lillian Gish.

Cheng Huan settles in Limehouse, where contact between the races is shown to have a corrupting effect. A magnificently composed establishing scene (a detail from which appears on the cover of this book) shows white women in an opium den, surrounded by Chinamen and other men of colour. Opium dissolves the natural barriers between the races; the focus is unequivocally upon the willing absorption of the women into this smoky promiscuity.

A series of close-ups show, first, white women seated with examples of different races; then the woman at the centre of the composition is shown reclining alone. Her eyelids close, her lips part and her head tilts back in voluptuous abandonment, the cause emphasised by cuts to the Chinese man with his pipe in the foreground of the tableau. In the middle of this company, her solitary, self-gratifying pleasure is more shocking still than the intercourse – the social form implying the possibility of the sexual – between the other women and the men. Griffith shrewdly identified an aspect of drugtaking that remains an unspoken source of distaste for outsiders, the attainment of ecstatic sensual states in company. It reasserted the continuity of dope with other forms of vice: for those who made the connection, the opium pyjama orgies of Mayfair must have seemed all the more depraved.

Lodged in this sinful world, his mission making no headway, Cheng Huan – referred to as the Yellow Man – runs a shop in Limehouse. One day he finds Lucy in the street after a beating, and takes her in to tend her. The love that begins to flower is both pure and impossible. Battling Burrows finds Lucy, takes her home and beats her to death. Cheng Huan kills Burrows, takes Lucy's body back to his room, and stabs himself in front of his altar. At the very moment when his encounter with Lucy allows the nobility of his spirit to be expressed, her murder leads to an act that is the antithesis of the values he had hoped to bring to the West. His Oriental enlightenment is overwhelmed by an explosive Western rage. (The opposition of qualities is emphasised by the use of a revolver in the film, whereas the short story has him place a snake on Burrows' couch – a subtle, Oriental sort of assault.)

It has been suggested that Lucy's abject submissiveness represents a masochism resulting from twin impermissible desires; the incestuous desire for her father, and that for the Yellow Man. She belongs to a Victorian character-type, the child prostitute.[12] This was a species in which the contradiction between sympathy and moral disapproval could be resolved, although her innocence was necessarily fatal. Billie Carleton posthumously became a sort of cousin to the likes of Lucy.

Another notable fiction of 1919, though lacking the artistic qualities of *Broken Blossoms*, was Sax Rohmer's *Dope*.[13] Rohmer began life as Arthur Henry Ward and adopted a 'Saxon' pen-name; although many Britons from the Royal Family down were shortly forced to discard their genuinely Germanic names, Rohmer survived the war through his fictional conflict between West and East. He claimed that, when he asked a ouija board how to make his living, it spelled out 'C-H-I-N-A-M-A-N'; the secret of his success, he said, was that he knew nothing of the Chinese.[14]

His Chinatown in *Dope* certainly illustrates the bliss of novelistic ignorance. Rohmer understood the potential of mixing unrestrained fantasy with elements of the *roman à clef*. The result is a panorama of dope mythology extending from a narrative inspired by the Carleton case. Rohmer sketches the terrain of the post-war drug panic with florid cameos of Limehouse and the West End. There are nightclubs, flagrant in their social promiscuity: 'The peerage was well represented, so was Judah; there were women entitled to wear coronets dancing with men entitled to wear the broad arrow, and men whose forefathers had signed Magna Charta dancing with chorus girls from the revues and musical comedies.'

The female lead in the narrative is Rita Dresden, an actress who aspires to a better stage than that of musical comedy. She finds that advancement in the theatre depends on the favour of powerful men, and is forced to let the influential Sir Lucien Pyne court her. On the first night that she is due to play the leading part that this dalliance secures, she is seized with stage fright. Sir Lucien produces a small gold box from his waistcoat pocket ...

Dresden becomes dependent on cocaine to perform, and thence drifts into the drug underworld, with opium parties in Mayfair, purchases from an Egyptian dealer and excursions to Limehouse, the lair of the drug trafficker Sin Sin Wa. His influence extends to the West End through his wife Mrs Sin, the 'officiating priestess' at the Mayfair

'Regretted By Many: The Late Miss Billie Carleton.' (*The Sketch*, 11 December 1918. By permission of the British Library.)

parties. In his ornate disclaimer, Rohmer denies that the novel is inspired by any *cause célèbre* – though he does allow that his Chief Inspector Kerry is based on an ex-CID man.

The prototypes have certainly undergone extensive elaboration, the Lau Pings most spectacularly. Sin Sin Wa has one eye, a pigtail and a raven that perches on his shoulder; Lola Sin is a voluptuous Cuban Jewess from Buenos Aires, characterised by a magnificently rolling mixed metaphor: 'one of the night-club birds – a sort of mysterious fungus ... flowering in the dark, and fattening on gilded fools'.

On the other hand, Rita Dresden seems truer to the spirit of the real Billie Carleton than the Victorian waif that the actress became in death. Dresden was an ambitious young woman who appreciated that she had to be nice to men to get on, and wanted to marry a wealthy specimen. Rohmer is matter-of-fact about his heroine, who is worldly but not wicked. The essential tragedy of Billie Carleton, it was suggested, was that she was too delicate for the world. The theme of the girl with the 'fairylike figure and face' was struck up as soon as Carleton died, before the circumstances were known.[15] 'She had a certain frail beauty and delicate art of her own. It was all of that perishable, moth-like substance that does not last long in the wear and tear of this rough-and-ready world.'[16]

Despite the connotations of innocence, this line did not have to be abandoned on the revelation of her secret vice. Its dominant image of frailty was at the heart of the idea of young womanhood that was to animate the drug hysteria of the next few years. The metaphor of moth or butterfly remained popular, both for Carleton and her successors. The *News of the World* incorporated it into the hyperbole of scandal:

> Admired by thousands, loved by many, her picture in hundreds of albums, earning the salary of a Cabinet Minister – £100 per week – light-hearted, gay and apparently happy. This was Miss Billie Carleton, the famous musical comedy star. Today she lies in the cold, dark tomb, her butterfly existence cut tragically short, her brief life ended.[17]

Three years later, another woman drugtaker's death prompted the memory of the *World's Pictorial News*: 'We have but to close our eyes to conjure up visions of bright, beautiful Billie Carleton, flitting through life on butterfly wings, fragrant as a lovely flower, but all the time a child gripped in the fiendish clutches of the devil of cocaine.'[18] And when Charles B. Cochran came to write his memoirs, he averred that 'a more beautiful creature has never fluttered upon a stage. She seemed scarcely human, so fragile was she.'[19]

Like Lucy of *Broken Blossoms*, and the Victorian fictional child-prostitute type in whose tradition Lillian Gish's character stood, Billie Carleton became a paradoxical figure in whom innocence and vice could co-exist. The contradiction is resolved by death, and the characterisation tends to the iconic. Reminiscences of her consistently drew upon a stock repertoire of exemplary feminine qualities. A piece on 'stage butterflies' described her as 'a woman of infinite humour, generosity and kindness'.[20] Cochran remembered 'a young girl of flower-like beauty, delicate charm, and great intelligence'. For the dancer and model Dolores, 'Billie was just the most fragrant specimen of womanhood it was possible to meet. Fond of outdoor sports, she loved animals, whilst children were an absolute passion with her. She was in fact, the very essence of English girlhood.'[21]

The reduction of this complex young woman to an essence also reduced her to her origins. Billie Carleton was a bright young thing a few years ahead of her time; Florence Stewart was the illegitimate daughter of a Victorian chorus girl – the spiritual cousin of Lucy Burrows. Despite that, or because of it, she got to the Savoy and the Haymarket through her own efforts. Rewritten after her death, she was put back more or less where she started.

Her name was also appropriated by one or two non-canonical elements, as if to pay a sort of backhanded homage to some of the unapproved strands of femininity to be found in her narrative. In 1920, a twenty-three year-old woman calling herself Teddy Carleton (among other aliases) embarked on a flamboyant crime spree in the characteristic style of the Aftermath; travelling restlessly, thieving by deceit rather than violence. She took cocaine as well.[22] The post-war landscape was dotted with hustlers and drifters, but what marked Teddy Carleton out was, of course, her sex. She marked a new extremity in the growing unwillingness of women to be satisfied with their lot, a refusal that increasingly had overtones of the perverse.

The traditional reason for women to dress in men's clothes was disguise to help them commit crimes: it was thus fitting that Teddy Carleton should have adopted the symbolic transvestism of a male forename.[23] She had a crudely symmetrical counterpart in the man who blackmailed a country vicar for £1367 – a last distant echo of De Veulle's blackmail episode – using the name Billy Carlton.[24]

The major application of Billie Carleton's name was as a point of departure for drug stories. Until well into the 1950s, these narratives conventionally began with a reference to tragic Billie Carleton, who epitomised the sorry fate of the drug victim. As new villains were identified, they were linked to the original legend by claims that they had supplied Carleton with cocaine.

Against the obdurate current of this refusal to let Billie Carleton rest, it seems apt that her ghost was said to haunt the rooms where she died at Savoy Court, which had subsequently become part of the BBC's original offices. 'A graceful woman, light as air, moves slowly past,' it was reported, 'to vanish as suddenly as she appeared.'[25]

And what about the rest of them? The dramatis personae of the Carleton case were not the sort of people to leave many traces after them, either in documentation or descendants. Nonetheless, a few fragmentary postscripts remain. Their various fortunes were mixed; they tended to continue, or finish, as they had begun.

Reggie De Veulle disappeared from the public eye when he went through the gates of Wormwood Scrubs. The London theatre records for the 1920s contain a single entry for 'De Veuille', an oddly fussy variation on his name which he had used before; the credit is as costume designer for a 1926 musical called *Yvonne*. That, as far as the West End stage was concerned, appears to have been it. One might surmise he would have been tempted to go abroad, as he had done before the war, but his conviction may have forced him to try and resume a career in the place of his downfall. Olive Richardson also has one solitary entry in the post-war records, as an actress and choreographer for a show staged in 1921.[26]

Two of the secondary characters died during the court proceedings. John Marsh succumbed to pneumonia; he was said, romantically but incorrectly, to have been buried near Billie Carleton.[27]

Around the same time, Captain Schiff expired in more colourful circumstances. He died of complications after being beaten up by Alfred Nicholls, a Cornish tin miner, who was incensed by the attentions Schiff had been paying to his 'buxom' seventeen year-old daughter Norah, a barmaid. The *Empire News* obituary report enthusiastically disregarded the convention of not speaking ill of the dead. In fact, its account began 'If ever a man deserved death ...' Although Schiff had held a commission in the Royal Sussex Regiment, and had lost a son at Arras, the paper claimed that he supported the other side. His fingernails were cut to a point in German fashion, it claimed, and he 'invariably took his soup in the noisy fashion in the "art" of which the Hun stands supreme'. As well as being a womaniser and a blackmailer, he was said to have carried a revolver and a knuckleduster round the West End, and was hinted to have supplied Billie Carleton's cocaine. 'He was a cool and clever gambler, an expert in drugs, and a dope party of any note was seldom held without it was graced by the presence of Captain Schiff.'[28]

The briefest and most tragic epilogue was that of Ada Lau Ping. Testimony that she had a serious illness did not influence the outcome of her appeal, and so she was forced to endure the grim conditions of Holloway Prison while suffering from tuberculosis. She died of the disease in November 1920, aged twenty-nine; not in Limehouse, but Bournemouth, where she had moved with her daughter. On the death certificate, the daughter's name is given as B. Goodwin: 'present at the death', but apparently absent for much of her life. Ada's maiden name was McGlashan; on marrying Lau Ping, she was the widow of a seaman named De Brovitz. As well as having no provenance, the name of the one child that emerges from these data turns out, against the odds, to be too prosaic to be traceable.

Lau Ping You, who was also consumptive, remained at liberty until 1922, when he and a number of other Chinese men were caught red-handed smoking opium. The others got off with light fines, as he had before, but the police identified him as 'one of the principals in the opium traffic', and recommended his deportation.[29]

The public's introduction to the private character of Lionel Belcher, during the Carleton hearings, had been confirmed a few months later in the divorce action against him. Remarkably, he contrived a favourable portrayal of himself a few years later, in the same papers that had previously detailed his unpleasant marital conduct. Belcher was married again within a couple of years, to a Frenchwoman said to be a heavy drug user. When she died in 1925, the doctors certified the cause of death as tuberculosis, but referred the case to the coroner when rumours started to fly around that she died of cocaine. It was confirmed that she died of TB, possibly aggravated by chronic alcoholism, and Belcher was solemnly represented as a devoted husband who had done all in his power to wean her off dope.[30] Many years later, however, a Carleton retrospective (*Fallen Stars*, No.3) asserted that he was 'involved in other sordid episodes which brought him again into conflict with the law'.[31]

The uncomfortable scrutiny of the Carleton proceedings did not induce either Dr Stuart or the pharmacist Thomas Wooldridge to steer clear of actresses and drugs. Frederick Stuart continued his Knightsbridge practice, and was one of the doctors who treated Brenda Dean Paul, who in the 1930s became the first non-posthumous celebrity addict in Britain. She acquired an opiate habit as a result of medical treatment, and pioneered the technique of synergistic publicity for her stage career and her wrangle with the dependency. Unfortunately, the habit proved more durable than the career; in the 1950s, her attempt at a comeback failed, and her greatest distinction in her final days was as the only junkie in town who carried a lapdog with painted nails.[32]

Thomas Wooldridge prospered in the Aftermath, his pharmacy practice having survived the embarrassing revelation, during the inquest, of six ounces of cocaine that he had 'forgotten' having bought. By 1926, he had three shops in Lisle Street and Little Newport Street, which run continuously behind the great show-palaces of Leicester Square. One was a chemist's, and the other two sold the sensational new devices of radio (BBC broadcasts had begun in 1922). Above one of these were rooms Wooldridge let out to actresses. In June, Wooldridge appeared before Samuel Ingleby Oddie once again, to answer questions about the death, from septicaemia, of an Australian actress who had visited his expansive flat in Bloomsbury. 'Nursing is one of my fortes,' the chemist informed the coroner. 'Nursing actresses?' quipped Oddie. That, Wooldridge agreed, was so. His conceit was not misplaced: there was insufficient evidence as to the cause of death, and Oddie observed that Wooldridge had got the better of him this time round. Wooldridge's luck did not hold for very long, though. In 1933 he was found dead from poisoning, the most ironic of fates for a chemist.[33]

The one great survivor seems to have been the most shadowy of all the characters in the Billie Carleton drama. Not only did Don Kimfull avoid appearing at the inquest or the trial, he never faced charges himself. Little emerged about him other than that he was said to sell drugs, and to be an Egyptian. Yet he may have been the most flamboyant, fantastical and famous of the entire coterie. A mirage it might have been, but the last images of Don Kimfull were refracted through the glasses of the legendary Dean's Bar in Tangier. In the latter days of the International Zone, after the Second World War, Dean's Bar became the honeypot for the louchest of a notoriously louche expatriate crowd – as well as attracting celebrities such as Ian Fleming,

Errol Flynn, Ava Gardner, Cecil Beaton, Helena Rubinstein, John Gielgud and Francis Bacon. Dean took against William Burroughs on sight, however, and was reluctant to serve him. Burroughs' 'Interzone', under the theoretical rule of nine powers and the effective control of none, was where people went to practise vices not tolerated in their own countries, or to escape from the consequences of having done so.[34]

As a host for the Tangerino set, Dean had an outstanding curriculum vitae, the more so for its lack of self-consistency, and the conviction with which different authorities upheld different versions of it. Dean was dark-skinned and had a Southern English accent. One account explained this as the result of a union between a Ramsgate lodging-house keeper and a transient West Indian. Another claimed that he was born in Hastings – like Lionel Belcher – to a businessman's wife, a Frenchwoman, who had strayed on a visit to Egypt. This version was embellished with the claim that after the businessman's death, the widow had gone back to France to live with her friend Cléo de Mérode, a celebrated dancer and courtesan.

Dean arrived in Tangier during the 1930s, and became head barman at the El Minzah Hotel. His part in the war, it was rumoured, was to act out in real life the role of Rick in Casablanca, eavesdropping in the cockpit of spies that his bar became, and passing on information that might lead to, say, a ship blowing up in the harbour. He was also said to be an opium addict, and to have been jailed for drug trafficking.

No doubt the principal source of all these stories was Dean himself. In a colony of fantasists and dissemblers, a talent for the bogus was a powerful aid to social success. There is, however, one account which claims to rest on first-hand knowledge of Dean's past – albeit related second-hand by the novelist Robin Maugham, in his autobiography.[35] Maugham recalls a conversation with the roguishly camp Gerald Hamilton. Who, Maugham inquired, was the wickedest man Hamilton had ever met? 'It's Dean, of Dean's Bar, without any doubt,' Hamilton replied. 'His real name isn't Dean anyhow. It's Donald Kimfull. He's a naughty baggage, and he always was.'

Hamilton went on to tell Maugham that he first met Kimfull around 1913, in London, when Kimfull was 'a gigolo about town'. The pair had been partners in crime; on one occasion, he recalled, they had collaborated in the theft of jewels from a millionaire's wife in Marseille.

It proves nothing, of course. But Hamilton clearly knew Don

Kimfull to have been a dubious character in pre-Great War London. He told the story as a participant, rather than as a friend of a friend who had been involved. The name of Kimfull was long forgotten, so it was not a question of identifying Dean as a known figure of notoriety, like Lord Lucan; the anecdote seems to serve no ulterior purpose. As supporting material, there were the stories about Dean and drugs; while suggestive, though, these were par for the course in a town of hashish and smugglers like Tangier. Much more impressively, there was the common thread of belief, from the Carleton set to the Tangerinos, that the individual identified as Don Kimfull was of Egyptian descent. The simplest explanation is that Dean was indeed Don Kimfull. And a very naughty baggage he would appear to have been.

In his latter days, however, he acquired stateliness. The journalist Michael Davidson depicted him as 'a gracious and lovable dignitary who, with the hauteur of a Versailles duchess, the cortesia of a Papal chamberlain, a heart made of honey and, often, a tongue like a scorpion's sting, rules over Dean's Bar'.[36]

One may surmise that the style of the valediction suited Dean, an indefatigable gossip whose favourite subject was himself, and who at the very least incorporated Kimfull's cryptic narrative as part of his own promiscuously ramifying story. It is as if a little part of the Billie Carleton story escaped and flourished in the sun, beyond the dull horizons of England. One imagines Kimfull, behind Great War blackouts, presiding at dinner with his scorpion's tongue, Reggie De Veulle straining to match it with his theatrical flippancies; and then, in another scene and another world, exchanging droll pleasantries with the Flemings, Flynns and Beatons.

All that remains of Dean's Bar today is a sign above an otherwise inconspicuous doorway in a street near Tangier's Grand Socco. Acquiescing for a moment in the romance of expatriate Tangier – a colony all but vanished now, and always largely imaginary anyway – it would be charming to imagine that somewhere among the proprietor's effects was an old book that related the adventures of Maurice and Reggie, and the tale of their cross-dressing party by the Thames.

8

COCAINE GIRLS
IN THE WEST END

It's women, women everywhere; and, as Mr George Robey would say, berlieve me – berlieve me not, but it's mighty few of them are really looking very war-worn. On the contrary, as everyone who runs has read, never have there been such weeks as these of Armistice for the doing of all those things it is pre-eminently feminine to do – dancing, shopping, love-making, marrying, sight-seeing, theatring, and the rest.

They say the night clubs are opening up in rows, and dressmakers say they're dizzy with the orders for dance frocks that keep on pourin' in. And they just can't have enough niggers to play jazz music, and I hear are thinkin' of hiring out squads of 'loonies' to make the mad jazz noises till there are more ships 'vailable to bring the best New York black jazz 'musicians' over.[1]

Instead of exhaustion and sadness, exuberance and frivolity; instead of Englishmen, women and black men were to the fore, bubbling with a Dionysiac energy that was, if the truth were admitted, a little unseemly – but the acute Eve, of the *Tatler*, sensed that flippancy was about to come into its own. The overarching order of reason had produced the war: what harm could the madness of jazz do, compared to that?

After what had passed, everything classical was diminished. In the long interval before a deep reckoning of the tragedy was possible, wisdom was replaced by cleverness, elegance by brittleness, idealism by cynicism. The jazz craze was an early episode of self-conscious bad taste. It had to be, because the notion that black culture might have intrinsic value was preposterous. 'Niggers' did not come in quotation marks; 'musicians' did. Jazz was not only other, in the symbolic sense; it was something other than music. 'Crude and vulgar, it is performed by niggers to the accompaniment of two or three banjoists and a drummer, whose chief business it is to make noises,' the *Observer* reported. 'In fact, the dance has been defined as "a number of niggers surrounded by noise".'[2]

The modern nymph makes the sign of the Pan-pipe.

The women, too, were surrounded by this noise, as it spread through the rows of new nightclubs, and out into the more plebeian dancehalls, such as the Hammersmith Palais, that were opening to cater for the dancing craze. A new kind of woman sprang to life in contemporary imagination and iconography. She was a Futurist creature, starkly painted in stylised geometries of black, white and scarlet; glossy and sharp. Or she was a gay wanton; barebacked, stockinged, brazen and glamorous with her cocktail or cigarette-holder. Unequivocally, she was modern. Soon she would be challenged by her antithesis, personified in the form of William Joynson-Hicks, a man who proudly boasted that he still wore 'the reactionary frock-coat of the Victorian Tories'.[3]

Nobody contributed more to the fuelling of that conflict than Kate Meyrick, a nightclub entrepreneur who became a celebrity in her own right. She got into the club business in 1919, after her husband left her with two sons at Harrow and four daughters at Roedean to support. As she told the story, she was in London nursing a daughter who had influenza, when she saw an advertisement placed by a man named Dalton Murray, who wanted a partner to help him hold tea dances.[4]

Dalton's, next to the Alhambra in Leicester Square, attracted just the sort of mixed clientele, from villains to Continental royalty, that made a classic club. It accordingly attracted the attention of the police as well, and Sergeant George Goddard was assigned to conduct undercover surveillance. When charges were brought, Goddard told the court that he had counted precisely 292 women of the unfortunate class leaving the premises. He boasted that he had been so cleverly disguised, if he might say so, that his own colleagues failed to recognise him; he made notes on the cuff of his shirt.[5] Raids by policemen in top hats and evening dress were to be a perennial feature of the 1920s club scene.

Herbert Muskett, the prosecuting counsel, called it a 'sink of iniquity' and a 'noxious fungus growth upon our social system'.[6] In her memoirs, Mrs Meyrick claimed that the closure of Dalton's, and her £25 fine, changed her attitude to the law. Her relationship with Sergeant Goddard flourished, however. In 1929, the Vice Squad officer was jailed on corruption charges. He was alleged to have amassed £18,000 in savings, a luxury car and a large house in Streatham, although his police wage was £6 15s a week. He claimed to have made £7000 or £8000 at the races during the war, £5000 from music publishing, £2000 or £3000 speculating in foreign currency, and £4000 selling rock at the Wembley Exhibition.[7] Kate Meyrick was sentenced to fifteen months' hard labour for bribing him.

By that time, she had launched a string of successful clubs; most famously the 43, at the house in Gerrard Street where Dryden had once lived. Her autobiography appeared shortly before her death in 1933; in it she estimated the total turnover of all her clubs since 1919 at half a million pounds.

After her blooding at Dalton's, her stepping stone to Soho had been Brett's, a dance hall in a Charing Cross Road basement, decorated in pink and gold, and equipped with a band of female musicians. Brett's Dance Hall stayed in business after Mrs Meyrick sold her stake in 1920, employing the Meyrick innovation of 'dance instructresses', professional dancing partners who were paid a small wage that was augmented by tips. It was one of Brett's dancers who precipitated the drug panics of 1922, the year of the Cocaine Girls.

Freda Kempton was born in 1899, the daughter of a jute arbitrator – an assessor of the fibre, and said to be one of the finest in the industry. The family had a comfortable house in Stoke Newington, with several servants, but the household began to suffer from George Kempton's wayward behaviour. He began to spend his time in nightclubs, seeking out the company of actresses. A trip to Canada ended ignominiously when George ran off with a woman and was deported. The marriage broke up in 1919.[8]

Freda remained close to her mother, but led her own life. Attractive and fair-haired, she was a natural Meyrick foot-soldier. According to Mrs Meyrick, some dance instructresses took home up to £80 a week, and ended up marrying aristocrats. Like aspiring actresses, their fortunes depended on looks, charm, stamina and male favour. They had to be able to draw attention to themselves, dance all night, and be charming as long as they were awake.

The surroundings were not especially conducive to an elegant demeanour. Freda's zone was the layer of clubs just above ground, legitimate but tawdry. Brett's itself was prosecuted after an undercover surveillance officer reported an incident in which a drunken man pulled down the top of a woman's dress. He also said he overheard a woman say 'Do get me some heroin, it is so good for me.' Sir Henry Curtis Bennett defended the club against these and other allegations, such as the claim that a woman had been seen sitting with her legs crossed, exposing her knee.[9]

Freda Kempton. (*Illustrated Sunday Herald*, 23 April 1922. By permission of the British Library.)

Freda's own way of getting noticed was her dancing style. 'Freda was a clever dancer, though personally I used to think her steps of an exaggerated type,' an acquaintance condescendingly remarked later, according to the *Evening News*. 'Always full of energy, even at four or five in the morning she would still be dancing and showing very few signs of fatigue.'[10]

The source of her energy was entirely predictable. Cocaine answered the nightclub dancers' need to stay appealing and lively through long nights. They shared this requirement, to some extent, with actresses and prostitutes; but theirs was the occupation for which 'snow' seemed tailor-made. Freda Kempton used to chew gum to mask the involuntary tooth-grinding that the drug induced.[11]

The euphoria of cocaine is often followed by depression, to which Freda seems to have been prone anyway. In early 1922, she had some disappointment in love. Kate Meyrick fancifully claimed that it was an unrequited infatuation with a married peer. A more plausible version held that she had left the man she had been living with, after he became infatuated with another woman.[12] By a tragic mischance, this distress coincided with the suicide of a friend, Audrey Knowles-Harrison.

Freda appeared at the inquest in January 1922, testifying that the dead woman had recently taken to drink, and had spoken of being 'fed up'; an understatement which covered her feelings about her impending divorce and the recent death of her child.[13] Later, Freda remarked to her friend Rose Heinberg how funny it would be if she committed suicide as well.[14]

On another occasion, Rose stayed the night with Freda, who opened her powder puff case to show her friend thirteen packets of cocaine.[15] If her habit was so heavy that she required at least thirteen times the basic unit of sale, one would expect her to have a single box or bottle containing the whole amount. The more likely explanation is that she was retailing the stuff herself.

The two women were members of the new breed that lived their lives after dark, making nightly processions from club to club, finishing up with an early breakfast and home with the milk. Freda was lodging with a woman named Sarah Heckel and her daughter Sadie, above a furniture shop in Westbourne Grove. Sadie had an idea that Freda's stamina might be artificial, and at one point asked her if she had ever taken drugs. Freda admitted she had tried cocaine, but said she would never do so again. Three weeks later, encountering Sadie after returning home at six in the morning, her jaw twitching, she was forced to claim she thought she had been drugged without her knowledge.[16]

The notion, like her life in general, was a long way adrift from reality. Her milieu was the negative image of daytime society; its hours the reverse of the conventional order, its values attuned to the pleasure principle, its economy only tenuously and dubiously connected with the authorised fabric of wealth creation. Her own bodily economy operated on cocaine credit; the precariousness of her emotions was apparent in the way she toyed aloud with death. The one member of her family to whom she was close was her mother, Jessie Kempton: she told Rose Heinberg that she would not live ten minutes if her mother were to die.[17]

Her family had broken up, as had her relationship with her lover; her occupation was marginal and essentially anonymous. The night world being to a significant extent imaginary, Freda Kempton was a woman of no fixed place. In its last few weeks, her life was overshadowed by the presence of a man so radically placeless as to seem hallucinatory. Freda's role in the drug drama would be to herald, by her own self-sacrifice, the entry of the 'Dope King', Brilliant Chang.

One night, past three o'clock, Freda and Rose were in the New Court

The last picture of Freda Kempton (arrow) taken at a night club carnival a few days before the tragedy.

Evening News, 24 April 1922. (By permission of the British Library.)

Club, off Tottenham Court Road, when a man named Micky took Freda to one side and told her that Billy wanted to meet her.[18] Billy – short for Brilliant – Chang was a unique figure in the night landscape. The scion of a wealthy family with mercantile interests in Shanghai and Hong Kong, he was said to have come to England in 1913; he was now in his mid-thirties. He had a City office from which he looked after his uncle's business affairs, which included contract work for the Admiralty, and a share in a Chinese restaurant in Regent Street.[19]

It was here that Freda, Rose, Chang and his friends ended up, Freda drinking port from a glass that Chang kept topped up. After a while, he asked her to go outside with him. When she came back a few minutes later, Rose saw that her mouth was twitching.

According to Rose, she accompanied Freda back to the restaurant in the small hours a week later, but Freda insisted on going in alone. She returned shortly after with a small blue bottle.[20] According to Chang himself, Freda had begun to ask him for money almost since their first meeting. He said he supplied it, but did not mention what, if anything, he got in return. Naturally, he denied having anything to do with cocaine. Part of his account at least was supported by Sadie Heckel, who said that Freda told her she was kept by the Chinaman.[21]

On 5 March, Freda's Sunday night began with a birthday party for a friend at the Westbourne Grove flat. She went out to Brett's at midnight, where she met up with Rose; at half-past three, they went on to the New Court for breakfast with a couple of men friends. Their escorts left, and Freda tried unsuccessfully to get hold of Chang on the telephone. The next port of call was the 43, where they found Chang. The night finished with whiskies at the Regent Street restaurant.[22]

Here, according to Rose, Billy Chang gave Freda another little blue bottle of powder. 'Can you die while sniffing cocaine?' Freda asked. 'No, the only way you can kill yourself is by putting cocaine in water,' Chang replied. On the way home in a taxi, Freda said she was going to drink the cocaine. Rose told her not to be silly.[23] When she got home, Freda added the bottle to the two others she had concealed in a pair of long white kid gloves.

Freda spent most of the day in bed, getting up when her mother called round with her nephew. Jessie Kempton recalled Freda running along the corridor in her pyjamas, dancing, singing and playing with the child. She ironed a frock and washed her hair, then went to take an hour's rest at teatime, setting the alarm for seven; Jessie left.

At seven o'clock, Freda emerged and asked Sarah Heckel for a glass of water. An hour later, she came down the passage, crying out from pain in her head. Sadie arrived home shortly afterwards to find Freda sobbing and dashing her head against the wall in agony. Around nine, Freda went into convulsions and foam appeared at her mouth. She died with her head resting on her landlady's arm.[24]

The cause of this scene, so sadly reminiscent of the Yeoland sisters' death in 1901, was confirmed as a cocaine overdose by Sir Bernard Spilsbury. Sadie Heckel said that Freda had left the beginning of a note, though the evidence was unverifiable, as she said she had burned it. According to Sadie, it read, 'Mother, forgive me. The whole world was against me. I really meant no harm and' – here it broke off. The inquest returned a verdict of suicide during a state of temporary insanity.[25]

The drug, it recorded, had been supplied by a person or persons unknown. There was insufficient evidence to bring charges against Chang. The frustration was most visible in the press, whose efforts to imply Chang's guilt without an underpinning of verifiable fact only served to make the Chinese night-bird seem like some sort of being from another realm. It was as if, having been compelled to testify, he turned the power of the law into the means of his glorification. After the verdict, it was reported, 'some of the girls rushed to Chang, patted his back, and one, more daring than the rest, fondled the Chinaman's black, smooth hair and passed her fingers slowly through it.'[26] The thick black hair, the blue overcoat with its luxurious fur collar, the grey suede shoes; all were noted, all added to a potent aura of sensuality.[27]

Brilliant Chang's appearance in the witness box thus gained a theatrical undertone, a theme developed in the description of how Chang made a grand entrance in his familiar surroundings:

> Let me describe him as I saw him a few months ago. It was at a night club. A dance had just finished, and the little tables were crowded. Suddenly the curtain covering the door was pushed aside, and 'Brilliant' Chang stood at the entrance. He paused a moment, silhouetted against the dark curtain, while his eyes searched the room.
>
> A murmur ran round the tables. 'There's the rich young Chink!' Half a dozen girls rose to greet him. Nodding slightly, he advanced and spoke to one of them. The others, shrugging their shoulders, sat down again.[28]

This particular correspondent claimed that Kempton's death had unsettled Chang, who was planning to return home as a result. He seriously underestimated Brilliant Chang's tenacity.

The account itself echoed a narrative published the previous month, as part of a campaign against drugs and 'dance dens', launched by the *Daily Express* within a few days of the tragedy. Under the headlines 'Nights In The Dancing Dens – When The Chinaman Takes The Floor', another special correspondent described a Sunday night excursion from the West End to 'a forbidding neighbourhood not very far from the Marble Arch'. His companion tells him to stop the taxi before it gets too close, and they walk the backstreets to the door in the wall of some industrial premises – they pass rows of stables and carter's vans – where a sinister figure in black relieves him of £2 and bundles the pair of them into a large unlit building. In today's terms, it was a warehouse party.

At the end of a dark passage, they descend to the cellar. Here a genuine den is revealed, dimly lit, smoky, and 'decorated on the incoherent Futurist lines usual in such places'. The band, however,

> crashed out a really good foxtrot ... My companion slipped off her cloak and we danced. Round us danced the same old sickening crowd of under-sized aliens, blue about the chin and greasy, the same predominating type of girl, young, thin, underdressed, perpetually seized with hysterical laughter, ogling, foolish.
>
> Here and there were a few well-groomed men with extravagantly-dressed women, and there were also a number of women whose appearance would have passed unnoticed in any smart hotel dancing with rough-looking men who, to a casual observer, appeared very much beneath them in social position. There was a noticeable absence of the shy, rather thrilled casual visitor, the silly subaltern on the spree, the vacuous young man 'seeing life', the elderly man with the late crop of oats. All these were absent. This crowd had been carefully admitted.

The scene set, the correspondent describes a sudden buzz of excitement. A Chinaman has appeared at the top of the stairs.

> He was not the 'Chink' of popular fiction, a cringing yellow man hiding his clasped hands in the wide sleeves of his embroidered gown. This man's evening clothes had been made up not far from Savile-Row. His long, thin hands were manicured, his manners were too perfect to be described as good. The picture he made as he stood there framed against the dark stairway, smiling round the room with that fixed Oriental smile which seems devoid of warmth and humanity, was so typical of the novelist's ideas of dopedom that he seemed like a vision conjured up by the surroundings.
>
> 'Everything going strong!' he laughed, as he stepped down. A young girl ran up to him, held her arms out, he clasped her closely to him, and

they danced. Not only did he dance in perfect style, but he also revolved in an atmosphere of general approbation.

Who are these smiling yellow men? They are to be met wherever men and girls dance when the normal night owls of London have gone home to bed. Are they students out for a rag? Are they wealthy Chinese businessmen? Are they ... what and who are they, and why are they so popular with frail white women?[29]

The plural was no more than a conceit, multiplying the threat while minimising any risk of litigation. Chang inspired awe and excitement because of his singularity, not because he was a specimen of some Oriental brotherhood.

The remarks about the Chinese man's clothes are not trivial. Orientals were understood to share not only their status as the white man's other with women, but also their femininity – as expressed in submissive posture and a feminine form of dress. The Chinaman's cross-dressing as a European thus entailed an element of transvestism in the conventional sense. The theatricality of the scene emphasises the implication that he was in costume, acting a part; its falsity betrayed by his effeminately long and manicured hands – and the punctilious courtesy which Englishmen believe to be profoundly un-English.

The Chinaman was indeed like a vision conjured up by the surroundings. His hallucinatory quality derived not so much from resemblance to fictional stereotypes, however, but rather from his inherent contradictions. Though the questions were posed as rhetorical innuendos about the drug traffic, they addressed a genuine mystery. Who was he? What was the secret of his attraction for white women?

This is not to say that the smiling yellow man was shaped entirely without a fictional model. Politeness and disguise were hallmarks of the most successful Oriental in fiction, Dr Fu Manchu, the evil genius at the centre of a great criminal web. Sure enough, the *Evening News* claimed that a man known to nightclub women as the 'Chinese dope king' controlled the drug traffic, through a network of 'porters, cloak-room attendants, railway officials, milliners, coffee-house proprietors', taxi-drivers, manicurists and, of course, women victims who recruited other women into drug slavery.[30] The Kempton tragedy was only the trigger for a story that had been building up anyway. This account was an elaboration of a story the paper had run ten days before the death, in which actresses and fashionable women were said to acquire their drugs through shady antique shops in Kensington and Holborn, Oriental *objets d'art* being placed in the windows as coded signals. The head of the trafficking organisation employed 'chiefly women of all classes from manicurists in reputable parlours to attendants in cloak rooms'.[31]

In the Dope King, the conspiracy myth was invested with a disquieting erotic force. The fascination he exerted over white women was the more mysterious for being so totally at variance with European ideals of male attractiveness – Chang was not only the wrong colour, but barely more than five feet tall. There is a prototype for this sort of attraction: the mythology of vampirism. The vampire is marked by pallor, rather than Oriental colouring, but 'yellowness' has a similar connotation of unhealthiness. His female followers are distinguished by their wantonness and their need to recruit further victims.

The *Evening News* published its own account of an expedition into the London night, headed 'Cocaine Girls In The West End', later the same day that the *Express* story appeared. As in the *Express*, the word was that clubland was terrified by the heat brought down on it by the Kempton tragedy. The reporter could not persuade a single hotel porter to sell him a bottle under the counter after hours, though he got into a club near Cambridge Circus which served watered-down whisky at two shillings a glass. At half-past three, he went on to another club off Shaftesbury Avenue, where breakfast but no drink was available. Here, however, his

> companion pointed out three girl-addicts to cocaine.
> One was a frail-looking creature of about twenty in a flimsy frock that left three-quarters of her back bare.
> During the intervals of her vivacious dancing in an underground room, she gave herself over to almost hysterical attacks of inane, purposeless laughter, and now and then stroked the man sitting with her.[32]

This was another example of the 'predominating type' that the *Express* correspondent observed: young, frail, underdressed, given to hysterical laughter. They belonged to a subspecies of the consumptive type; thin, sickly, prone to alternate between feverish overexcitement and exhaustion.

The factor of youth had a wider resonance. After all, the idea that young women were distinguished by immaturity was endorsed in the restriction of the franchise to women over thirty: advocates of universal adult suffrage were ridiculed for demanding 'votes for flappers'. (A 'Flappers' Bill' was passed in 1927.) And in a distinctively modern fashion, nightlife was seen as a youth issue. The mainstream press depicted it as a problem; a magazine like the stylish *Pan*, 'a journal for saints and cynics', was exceptional in nailing its colours to the mast of youth.

In addition to cultural conflict, dope posed the threat of neurosis and racial degeneration, an issue thrown into stark relief by the alleged involvement of the Chinese. On the one side was the model young woman, fond of children and outdoor sport; on the other was the cocaine girl, wanton, sickly, hysterical and worse. An *Evening News* leader, calling for stiffer penalties, observed that 'the victims are often beautiful girls whose sensitive temperaments have become neurotic from the adoration they receive, and the night life to which that adoration has brought them.'[33] The night world was intrinsically unhealthy; its sudden mushrooming seemed to pose a threat to a whole new generation.

That included the daughters of the ordinary people who read these newspapers. Across the suburbs, young women craved excitement and glamour. The *Evening News* described a nightclub encounter with a seventeen year-old 'dope girl', a 'common, insignificant girl changed into a creature of almost dazzling brilliance'.[34] The Rev. J. Degen, comparing Freda Kempton's life to an episode from the Satyricon, deplored the 'slang and explosive golf language' favoured by young women, along with other unfeminine traits. 'Jazz-bitten Muriel or Daphne does not mind taking big risks. In fact, she will put her head – metaphorically speaking – right into the lion's mouth with high-pitched laugh and frivolous joke.'[35] He called for the flogging of drug dealers, a demand also raised in Parliament.[36]

Every columnist and opinioniser in the country had their say on the drug question. James Douglas reran the Billie Carleton obituaries with Freda Kempton's name substituted. Where not word for word identical – 'only a child in years' – the imagery was the same: 'She was young, she was beautiful, and she danced. She called herself a dance instructress, but it is evident that she was a foolish little moth whose wings were scorched by the flame of vicious luxury.'[37] The metaphor of the moth or butterfly brought out the frailty of the flapper.

Naturally, Douglas called her 'beautiful'; interestingly, he claimed she was the daughter of a clerk, so that she stood as a warning to the swarm of young women of humble origins fluttering towards the artificial lights. He said she had spoken of being 'fed up' on the night of her death, just like her friend Audrey Knowles-Harrison, wringing his hands over the pathos of the modern young woman's condition.

THE SHADOW OF DEATH.

Daily Express, 14 March 1922. (By permission of the British Library.)

The theme was echoed by George Overton, one of the policemen who had been called to the scene of Billie Carleton's death. In his serialised memoirs, he included the story of Laura Grey, who took an overdose of veronal and left a note saying 'I am simply very, very tired of things in general.' No single case contained more elements of the cautionary drug tale than Grey's. She was said to have left home to seek her independence under the influence of suffragist ideas; but she failed to make a career for herself on the stage, descended into the underworld of nightclubs and drugs, and finally killed herself after becoming pregnant by a man who spurned her.[38]

A different line was taken, unsurprisingly, by Rebecca West. She objected to commentaries that put the blame on women, such as the press claim that 'The dullness of the average married woman of the suburbs is largely responsible for the hectic night life of the West End.' Her verdict on the nightclub was categorical:

> It exists for the purpose of trading in drink and drugs; and the more important of the two is the trade in drugs. One has only to go to any night club and see the Chinese and South Americans, and aliens of all degrees of colour, to see that the best brains of every country's roguery are attending to these things.[39]

What all the commentators agreed on was the scale of the problem. Drugs and clubs, going hand in hand, were everywhere. The extent of coverage was unprecedented, far exceeding the spin-offs from the Carleton case. As in more recent times, a 'war on drugs' was declared. Under such a headline, it was reported that restaurant staff, watching hawkishly for drug fiends, had pounced on an innocent diner unwise enough to take his medicinal tablets without heed of the prevailing atmosphere.[40]

The drug flap was not confined to the print media. Cinema was conspicuously modern not only in its technology, but also in its publicity reflexes. A production could be completed in a few weeks, allowing the medium to follow hard on the heels of a news story – and to claim the credentials of the press. The Birmingham director Jack Graham-Cutts (with whom Alfred Hitchcock served an apprenticeship the following year) declared that his film *Cocaine* was a pioneer work of 'screen journalism'. Made in six weeks at studios in Teddington, it was released at the beginning of May, two months after Freda Kempton's death.[41]

Cocaine's distinction today is that, perhaps uniquely among British drug films of the period, it has survived. At any rate, some of its footage has – but in no particular order. The British Film Institute's archive reel is a hectic collage of sequences and corroded intertitles, apparently compiled at random from lengths of film no more than a few yards long. But *Cocaine*'s major distinction in cinema history is as the subject of a censorship row. The Public Record Office file still exists, and thanks to a diligent civil servant, we have a synopsis with which to make sense of the chaotic reel.[42]

The plot revolves around nightclubs, a drug syndicate, and the threat posed by both these elements to a young woman, played by Flora Le Breton, who comes to the metropolis from the large house in the country where she lives. These prosperous surroundings are actually the fruits of the drug traffic, for the head of the syndicate, known as 'Number One', is none other than her own father.

In London, an actress friend (played by Hilda Bayley) takes the daughter under her wing. She introduces the *ingénue* to the world of the nightclub, with its exotic tango displays and pastiche-Futurist decor, but conceals the powder that she sniffs as she gets dressed up for the evening: 'Cocaine! ... The Mirage of Life ... The Poison which promises Spring and brings Winter ... that destroys Life and Love ... glorifies the Devil ... and scoffs at the Peace God alone can give.' In the corner of the caption, as if the point were not sufficiently made, there is a skull and crossbones.

At the club, according to the *Daily Express*, the women see 'Sleek young men and thinly clothed girls (many of them the 'real thing') jazz and shimmy and fox-trot under the influence of late hours and excitement, nigger-music and cocktails, drugs and the devil.' S.W. Harris, the civil servant, reported that the depiction of the nightclub bordered on the indecent. Despite the wholesomely bright lighting, the images of revelling men and women together on sofas were heady stuff. The nightclub scene climaxed with the actress undergoing a paroxysm of cocaine craving, her hair dishevelled, as though by electric current, her hands outstretched in supplication. The manager of 'The Limit' finally lets her have what she wants.

The syndicate has a Chinese agent, played by a white man who brought a Quasimodo touch to the part, walking with a stiff leg and one shoulder hunched. 'Chief histrionic honours are carried away by Mr. Tony Fraser as a 'Chink' of low degree, a walking embodiment of evil,' said the *Express*. After being arrested, Lo Ki vows revenge on Number One; hearing about the daughter from a crony – actually played by a Chinese man – in an opium den, he decides to engineer the woman's enslavement to cocaine.

He goes to the club and tricks her into taking the drug, whereupon she abandons herself to the predatory manager. Number One's nefarious activities have come home to roost. 'Daddy, I've had some cocaine,' she simpers flirtatiously. Number One shoots Lo Ki and then commits suicide in the club, as the police arrive on a raid. The actress takes an overdose and expires, repentant, in the High Church chapel conveniently located next door. The daughter's future is saved by marriage to her faithful suitor.

Hilda Bayley gave interviews describing the dreadful experience of researching the role in dance dens, and piously expressing the belief that the film would help extirpate the evil.[43] Within the trade, by contrast, the film was promoted with modish cynicism. The *Film Renter & Moving Picture News* jauntily reported that a distributor had been 'snowed under' by demand, and carried advertising copy in the same vein:

If you're down in the mouth,
dull, depressed and feel like
nothing on earth, take a dose of

COCAINE

It will 'buck up' your box-office receipts.
It will drive away depression.[44]

Copy in the *Bioscope* emphasised the box-office bottom line without the archness:

HOW GIRLS BECOME 'DOPE FIENDS'!!
A Sensational Story Of London Night Life

&

THE BIGGEST MONEY-MAKER WHICH HAS BEEN
OFFERED TO EXHIBITORS THIS YEAR
THE NEWSPAPER TOPIC OF THE MOMENT[45]

The one obstacle to the profits was the Board of Film Censors. At this stage, the Board was an advisory body, but one which was increasingly keen on flexing its muscles. In its early days, it had assigned U or A certificates to nearly any film that came its way, but had taken a tougher line since its chairmanship had been assumed by the MP and journalist T.P. O'Connor. Its authority had recently been strengthened by the London County Council, which had decided to ban the showing of films refused BFC certificates.

The Board persuaded the Home Office drugs campaigner Sir Malcolm Delevingne to view *Cocaine*, along with his colleague S.W. Harris, who reported their conclusion that refusal to grant a certificate would be justified. They felt that, firstly, 'apart from the sensational and sordid character of the film it was entirely unscientific in its treatment of the subject, as the effect of cocaine is not that which the film alleges – a single dose would not have the effect of turning a modest girl into an abandoned hussy.' But they apparently thought that might come as a disappointment to the class of young woman in question, since their second objection was that the film would 'encourage rather than dissuade a girl from experimenting with the drug'.

It was not difficult to find a reason to ban a film. The BFC had seventy, including 'inflammatory political subtitles or scenes likely to engender racial hatred, disparage friendly relations with our Allies, or offend religious beliefs and susceptibilities; scenes of cruelty to children or animals; irreverence; drunkenness; realistic murders; executions or crucifixions; or impropriety in dress or action'. This encyclopaedic approach to censorship was regarded with some distaste by the press. *The Times* damned it by cool implication, the *Daily Express* by declamation: 'There are forces at work in this campaign against the photoplay which may ultimately end in the downfall of Anglo-saxondom as the repository of liberty.'[46]

Beyond the metropolis and its 'dancedope dens', the authorities were less inclined to see *Cocaine* as a menace. After it had been refused a licence, the Home Secretary, Edward Shortt, wrote to the Chief Constables of Manchester and Cardiff, where the film had been passed for exhibition. In Manchester, an Inspector Fisher had concluded that it would undoubtedly deter drugtaking, though he had six feet of a sofa scene excised before passing it. Replying to the Whitehall letter, Cardiff's Chief Constable argued that as the city had no nightclubs, the facilities for the drug traffic were so limited as to be non-existent.

There was, however, an objection from another quarter of Cardiff. The Bill Posters Association had already barred the Astra film company from using the *Daily Express* cartoon of Death as a nightclub doorman. The lure of topicality was too much for the Capital Picture House, though. Low Hing, a Chinese resident of the dockland area, sent a letter to the Chinese Consul-General complaining that

Too dangerous for the British public to see: a still from: *Human Wreckage*. (British Film Institute.).

The name of this picture is Cocaine and it is an insult to the Chinese people, also they have newspaper cuttings of the dancing girl and Mr. Chang's photo. outside and over all the newspaper cuttings they have written in blue lead:

READ THIS FIRST THEN COME AND SEE THE FILM

and the picture of the Chinaman is put very ugly and leering and I think such pictures should be banned everywhere as this same picture was banned in London.

Low Hing was interviewed by a police inspector, who reported the letter-writer's specific objection to the portrayal of Lo Ki as an 'ugly cripple', and the general offence that the film had caused to the Chinese community. A week later, the Chief Constable reversed his position and banned it.

The *Cocaine* furore had a sequel two years later, involving the American drug film *Human Wreckage*. After it was refused a certificate, the US distributor threatened to stir up publicity by staging a private screening, to which celebrities from royalty downwards would be invited. The British Board of Film Censors took the line, familiar today, that allowing images or narratives about drugs to be presented to the public would encourage their use: 'It appeared to us to be a pernicious and dangerous film calculated to impede the efforts of the Authorities in their desire to check the growth of the drug habit in this country.'[47]

Calculated it was, but hardly in the direction suggested by the British censors. *Human Wreckage* was the brainchild of Florence Reid, the widow of the Hollywood star Wally Reid, a morphine addict who died in 1923. Notable cinematically as a rare example of the 'Caligarist' design style in a Hollywood film, it received behind-the-scenes support from Will Hays, the purity crusader who purged American movies with censorship codes for directors and morals clauses for casts.[48]

The British Board was evidently unpersuaded of 'Czar' Hays' powers – or perhaps it was suspicious of the company he kept. In support of its case, it submitted two extracts from American pro-censorship commentaries for the Home Office's attention. One warned of 'five or six unmoral men, all Hebrews, who are the real censors of motion pictures throughout the world. They have and are using tyrannical, despotic power in foisting demoralizing pictures upon all Nations of the world.' So did the second, describing the 'despotic dictation of ... the Owners, a small group of "Super-Censors" (five Jews), who reserve the right to say what shall be produced for the mental consumption of not only the people of the United States, but for practically 90 per cent of the world consumption of motion-picture films.'

Whatever S.W. Harris thought of these documents, he refrained from comment. But that year, the climate at the Home Office became much more favourable for such views, with the appointment as Home Secretary of William Joynson-Hicks; anti-Semite, admirer of Mussolini, detester of aliens in general – and scourge of the nightclubs. 'But what do you do here?' a visitor to his Whitehall citadel once asked. 'It is I who am the ruler of England,' Jix replied.[49]

With the spectre of the Victorian frockcoat haunting the Home Office, this was the stage at which the two sides evolved into their full archetypes. Having worn their hair bobbed for a number of years, young women now adopted the boyish look as a whole. 'The short skirts, bobbed hair, and flat chests that were in fashion were in fact symbols of immaturity,' Quentin Crisp pointed out; '... They knew that they looked nothing like boys. They also realised that it was meant to be a compliment. Manliness was all the rage. The men of the twenties searched themselves for vestiges of effeminacy as though for lice.'[50]

Young women thus reflected the immaturity ascribed to them by opinion and by electoral law. The questions of citizenship and sexuality were intertwined: the principal symbolic quality of young womanhood is nubility, which casts an interesting light on the denial of the franchise to younger women. Politically conscious women of all ages saw the restriction as demeaning, and demanded universal adult suffrage. Young women also made an unformulated demand for autonomy in the shape of a style that identified freedom with the absence of adult responsibility. Its androgynous aspect emphasised that this was the active freedom of boys, rather than the traditional sequestered passivity of girls.

Against this movement, the forces of reaction were not only weak, but arguably counter-productive. Churchill remarked that it was Joynson-Hicks who got young women the vote. And as James Laver's contemporary verse suggested, there were other ways of voting besides the ballot box:

Mother's advice, and Father's fears,
Alike are voted – just a bore.
There's negro music in our ears,
The world's one huge dancing floor.
We mean to tread the Primrose Path,
In spite of Mr. Joynson-Hicks.
We're People of the Aftermath
We're girls of 1926.

In greedy haste, on pleasure bent,
We have not time to think, or feel,
What need is there for sentiment
Now we've invented Sex Appeal?
We've silken legs and scarlet lips,
We're young and hungry, wild and free,
Our waists are round about the hips
Our shirts are well above the knee

We've boyish busts and Eton crops,
We quiver to the saxophone.
Come, dance before the music stops,
And who can bear to be alone?
Come drink your gin, or sniff your 'snow',
Since Youth is brief, and Love has wings,
And time will tarnish, ere we know,
The brightness of the Bright Young Things.[51]

Back in 1922, Jix and short skirts were still on the horizon. The campaign against dancing and dope was being conducted at ground level, by the police and organised puritans. Both worked undercover. It was reported that secret vigilance committees had been set up to combat nightclubs in the strip west of Tottenham Court Road, a notably cosmopolitan district. Today, that character survives in the restaurants of Charlotte Street; then, it was not only a polyglot area, but favoured (along with the Seven Dials area of Covent Garden) by black men in particular. 'White girls are being lured in increasing numbers by black men, Scandinavians, Italians, Belgians, Frenchmen, Austrians and Germans of the worst type,' claimed Rev. S. Maurice Watts, revealing that his committee planned to infiltrate the shebeens of the district.[52]

As well as Sergeant Goddard and his colleagues in dress shirts and tails, women played a significant role in drug surveillance. Women police had developed from voluntary patrols mounted during the war, by feminist campaigners – some pursuing suffrage, some fighting the cause of purity – who had seized their opportunity by asserting the need to keep an eye on the female population. Some later came to feel that they were being used to protect men from an imaginary female threat, rather than to protect their sisters from real male ones.[53]

Drug policing had been associated with women police from the very start: when women were permitted to undertake police duties by the 1916 Police Act, the Metropolitan Police Commissioner announced that he would be engaging women patrols to investigate the sale of cocaine to soldiers by prostitutes, and to help stamp out indecency in the parks. While women patrols appear to have devoted much of their time to ticking young women off for flirting with soldiers, drug surveillance gave female police their first opportunity to take part in the kind of operation that enjoys high status within police culture. Two of the first women police, Violet Butcher and Lillian Dawes, are believed to have been involved in these activities. It is thought that one or the other was assigned to pose as a prostitute in West End lavatories, used as dressing-rooms in the evenings by street prostitutes, to break up cocaine dealing among them. Dawes, a traditional beer-and-fags cockney, was said to have been assigned to drug and nightclub observations.[54]

The police spent much of the year watching and pouncing on the street dealers. The individual cases confirm the sociology of the drug traffic, and supported the stereotypes of dope. There was Britannia 'Gypsy' Yettram, of no fixed abode, apprehended after women were seen to come up to her in the Shaftesbury Tavern, Holborn, asking for 'snow'.[55] There was William Mitchell, a bookie, partially paralysed and nearly blind, caught passing a packet of cocaine to two women in a Little Newport Street cafe; or George Charles, a sixty year-old seaman whom Police Sergeant Marks saw approached by two women in search of 'Tokyo'.[56]

Sometimes different sorts of powder were discovered. Sergeant Owen arrested Nathaniel Wiseman, a Romanian, after hearing him offer drugs in a Regent Street café, but what Wiseman was found to be in possession of was soap powder.[57] A detective was offered cocaine that turned out to be sugar, by a man at Holland Park Underground station – which suggests that the street traffic extended rather a long way beyond the heart of the West End. The culprit got six weeks' hard labour for trying to obtain money under false pretences.[58] Most outrageous, however, was Jack M'Lean, a young man caught soliciting in Piccadilly by Sergeant Pearce. The powder in his pocket was not white, but pink, and intended for the cheeks rather than the nose. On an impressive number of counts, M'Lean exemplified the 'burglars, thieves, prostitutes, sodomites, men living upon the earnings of women and other nefarious persons' that the Metropolitan Police Commissioner had claimed were selling cocaine in 1916 (see page 43). His previous form included living off immoral earnings, impersonating a police officer to demand 'bribes' from women in Hyde Park, and, indeed, an arrest for cocaine dealing.[59]

Sometimes a slightly better class of trafficker was netted. Detectives Owen and Haines trapped Sitaram Sampatrao Gaikwar in a sting operation, meeting the young nephew of the Maharajah of Baroda off the boat train at Victoria and posing as cocaine buyers. They agreed on a price of £750 for twenty-eight ounces, then arrested him in a taxi after he collected the parcel from a Lyons Tea Shop near Waterloo. 'Oh, you are police. What rotten luck. But, still, I understand,' he was reported as saying. Gaikwar used cocaine profits to make up for the shortfall in the allowance he received from his uncle, which had been cut from £5000 a year to £50 a month. He got his supplies on trips to the Continent: Germany, with its highly developed pharmaceutical industry, was the principal source of cocaine during this period.[60]

Gaikwar's level, not to say sporting, attitude was out of key with the tone of the times. Molly Gibbons, a domestic servant of twenty-one, hit the note with her hysterical laughter as she sniffed cocaine at midnight in a Soho doorway; at that point, Constable William Pearse moved in on the emblematic dope girl.[61] A freelance vigilante was arrested after going in pursuit of 'dago dope merchants' armed with a hunting knife and a loaded revolver. The ex-sailor, who was sentenced to three years' penal servitude, blamed Jews and Italians for his wife's addiction. 'She was one of the many victims of the war,' John Ross said. 'She did not care for domestic drudgery, although she came from a working-class home. Apart from that, she got into the hands of dope merchants. During the war I discovered she was using a hypodermic syringe.'[62]

The police campaign appeared to be directed at the retail and lower wholesale end of the trade, rather than at the vast syndicates described in the press. In one case at least, though, the detectives were trying to attack a bigger fish by picking off the small fry. Convinced that Brilliant Chang was a major trafficker who had eluded them at the Kempton inquest, the police kept a close eye on the staff of his restaurant. Ah Sing, said to live on the premises, was overheard promising 'the real stuff' to a woman in a side-street a few yards away. Lo Li Foo, a man of twenty who had lived in Britain for ten years, was caught with a silver matchbox containing cocaine. His room off Seven Dials was described as an 'opium den', with blankets and pillows strewn on the floor.

The pair were convicted in August, but both Chang's staff and the police continued their operations. In November, Pearse arrested a man of fifty-two called Sin Fong, after seeing him offer a £5 packet of cocaine to a woman in Glasshouse Street. Sin Fong said he had bought it from friends in the restaurant, which was, again, no more than a stone's throw away. There Pearse surprised a cook, Lon Chenk, showing another packet to two women. A second cook, Yong Yua, tried to throw away two more packets.[63] It became clear that Brilliant Chang would have to get out of the restaurant business.

A couple of weeks after the conviction of Chang's cooks, the year of the Dope Girls had its finale. It involved a Chinese man and white women; it was set in Cardiff, not the capital; and it was the most bizarre incident – as told, at any rate – of the entire drug panic.

A smell like burning sulphur was the first inkling Mr J. Haggett, a butcher, had of the drama that was unfolding next door to him. Then a Chinese man entered his shop in Lower Cathedral Road. The visitor did not ask for meat, but inquired, 'Do you know when a man is dead?' The young butcher accompanied the man next door to the Hop Sing Lung laundry. Upstairs, opening the door to a back bedroom, Haggett was confronted by 'a sickly smell as of carnation scent' and an extraordinary spectacle. On the bed were four bodies, of a Chinese man and three young white women, though '... the features of the women were so yellow that for a time Mr Haggett did not realise they were white girls.'[64] The Chinaman was dead, the women unconscious.

The miasma was nearly too much for one of the policemen called to the scene, according to a report based on an interview with a police chief: one of the most powerful officers in the force was said to have been almost knocked out by the fumes in the room. As he and his colleagues carried the scantily-clad women to the back yard, 'they were assailed and sickened by the opium-laden breath of the victims, and the bending of the bodies caused the noxious vapours from their lungs to come with greater force.'[65]

In the yard, they responded energetically to medical instructions that the women be prevented from resting. The victims were stripped,

YEE SING.

THE DISCOVERY.

HOP SING LUNG LAUNDRY

SCENE OF THE TRAGEDY.

No way to run a laundry. (*Illustrated Police News*, 30 November 1922. By permission of the British Library.)

slapped, and marched incessantly around in circles. When the policemen were exhausted, the process was continued at the hospital; when the hospital staff themselves were spent, 'police matrons of the finest physical type' were dispatched to help. In all, the young women underwent almost fifty hours of continual pummelling and massaging.

At the inquest on Yee Sing, known as Johnny Hop, the three women were hardly capable of coherent speech. They were sisters; Florence, Gwendoline and Rosetta Paul, aged twenty-five, twenty-three and twenty-one. Gwendoline, seeming barely conscious of her surroundings, said that she had been 'intimate' with Yee Sing. She had a nine-month-old child by another Chinese man. The coroner gave up trying to question Florence, who said that they had gone with three different men on the night in question; Rosetta's manner was even more vacant, and her speech more rambling.[66]

The death itself was mysterious. It was suggested that hashish, used as a love potion by the Chinese, was to blame. The antidote was made from geraniums – though it was also asserted that harem women found guilty of infidelity were killed by being placed in a room full of the flowers, which emitted lethal fumes. Another suggestion was that the lethal agent was a secret drug made from onions.[67] The inquest itself settled on a verdict of heart disease accelerated by opium poisoning. A kettle that had been used for the preparation of opium was found; it was conjectured that the dead man and the women might have drunk tea containing the drug.

According to neighbours where the Paul family had originally lived, the household had broken up after the death of their father in 1918. Like Gwendoline, Rosetta also had a baby and a sexual association with a Chinese man; Florence had looked after Rosetta's child while sleeping rough. On the night of Yee Sing's death, they were said to have tried to get a roof over their heads at several other Chinese laundries.

In the nineteenth century, the Paul sisters would have been seen as part of the 'submerged tenth' of society; late in the twentieth, they would have been identified as members of the underclass. This was long before welfare, though. When they were removed into the care of the authorities, the medical apparatus and the police collaborated in relays to inflict what, even allowing for the obvious exaggeration in the reports, amounted to a merciless campaign of physical assault and sleep deprivation. The disorientation and confusion displayed by the sisters in court is just what would be expected to result from such punishment. Yet the accounts are quite blind to the possibility that the treatment, rather than the narcotic, was responsible for the women's pitiful condition.

The Paul sisters, rendered unable to speak, were submerged in a controversy that flared above their heads. The issue became politicised, as, on a far lesser scale, had the screening of *Cocaine* earlier in the year. In the press, the incident was used to link the spread of coloured men beyond the dock area – the laundry was in a 'superior residential quarter' – and allegations that girls from the hills were lured into white slavery by black and yellow men.[68] The Sey Yup, or Chinese Protection Society, countered such allegations by sending a solicitor to the inquest with a brief to show that the women were members of a certain class of white girl that were apt to pester Chinese men.

Away in London, the House of Commons heard demands for greater powers of inspection over premises suspected of harbouring the drug traffic.[69] 'I hope and pray that every Chinese laundry worker will be repatriated right away,' a magistrate named J.R. Llewellyn told a meeting of the Board of Guardians back in Cardiff.[70] There was talk of an anti-Chinese demonstration being held at Yee Sing's funeral.

In the event, the furore died down without serious consequences. It could easily have been otherwise. Three years before, in the interregnum between the Armistice and the Treaty of Versailles, the fractures in British masculinity had burst into a drumroll of violence across the country. Men in uniform were impatient to recover their civilian identities, but feared for their prospects in the post-war world. Most of the disturbances were camp mutinies: 10,000 soldiers demonstrated at Folkestone in January 1919; thousands of others did likewise at other camps. In March, five men died when Canadians rioted at Rhyl; in June, the peak of the 'khaki riots', several hundred Canadians burned down the police station at Epsom in Surrey, killing a policeman. Three regiments mutinied at Sutton in the same county. The following month, Victory Day was marked by clashes between civilians and servicemen or ex-combatants in a number of towns. In Luton, ex-servicemen burnt down the Town Hall after being refused permission to hold a memorial service.[71]

This was the reverse of the post-war coin. The uppermost face was of the flapper – 'women, women everywhere'. Her new identity was being crystallised and polished; while underneath was her male counterpart, his heroic role as soldier now redundant, his civilian identity profoundly uncertain. 'They were subject to queer moods and queer tempers, fits of profound depression alternating with a restless desire for pleasure,' Philip Gibbs observed. 'Many were easily moved to a passion where they lost control of themselves, many were bitter in their speech, violent in opinion, frightening.'[72]

The khaki riots of that spring were accompanied by a wave of race riots in major port cities – London, Liverpool, Tyneside, Glasgow, Newport and Cardiff – where fears over shortages of jobs and housing could be turned into aggression against coloured scapegoats. In Liverpool, a black man was thrown into Queen's Dock and stoned until he drowned. Mobs, thousands strong, terrorised the city's black population for the next three days.

The worst outbreak was in South Wales, where three men were killed. It was said to have triggered by a sexually loaded remark or gesture, made by a black man in Newport to a white woman. Chinese laundries were among the properties wrecked in the ensuing riot. Mobs formed a few days later, after the arrest of a demobilised soldier who stabbed a black docker to death. Some of these were led by Australian soldiers, uniformed and armed with rifles, who used military assault tactics as they opened fire in the Cardiff streets. Some of the defenders also had guns: one Arab shot a Mons veteran, who died wearing the medal ribbon commemorating that battle.[73]

The capacity for organisation in self-defence, displayed physically by the men of colour during the 1919 attacks, was also evident in the response of the Chinese community to the Paul case. By that time, the temper of the country was cooler, and solicitors could replace sentries.

Perhaps the most remarkable aspect of the episode, however, was not so much its abstraction into the realm of debate, but the extent to which its trajectory continued on into the realm of fantasy. The embellishments have a flavour which distinguishes them from other accounts arising from the dope panic: possibly the location of the incident, away from London, allowed a different group of themes to attach themselves.

What is most striking is their proximity to the supernatural. The butcher smells something like sulphur, with its obvious connotations of hell. In the room, there is an uncanny scent of carnations; another account describes the lethal effect of geraniums and onions. The intimations of secret lore suggest witchcraft; the mysterious aroma may betoken spirits. The alternative version, in which a stout policeman is nearly overcome by opium fumes – that also issue from the women's lungs, although the drug has not been smoked, but swallowed – is equally supernatural in mood. Another sinister touch is the yellowing of the women's skins, that makes them nearly unrecognisable as European. A literary precedent exists in Dickens' *The Mystery of Edwin Drood*, in which an old Englishwoman is said to have 'opium-smoked herself into a strange likeness of the Chinaman'.[74]

In this light, the nature of the sisters' ordeal becomes apparent. It was an exorcism; a ritual in which the victim is frequently crushed in order to save her. The forces of orthodoxy, secular or religious, engage the enemy through the bodies of the possessed women, whose fates are secondary to the goal of casting out the evil spirits. Joynson-Hicks, the self-proclaimed Victorian reactionary, was trumped by the Cardiff authorities, who summoned up a medieval reaction to the phantasms of modernity.

9

PAN AND FU MANCHU

Despite the efforts of the police, Brilliant Chang remained at liberty throughout both 1922 and 1923. Unconvicted, he could not openly be entitled the 'Dope King', but another figure was available to act as regent. They complemented each other: in the drug legends of the 1920s, both a Yellow and a Black Dope King reigned over Britain.

Like Chang, Edgar Manning was a highly sexual figure. The earliest episode in his life to be recorded in detail describes how, after being seduced by Manning, a young white woman of nineteen exchanged her modest but desirable job, as a clerk at a paper manufacturer's in Hertfordshire, for the life of a prostitute in the West End. No case could have been more baffling to those who agonised over the inexplicable fascination that men of colour held for white girls.

It was in 1918 that Doreen Taylor came down to London for the day, from her home town of Hemel Hempstead, and was accosted by a well-dressed black man in St Martin's Lane. Would she like to come and live with him? he asked. She went up to his room, where, as the witness statement puts it, intimacy took place.[1]

Taylor returned to Hemel Hempstead, but she was summoned back by a letter from Manning two or three days later. A few days after that, she bumped into a friend from home called Maisie Kitchener, who was now getting her living on the streets of the West End. Doreen Taylor thought she would do the same. Eventually she moved out of Manning's room and got her own lodging in Little Newport Street, the Soho passage in the shadow of the Leicester Square theatres. Her relationship with him persisted, though; she called herself Peggy Manning, and he would visit nearly every day. Sometimes he would hold rehearsals for his jazz band – he played the drums – in the building.

One afternoon in July 1920, however, someone else turned up in his place. A stranger with an American accent handed her a note: 'My dear Peggy, this gentleman is a friend of mine and will speak with you confidentially. I am alright, Yours Edgar.'

Taylor knew of a number of reasons why Edgar Manning might be in trouble. She gave him money on occasion: although he would return the favour at other times, taking money from a prostitute made him guilty of living off immoral earnings. Some other reasons lay around her room: cocaine, parcelled up into paper wraps for sale at five shillings apiece, and a loaded Colt revolver. Manning had a second Colt, a .38. This one had now been emptied.

Manning's public debut as a hoodlum was nothing if not spectacular, and aptly located in London's theatreland. The sequence of events had begun in Mrs Fox's restaurant, at 9 Little Newport Street. This poky establishment was a rendezvous for the underworld; a haunt of resting actresses and idling crooks. Elizabeth Fox, who had kept the establishment for twenty years, was an aunt – a 'fairy godmother', one account said – to the West End criminal community.[2] The previous weekend, she had gone to the races at Lingfield with a party of her friends and customers, including Edgar Manning. It had been a good outing for her; at the end of the first day, she had been £70 up.

Manning's luck had been more modest, but that did not stop an acquaintance named Frank Miller, known as Yankee Frank, from coming up to him in Mrs Fox's and demanding a pound of it. 'I have not a pound to give you,' Manning replied. 'You're a fucking thief,' returned Yankee Frank. 'I know how you're earning your living.' Manning still refused. 'You're a fucking shitpot,' Frank added. He then turned his attention to a woman called Molly O'Brien, who was sitting nearby. 'You're a bloody prostitute,' he told her, chewing on a cigar.

According to O'Brien, she was in fact an actress (and a solitary entry in the records, ten years before, supports her claim). Her actual rejoinder was, 'It's a pity you don't go and work for a living, you're only a ponce,' (which, according to the police, was perfectly true, though Miller called himself a motor mechanic). Yankee Frank flung a coin and his cigar at her, then punched her in the eye. 'If there wasn't so many people in here, I'd do something else to you,' he exclaimed, and ran out. Manning asked if she was hurt, and left soon after.

A while later, Molly O'Brien saw Frank in the street with a companion; his brother, though the man went under the name of Charles Tunick. She remonstrated with him again, this time receiving a blow to the stomach for her trouble. The two men ran off and turned up Charing Cross Road, where they met a friend, Robert Davis. The trio walked on to Cambridge Circus and turned left down Shaftesbury Avenue, stopping on a corner opposite the Palace Theatre. While they were chatting, Edgar Manning appeared. They rushed him; he ran round a passing bus and opened fire, hitting all three in the legs. None was seriously hurt, even Miller, who had been shot in both thighs.

The police found Manning in his room in Margaret Street, the other side of Oxford Street. It was the front room on the ground floor; the preferred perch of villains, since they could see trouble coming and escape out the back. But Manning made no attempt to flee. He was sitting by the bed in his shirtsleeves, talking to a friend. 'That's quite right, Guvnor. I shall give you no trouble,' he told the arresting officer.

All right, guv, I'll come quietly ... Perhaps words like that were yet to become stilted. At any rate, the mood conveyed by the dialogue was consistent with the testimony as a whole. Manning's general demeanour was polite and equable. A posthumous account recalls the immaculately dressed Manning strolling the streets and greeting women 'with an old-world courtesy, ironical when one realises what his association with them was'.[3] His note to Doreen Taylor had a degree of elegance in its formality, rather remarkable in the heat of the moment. The waitress at Mrs Fox's confirmed that he had always been orderly; Taylor's landlady affirmed his quietness and courtesy. So did his own landlady, though she added that he often drank a bottle of whisky a day, and had a habit of leaving his revolver lying on the washstand. He had a licence for it, though.

The one exception to this pattern of public civility, in fact, was the gunning down of the three men in a major London thoroughfare. But even here, he expressed regret – to a degree – on arrest. Although Miller was a 'gorilla', and 'ought to be out of the way', Manning said he was sorry about the others, and had deliberately shot to wound rather than to kill. Hoping to hang on to the revolver, he claimed to have thrown it away; the police promptly found it under the bed.

The episode was a cameo of Edgar Manning in action. A triple kneecapping, in broad daylight, in the heart of the West End: it was stupid, carried out without regard to the consequences – and had an undeniable panache. Manning's subsequent notoriety derived in significant part from the combination of a style that made him visible, and the strategyless excursions that draw a small-time crook back into court as inexorably as gravity. Each time police action put him in the papers again, the Manning demon grew.

On this first occasion, however, it was as if good manners paid off.

Manning was initially charged with attempted murder, but this was reduced to unlawful wounding – another triumph for Huntly Jenkins, the man who successfully defended Reggie De Veulle's manslaughter charge. At the Old Bailey, Edgar Manning received a sentence of sixteen months' hard labour: it seems inconceivable that a sane person cutting loose with a firearm in the middle of the West End could be let off so lightly today.

One factor in his favour was that he had reached his thirties without besmirching his record, although the Flying Squad had identified him as a prostitutes' drug dealer in 1919. His origins in Jamaica were never precisely determined, but he appears to have been born in 1888 and christened Alfred Mullin. His parents, who were unmarried, were two former slaves called Benjamin Mullin and Cecilia Francesco; both were dead by the mid-1920s. Manning left Jamaica in his teens, probably going to the United States. Like many West Indian men, he came to Britain during the war and worked in a munitions factory. He gave satisfactory service as a labourer in the forging department of the Vickers cartridge works at Dartford, but left because of illness in August 1918. His condition required an operation that December, but he recovered sufficiently to join a touring theatre company for a few months. He was said to play in the jazz band at Ciro's, one of London's smartest nightclubs.

After serving his sentence for the shooting, he headed straight back to the West End and its drifting traffic of petty villains. Among them was a man named Eric Goodwin, the son of a wealthy Liverpool tobacco merchant. Goodwin had joined the Army in 1915, as a subaltern in the Lancashire Fusiliers. One of his comrades in the draft was J.R.R. Tolkien: while the latter's experiences at the Front found expression in the blighted landscapes of *The Lord of the Rings*, Eric Goodwin's war legacy was an opiate habit, acquired in the course of treatment for wounds. Addiction among veterans was not uncommon, and surfaced occasionally when one overdosed or fell foul of the law, but the ex-combatant addict was not attributed any great significance in the typology of the drug habit.[4]

Goodwin told his doctor that he had been gassed, and his horse had been killed under him. When the military hospital stopped giving him morphine, he got friends to smuggle it to him in boxes of chocolates. After the war, he funded his habit through cars; both by repairing them and by stealing them. The number of vehicles on the roads nearly doubled between 1920 and 1922, approaching one million, and providing many former soldiers with a source of income, legal or otherwise.

One night in January 1922, Goodwin and a friend called on Manning. While waiting for the latter to return from an errand, Goodwin gave himself an injection of heroin and passed out. Manning realised he was dead a few hours later.[5]

Suspicion naturally fell on the Jamaican, for whom Goodwin was said to have sold heroin in the better class of nightclub; Inspector Walter Burmby's constables Owen and Haines began to keep him under surveillance. Also keeping an eye on him was Sergeant Marks, who used to put bicycle clips on suspects to prevent them from disposing of drugs through holes in their trouser pockets.[6]

Manning's name also came up when Freda Kempton died two months later. The Paddington police were told he had sold her cocaine, albeit only once or twice. A couple of months after that, he was named as the man who supplied drugs to Maud Davis, a dressmaker and prostitute who died of an overdose in her St Martin's Lane lodgings.[7]

Manning pulled back from the West End after Goodwin's death. He now had a partner in crime, a Greek woman called Zenovia Iassonides. She and her husband ran the Montmartre Café in Soho's Church Street, to which women, from both better and worse classes, were said to flock in search of drugs.[8] Manning struck up with Zenovia, and they moved up to Primrose Hill to run a dope double-act. Edgar had a front room at 22 Regents Park Road, while Zenovia lived over the road at number 33. Manning's landlady, a Mrs Mason, was also suspected of cocaine trafficking. The press later claimed that in this neighbourhood, Zenovia and Edgar attracted a more discreet clientele, which would have been reluctant to venture into Soho. Customers could have injections on the premises, or take the drugs away; up to twenty doped girls might be unconscious in the dealers' rooms at any time.[9]

It was not only the press that alleged Manning and Iassonides were operating on a wholesale scale. Burmby's operation was disrupted in April, when a woman phoned S Division to tell them that Manning had two pounds of cocaine in his room. The police rushed straight round, but found nothing. Manning fired off an aggrieved letter to the Commissioner of Police:

> Honerable Sir:-
>
> I humbly beg your kind permission, to grant me a personal interview at your earliest convenience, so as to allow me to lay my grievance before you, wherein Justice is concerned.

Sir:- I humbly appeal to you, for I can no longer bear this torment Bullying and intimidating, action from members of the C.I.D. department:-

viz:- Seg. W Wilkins with two other officers of the same dept. also Seg. Marks with two other officers from Marlborough St.

My nerves are being badly strained, owing to the fact, that I have been a victim of Malaria, an at times, not quite responsible for my actions.

The fact is, I being by nature desine – Black seems to make my persecution the more unbearable, it is now making my nerves a total wreck and also interferes with my dayle living also my place of abode.

Thanking you in anticipation

'Sir:- Your Most humbly,

Edgar Manning.

With his repeated protestations of humility, and his posture as a debilitated victim of harassment, Manning seems to pre-empt the terms of his demonisation by defining himself as their opposite. In journalism and popular writing, he represented animal black potency, cunning and predatory; in his own humble missive, he exemplified the black man as victim of the authorities – and no more: he makes his colour seem like a source of weakness, not pride. His references to his nerves, of course, play on a theme traditionally feminine in connotation. That might have been an expression of his personality; or it might have been a form of deference, making himself seem less of a man.

The request for an audience was a distinctly colonial one, the traditional mode for a villager to pursue a grievance at the court of the District Officer. Naturally the meeting never took place. A week after writing the letter, Manning was apprehended at Zenovia's house. As well as fifteen tablets of morphine in his pocket, he had an attaché case stuffed with a complete kit of vice villainy: a bottle of cocaine, opium utensils, a syringe case and hypodermic needles, a pornographic book and photos, a revolver, and thirteen ounces of opium. Back at his lodgings were scales, a price list of injectable drugs, and the *pièce de resistance*, a fashionable silver-topped walking stick, hollowed out to conceal an eighteen-inch glass tube in which drugs could be carried.

The police congratulated themselves on capturing a 'dangerous and notorious pest', who held opium parties and had a dozen prostitutes and others selling his drugs around the West End. In the eyes of the press, the black man and the alien woman made a pretty pair. 'Madame Tinovia' [*sic*], the 'cocaine queen', was said to have started her career

Edgar Manning in court.

drugging soldiers round Victoria. It was stressed that both she and Manning operated by recruiting proxies: 'Manning, in fact, was a man who had numerous white women agents who induced girls to try cocaine-sniffing, and thus led them to be victims and to be under the black man's influence.'[10]

This time, he got a month for the gun and six months for the drugs. It was the maximum sentence possible under the Dangerous Drugs Act of 1920 (which had made the temporary provisions of DORA 40B permanent), but meant that he was not out of circulation for long. The following months saw more effective prosecutions against Zenovia Iassonides, her husband and nephew, who, as aliens, were liable to deportation.[11]

After her release, Zenovia and her nephew went to Paris. She stayed in touch with Edgar; the police found a photo of her in his bedroom when they next arrested him in 1923. Manning had taken a flat in Lisson Street, near Marylebone Station. For an 'exceedingly cunning' scoundrel – Burmby's description – he was remarkably artless. Having struck up friendly relations with the neighbours, a married couple, through using their phone, he showed them a revolver in a cardboard box and asked if they knew anybody who wanted to buy it for £5. He incurred the landlord's wrath by not paying the rent, and drew more attention to himself with a constant stream of women callers, at all hours of the day and night.

When Burmby and Owen arrived on the inevitable raid, the door was opened by a woman called Peggy Pearce, who, like Doreen Taylor, called herself Peggy Manning. They found the usual cornucopia of evidence inside: the revolver, ammunition, opium utensils, a syringe, cocaine, opium and assorted paraphernalia. This time, the stakes were higher. The Dangerous Drugs Act had just been amended, raising the maximum penalty to ten years' penal servitude. Manning's trial at the Central Criminal Court was the first case on indictment since the amendment came into effect. (The fortunate consequence, from this book's point of view, is that Manning's entire police file is among the small percentage of criminal records saved from routine destruction because of their legal interest. That is why Manning's letter and Frank Miller's curses are preserved in perpetuity at the Public Record Office.)

For what Ernest Wild, the Recorder of London, called a 'vile and foul' offence, Manning was sentenced to three years' penal servitude; a 'lagging', in criminal parlance. Penal servitude was the most serious form of imprisonment, though by this time it was distinguished mainly by the length of sentences – three years was the minimum term – and the broad arrows on the uniforms of 'convict' prisoners, as they were known. The worst of them went to Dartmoor, the other male convicts to Maidstone or Parkhurst. The latter had the best hospital facilities, which may be why Manning, with his persistent poor health, was sent there.

The jail doors closed amid the clamour of the press. Under the headline 'Evil Negro Caught', the *News of the World* gloated over the conviction of the 'king of London's dope traffic'.[12] 'This negro was money mad, and he made it at the sacrifice of the souls of white women and white girls ...' the paper concluded.

Referring back, as was obligatory, to the original legend of Billie Carleton, the *News of the World* claimed Manning had been directly responsible for her death. And Manning himself put his name to a fantasy in which Carleton featured prominently. He was released on licence in November 1925; in February 1926, the readers of the *World's Pictorial News* were treated to a feature under Manning's byline entitled 'My Life As The Dope King Of London' – 'Eddie Manning, once known as the Dope King of London, describes the cravings which brought misery to himself, as to many others, and introduced him to the debaucheries of pyjama parties.'[13]

This was not the Eddie Manning known to Walter Burmby, Doreen Taylor, or, indeed, his parents. This one was sent to Britain in 1912 to read for the Bar, so as to fulfil his comfortably-off father's desire to see him become 'a member of the educated and official class'. He was seduced by a woman he met in a nightclub, who introduced him to a depraved and perverted set. It lived for drink, drugs and sex alone; its leading figures were a woman called Cocaine Daisy, and Billie Carleton. Later Manning introduced Brilliant Chang to the dope scene, and it was at one of Manning's parties that Chang and Freda Kempton met. Manning ended up in a sumptuous Mayfair flat, drinking champagne and going on to dope parties every night.

> The women there especially seemed to go utterly mad with excitement. Dope had sapped away all their feelings of modesty and restraint. The wild syncopated rhythm of Africa's pulsing music – translated into American jazz tunes – did the rest. On one occasion I remember a girl, little more than a child, leaped up from a low couch, and standing in the middle of the room, she began to tear off her clothes.
>
> Finally she stood before us like a demoniacal Greek statue of an

Amazon. Naked, lissom, and trim, with the figure of a boy, her eyes blazed, her hands clasped and unclasped convulsively, she stamped her feet on the carpet. Obviously she felt an impelling desire to do something – something startling – something big. But what to do she knew not.

She looked round the room wildly, then suddenly she realised her nakedness. With a scream she collapsed on to the floor sobbing hysterically.

This incident, startling though it may sound to those who have no personal experience of dope addicts, was ordinary enough in the circle in which I moved. I have selected it to tell my readers because it is possible to recount without offence.

The wildest orgies were the Carleton set's snow parties, at one of which the actress herself did a mad dance to the accompaniment of a world-famous violinist. This fantasy derived from popular fiction caricaturing the bohemian avant-garde; the naked young girl recalls, in particular, the nubile artist's model Macaiea in Lady Dorothy Mills' *The Laughter of Fools* (Duckworth, London 1920). The novel tells the story of a young war widow whose aristocratic bohemian friend, ensconced in a room 'like a hashish dream that has spent a weekend in Paris', tells her to live in a studio and wear her hair off her forehead. She soon finds herself listening to a woman reading poetry in the backroom of a working men's restaurant, or dancing at a party in a converted garage. The ringleader of the set is an artist with a weakness for women and opium. One of his protegées is the fourteen year-old Macaiea, who recites Swinburne's 'Atalanta', is plied with drink, and does a Greek dance. She is eventually found half-drowned in a bowl of wine when an opium orgy is raided, along with a huge black man seated on a dais, smoking opium from a pipe with a skull-shaped bowl. The artist's name happens to be Manning.

The girl's outburst in Edgar Manning's story is symbolic: the London night seemed full of young women, little more than children, possessed with artificially incandescent energies but lacking the understanding with which to direct them, impulsively stripping themselves of virtue, and realising their exposure too late. At a deeper level, she represents a non-viable type; her femininity subverted by an androgynous immaturity and the sort of neo-classical Maenad wildness that D.H. Lawrence found so worrying.

The absurdest aspect of the piece is Manning's received pronunciation. Not a trace of blackness remains: he describes the effects of African rhythms like an explorer sending a dispatch back to his people in Surrey. The article breaks no new ground in terms of popular drug writing as a whole, but it marks one more inglorious stage in the evolution of drug journalism, with its use of the confessional mode to give fiction the bogus authority of a first-person narrative.

Unsurprisingly, the portrait of Edgar Manning as a sober young man seduced from his studies failed to supplant that of him as the evil negro. The real Manning fitted a stereotype that had already begun to enter popular consciousness. As with the Chinese, young white women were said to be prone to 'yield to the strange fascination of these cunning and vicious negroes, with their air of gaiety, their easy and infectious laughter, their gleaming white teeth and rolling eyes, and their passion for song and music'.[14] More benign accounts depicted black men as simple, childlike folk, concerned principally with amusements and show. They were said to 'dress like lords, in spats and spotless linen', and to be 'exceptionally fond of gramophones, billiards, music halls, jewellery, boxing'.[15]

The tone of such reporting ranged from condescension through contempt to open hatred. Under the headline 'Vanity Of Our Coloured Guests', another piece accused the black man of wearing coloured socks and not knowing the value of money. 'Swank seems to be interwoven in every little act of these men's lives. When they get their wages some of them act like little children and go nosing round the shops for things they don't want.'[16] There was a 'black peril' as well as a yellow peril, according to *John Bull*. It consisted essentially of the miscegenation threat, and concretely of black men inhabiting the area north of Oxford Street between Tottenham Court Road and Great Portland Street. Here they were said to pose as unemployed musicians at the Labour Exchange, and to hang around St Giles, Bloomsbury waiting for racing editions to come out. When not loafing, 'they run gambling houses, they trade in dope, they spread disease.'[17]

Edgar Manning thus epitomised a major folk devil, the drug trafficker, and a minor one, the black delinquent. He was also a forerunner of a type familiar in the drug iconography of the past twenty years, particularly in the United States; the black pusher-pimp. The stereotype comprises drugs, guns, aggression, flaunted wealth and flamboyant clothes. It serves to show just how placid 1920s London was by comparison. Though Manning seemed to feel undressed without a pistol, he is only known to have fired it on that one occasion in Shaftesbury Avenue. Nor were any other acts of violence attributed to him: he was not alleged to have beaten his women; only to have supplied them with drugs. His other crimes were against property. In this respect he was a man of his times, a period in which, for all its hardships, crimes against the person were at a low level.

Even Manning's clothes could only be faulted by quibblers – such as Robert Fabian, the policeman who became a household name in the 1950s as 'Fabian of the Yard'. A brilliant self-publicist, Fabian not only had a TV series based on his adventures, but oversaw the spinning Wheel of Fortune on a game show, and took advantage of his celebrity to beat the hanging-and-flogging drum into the 1970s. His fame arose from reminiscences of a career that began in May 1921, when P.C. Fabian ventured onto the streets of Soho for the first time, under the wing of an older bobby.

> We walked down Lisle Street, and my companion paused, drawing me into the shadows, as a tall, slim negro came out of a house. He was superbly well-dressed – perhaps somewhat overdressed – in a tightly tailored black overcoat with velvet collar and homburg hat, and cigar in his big teeth. He glanced alertly up and down the street but did not see us. A white girl was with him – a pretty, delicate little creature, but rather dishevelled and forlorn, I thought.
>
> 'Who is it?' I asked, when they had gone. The old policeman said solemnly: 'That, son, was Eddie Manning – called Eddie the Villain. And take my advice, son, if it means pinching that fellow, never go alone. If you get an urge to talk to him, don't. If he wants to give you a cigarette, refuse it. Never take a drink from him, never go to his place if you want information. Scrub him out of your life – he's the worst man in London.'[18]

Thus Fabian set the seal on the Manning legend. By that time, Manning himself was long dead, unable to sue, or to point out that in May 1921 he had been safely behind bars, half-way through his sentence for the shooting.

After the drug arrests among his employees, Brilliant Chang sold his share in the Chinese restaurant. Like his staff, who had been operating in the streets of Soho just over the road from the Regent Street premises, Chang did not venture far. He started up the Palm Court Club in Gerrard Street, to the discomfiture of Mrs Meyrick, based at number 43, who did not welcome the extra attention from the police that Chang would attract. Gerrard Street was not the high street of London's Chinatown that it is today. There are no Chinese names listed in the contemporary street directories (though these are biased towards ownership rather than occupation): Brilliant Chang might possibly have been the first Chinese man in Gerrard Street.

In her memoirs, 'Ma' Meyrick claimed that she would not let Chang into the 43, and had banned her dancers from visiting his restaurant after they started returning in a state of 'queer nervous excitement'. Similar problems arose, she said, when he started his club on her doorstep. From the safety of retrospection, Chang served to carry the blame for drug allegations which, at the time, were levelled at Kate Meyrick herself.[19]

Mrs Meyrick had a staying power – which is to say, a financial arrangement with corrupt police – that Chang lacked. The police kept up the pressure, and Chang's partnership in the club lasted only six months. In October 1923, he retreated to Limehouse.[20]

No doubt this appealed to the prevailing sense of racial tidiness, but Chang was as out of place as an Oxford undergraduate in a cotton mill. He was an educated, bourgeois, Westernised playboy, gone to ground among sailors, shopkeepers and artisans. The Limehouse Chinese community was stable and orderly, but was vulnerable to police pressure because of the illegality of two of its distinctive cultural traits, opium-smoking and gambling. Like Mrs Meyrick, those involved commercially in such activities would not have welcomed Chang, either as a competitor or as a magnet for the law.

Chang's new home was a flat at 13 Limehouse Causeway, between a derelict ground floor and a top floor let to Chinese sailors. He had two rooms, a dilapidated kitchen and a bedroom. In the latter, Chang was said to have recreated his West End lair: 'a nest of Oriental luxury. It was papered in blue and silver, with silver dragons rampant. The furniture was of the richest description, and the bed a great divan of luxury. A carpet which silenced the softest tread covered the floor.'[21]

Whatever effect exile from the West End had on Chang's involvement with cocaine, it did not diminish his erotic appetites. In his bedroom he kept a stock of letters, handwritten and identically worded, to pass to women who took his fancy:

> Dear Unknown – Please do not regard this as a liberty that I write to you, as I am really unable to resist the temptation after having seen you so many times. I should extremely like to know you better, and should be glad if you would do me the honour of meeting me one evening where we could have a little dinner and a quiet chat together. I do hope you will

consent to this, as it will give me great pleasure, and in any case do not be cross with me for having written to you.

Yours hopefully, Chang.

P.S. – If you reply, please address it to me at the Shanghai Restaurant, Limehouse-causeway, E14.

The police had some successes interdicting the drug traffic on the Limehouse – West End axis, such as the arrests of Jack Kelson, an American seaman who shuttled back and forth supplying cocaine to nightclubs, and May Roberts, the 'White Queen of Limehouse'.[22] Pinning Chang down was a different matter. They raided him twice, but found no drugs. On one occasion, in the daytime, they found two chorus girls in his bed.[23]

Eventually, they found a way of using a woman against him – which must have given them considerable satisfaction. Violet Payne was a failed actress who had come to the notice of the authorities in May 1923, when she was caught stealing clothes from a Marylebone hotel. These were to pay for drugs, which she bought at a chemist's run by a couple called Burnby, in Lisson Grove. (Edgar Manning was living nearby, in Lisson Street, at the time.)

Payne, who used the names Mary Deval and Ruby Duval, was a cameo study of abjection. For eight or nine years, the Burnbys had taken whatever money she could muster – Mrs Burnby also accepted stolen clothes – in exchange for cocaine and heroin. She used the drugs cyclically, taking cocaine in the day, and heroin at night to sleep. Mrs Burnby would give her injections on the premises.

In court, Payne recounted how she had also sold her own clothes to pay for cocaine. A few weeks before her arrest, Mrs Burnby had taken all her money – fourteen shillings – and botched the heroin injection. Payne's blood spurted all over the stove, and her face swelled up alarmingly. 'Don't die here, don't die here,' Mrs Burnby shrieked; the couple treated the young woman by holding smelling salts under her nose, and sent her on her way within an hour. Violet Payne's readiness to inform on her dealers is not difficult to understand. Mrs Burnby was jailed for six months and her husband for two.[24]

In March the following year, Violet Payne was spotted leaving a restaurant in Limehouse Causeway with Brilliant Chang. They went into a pub in Pennyfields, the other side of the West India Dock Road. Chang left, and she took two packets from her pocket, hiding one in her glove and the other under her skirt. She resisted arrest, struggling

Violet Payne. (*Empire News*, 9 March 1924. By permission of the British Library.)

in the charge room and trying to swallow evidence. But, as before, she talked.[25]

Chang's flat was raided again. This time, the detectives produced a single packet of cocaine from behind a loose board in the kitchen cupboard. Violet Payne and Brilliant Chang made a handsome couple together in the dock: she was pretty, and he was opulent in his fur-lined coat; enveloped, as always, in sensual luxury. Even his speech was erotic and tactile: 'a liquid, silken voice that was almost a caress'.

The case against Chang was, by contrast, less than elegant. The token packet was not a very plausible discovery on the premises of a man sophisticated enough, according to the police, to have controlled forty per cent of the London drug traffic. To nail the embarrassment, Chang was asked outright if he accused the police of planting it. Doubtlessly preferring a shorter prison sentence to a longer one, he answered that he did not; his explanation was that it must have been left by the previous occupants.

Violet Payne's function in the case against him was to testify that he not only took cocaine but dealt it, and to illustrate the web he was said to weave between drugs and sex. In terms of proof, her evidence left

Brilliant Chang, luxurious in his fur-lined coat.

something to be desired. She described approaching Chang in a Limehouse restaurant and asking for cocaine. Chang left; she went out separately, and a Chinese hand appeared over a wall, in Arthurian fashion, to present her with a packet of cocaine. She gave it a pound in return, and it disappeared.

Payne denied pulling up her skirt in the restaurant to show Chang the needle marks on her thigh – 'Good heavens, no!' – but admitted staying the night with him on at least one occasion when she called to buy cocaine.[26] The detective generalised from this example: 'This man would sell drugs to a white girl only if she gave herself to him as well as paying him. He has carried on the traffic with real Oriental craft and cunning.'[27]

The Recorder of London agreed. 'It is you and men like you who are corrupting the womanhood of this country,' he declared. 'Girls must be protected from this traffic, and society must be purged.' Chang was sentenced to fourteen months in prison, followed by deportation. Violet Payne was given three months' hard labour.

Although Chang was going out with a whimper, the press turned a rather mundane Limehouse drug case into a pyrotechnic display. 'The yellow king of the "dope runners" has been caught at last in the net of British justice,' the *Daily Express* announced. Running with the ball set in motion by police sources, it described a vast network, stretching across the Continent, with Chang at its centre. He only dealt with women, it said, and turned them into agents; one smuggled cocaine from Paris in her bloomers.[28]

Other accounts were more florid still. Freda Kempton was said to have committed suicide after he ensnared her with kindness and drugs, and then struck. When she asked him if cocaine could kill, 'He looked up quickly as he answered, but the happy light in the girl's eyes and the laugh upon her lips instantly killed the suspicion which had sprung to life in his brain. Had he only known it her happiness was prompted by the knowledge that death was very near at hand ...'[29]

The theme of a decadent, orgiastic sexuality was elaborated. Private dining rooms were an institution in plush and discreet West End restaurants: seduction was implicit, but had to take place on the sofa. At Chang's, it was related, these chambers were dens of soft, exotic, yielding luxury.

> Weird designs adorned the walls, great silken cushions in an infinite variety of colour littered the floor, which was carpeted with a covering into which the foot sank almost to the ankle. In the centre of each room

was a huge divan bed ... Sometimes one girl alone went with Chang to learn the mysteries of that intoxicatingly beautiful den of iniquity above the restaurant. At other times half-a-dozen drug-frenzied women together joined him in wild orgies.[30]

Another report stayed closer to the original police account of the two chorus girls in Chang's Limehouse lair. 'Recently two girls in the Tottenham Court-road district disappeared for four days. They came back at the end of that time with their clothes in rags, torn almost from their backs in the wild frenzy produced by Chang's opium pipe.'[31] A cigar might sometimes be only a cigar, but this was an instance in which a pipe was not only a pipe. And as well as its phallic connotation, a pipe could also be a musical instrument. Chang was Pan among the nymphs, piping them into intoxicated abandonment.

A streak of sadism ran through these perversities. 'He enjoyed the agony of the unfortunate woman of the streets until his victim was nearly frantic, enjoying her agony, gloating over her, and exulting in the eager clutching of her hands.'[32] The catalogue of depravity was not a random selection. While Edgar Manning represented the threat of alien savagery, Brilliant Chang stood for the menace of an alien civilisation. China was ancient, sophisticated; apparently in extended decline, yet radically different and therefore unknowable in the extent and nature of her challenge to the West. She was decadent, and probably cruel. In *Dope*, Sax Rohmer had alluded to a sado-masochistic element in the fascination of the Chinaman, with Molly Gretna's comical anticipation of bondage and whipping.

As well as echoing the orgies of Pan and Dionysus, the suggestions of group sex in the Chang accounts accorded with the general British understanding that outside Europe, polygamy prevailed. The sexual map for such regions was still marked 'Here be dragons'. Dick Carlish, the manager of a club Kate Meyrick opened in Montmartre, made the point vividly in his serialised memoirs: 'On rare occasions the Chinaman would open his eyes wide, to show twin pools, hinting, in some obscure, horrible way, at dark practices unknown to most Europeans, and beyond the imagination of nine-tenths of the most depraved of them.'[33]

The British also understood the Chinese to be a race whose mental development compensated for their slight physical forms. Chang made up for his five-foot stature with his education, his business abilities, and the meticulousness with which he approached seduction. The European races maintained that they had attained the pinnacles of both mental and physical development, but they feared that Orientals were more intellectually sophisticated, and Africans better physically endowed. Traditionally equating the latter with phallic power, European xenophobia conversely saw the Orient as feminine in cast. In China, therefore, the conventional order of gender was disrupted: Chinese sexuality, as represented in the figure of Chang, was intrinsically perverse. Could it even be that his erotic fascination derived from some strange sexual affinity with the women whom he drew to him?

Whatever the process, his corruptive power over white women was accepted as fact, as was the presumption of his leading role in the drug traffic. Yet there is no direct evidence to support the belief that he supplied drugs, other than to his girlfriends. At his trial, the police said that they had first come across his name in correspondence found when a Birmingham opium ring was broken up in 1917. They gave no further details, however, and the relevant Home Office files on drug cases of the period do not mention Chang. His employees certainly sold cocaine, but hawking packets of it in nearby streets suggests a sideline rather than a major trafficking operation.

The most striking evidence that Chang was a drug kingpin is the circumstantial fact of the dramatic fall in drug convictions from their peak in 1923 to the following year, in which Chang was jailed. The fall was a permanent one: between 1921 and 1923, there was an average of sixty-five cocaine prosecutions a year; between 1927 and 1929, the figure was just five. Opium prosecutions ran at 148 a year in the earlier period, and thirty-six per year in the latter.[34]

The simplest explanation why there were few prosecutions in 1924 is precisely that there were so many of them in 1923, rather than that the police were finally able to secure a conviction against Brilliant Chang. Though symbolically and culturally significant, the drug underground was small enough to be subdued by police action ... or to adapt to harassment and disappear out of sight altogether.

Whatever effect Chang's arrest had on the drug traffic, it undoubtedly marked the end of the Aftermath drug panic. Less tangible forces than Detectives Owen and Pearse and their colleagues rang the curtain down. The Aftermath itself was ending – with hindsight, Vera Brittain dated its demise to around 1925.[35] As the decade's edgy instability settled down into style, shock turned to ostentatious ennui. The day that the *Daily Express* reported Chang's imprisonment, it ran a piece very different in tone to its florid dispatches from the underground clubs of just two years before. 'London night clubs, with a few exceptions, generally remind you of an ill-assorted party gathered in a cellar to consume indifferent liquor bought with borrowed money at somebody's funeral,' it grumbled. 'A grim determination to pass the time somehow, far-fetched fun, and forced amusement are their elements.'[36] The revel had started with the Victory Ball, had flourished hectically and sometimes tragically in the metropolitan night, and now was over.

Or was it? The popular papers that created the Chang legend understood the fundamental principles of horror writing. If Fu Manchu and Dracula always survived to make a comeback, so could Brilliant Chang. Just as modern popular films often leave a gap in the end of the plot out of which the sequel can grow, the germ of the Chang apocrypha was implanted into the news of his conviction. 'Doubtless he will return and attempt to carry on his dreadful traffic. It is easily managed in the present state of our immigration laws, and to the average European official all Chinese appear very much alike.'[37]

After serving his sentence at Wormwood Scrubs, Chang was taken in a taxi to Fenchurch Street Station, and thence by train to the Royal Albert Docks. According to the popular papers, he was provided with a first-class stateroom by his relatives, and was seen off by some of his compatriots and 'several unhappy girls whose dope-sunken eyes and pallid cheeks told all too clearly the story of their downfall into the deepest abyss of all.' A voice was heard calling above the rest, 'Come back soon, Chang!'[38]

Sure enough, reports soon appeared to suggest that he had.[39] He had escaped from the ship briefly at Marseille, then again at Port Said; he was not on board when the liner docked in China. He knew his family and friends did not want him back: he would have been ostracised for his misdeeds and forced to live among the lowest of the low. Another account maintained that he was based in Zurich, from where he was planning a new drug campaign, aimed intially at Thames river resorts such as Marlow, Maidenhead, Hampton Court and Richmond.[40] Alternatively, he had returned from China and established his headquarters at Antwerp. Promoted from Dope King to 'Dope Emperor of Europe', he was reported to have been arrested in Paris, and then to have jumped bail.[41] The Germans had an extradition warrant out for him, in connection with the death by heroin overdose of Minna Spermel, a cabaret girl who had been friendly with the

Crown Prince. He was also wanted in Belgium.[42]

The following year, 1928, Chang's fortunes were said to have taken a different turn. He was back in China; blind, impoverished, and on the verge of madness.[43] But even this was not the end. The year after that, in one of those shameless somersaults so cherished by popular serial fiction, it was announced that Chang had circulated the report himself, and had employed a double to perpetrate the deception.[44] As late as September 1929, one more woman was identified as a victim of Chang's 'dope octopus'; Maria Orska, an actress, was now said to be confined in a German asylum.[45]

A week after that story appeared, Edgar Manning went down for the last time. His days as a Dope King were long behind him, though. Since his release from penal servitude, he had stayed firmly on the wrong side of the law, but he was never arrested for drug offences again. To a degree, he rested on his laurels, putting his name to the newspaper account of his adventures, and opening Eddy's Bar, a villains' haunt in a Soho backstreet. He struck up a relationship with a prostitute called Dora Lippack, a Russian national, which lasted his four years of liberty. In December 1928, he found himself in the dock at the Old Bailey, on charges of receiving stolen property from housebreakers, but was acquitted. He also received several summonses for harbouring prostitutes. Finally, he and Dora Lippack were captured in possession of goods that had been stolen from Lady Diana Cooper's car: Lippack was wearing a pair of Lady Diana's stockings when arrested. She was jailed for nine months and deported; he received a second and final 'lagging' of three years' penal servitude. It was during this trial that Detective-Sergeant Powell enunciated the verdict that stuck to Edgar Manning thereafter: 'He could well be described as the worst man in London.'[46]

Once back in Parkhurst, however, Manning lost his aura of menace. Outside, he represented the uncaged black beast; behind bars, the stereotype projected upon him was its opposite, that of the chained slave: simple, superstitious and submissive. Two ex-prisoners wrote about him in their memoirs, both depicting him as a childlike primitive with a profound awe of the supernatural. Val Davis said that Manning knew his Bible as well as a parson – and had a terrible fear of owls. When he heard one hoot, his 'body shook and his eyes rolled in abject terror.'[47]

His symbolic emasculation was underscored by the failure of his health, which had always been weak. He entered the prison hospital for the last time in October 1930, and did not leave it alive. When his condition deteriorated in mid-December, the prison's medical officer, Maurice Ahern, put him on a special diet of eggs, soup, jelly, and practically anything he fancied. It was the kindness of the nursery, but kindness nonetheless. And right to the end, Edgar Manning maintained the courtesy that had always distinguished him. Ahern affirmed that he was a very good patient, frequently expressing his gratitude.[48]

Manning died on 8 February 1931. The prison Death Book gives the cause of death as acute myelitis, toxaemia and heart failure.

One Dope King was consigned to a grave on the Isle of Wight, and the other existed in a phantom dimension of unverified apparition and rumour. In the absence of reliable sightings, the version that asserted Brilliant Chang's decline gradually came to be accepted. It had the aesthetic appeal of a folktale, and lent itself to a racial moral. Francis Chester said that Chang had died 'broken and blind'; he 'had neglected his own race in order to curry favour with the white folks, and it was said that he had a rich brother who refused to help him.'[49]

No canonical account emerged of Chang's life and nature as a whole, however. Despite the vehemence of the rhetoric directed against him, the stereotypy of the images used to describe him, and the basic consistency of themes in all versions of his narrative, he remained hallucinatory, elusive, and, indeed, inscrutable.

A couple of accounts outlined scenarios intended to resolve his anomalous position between East and West. One claimed that he had been married at thirteen – it was broadly accepted that he had a wife and three children in China – but soon 'fell completely and absolutely under that fascination which all white women seem to hold for men of the Orient'. He began to frequent the few streets or places of amusement open to both Orientals and Europeans, to the extent that he put his own safety at risk, and threatened to taint the family business with scandal. Talking to seamen, he learned of London, where proper boundaries between the races were not maintained: he asked to be sent there. Arriving in Limehouse, 'He started in the low Chinese cafés of the quarter, and was amazed to find white girls, beautiful to his eyes, eating and drinking with men of the Orient. He knew that they would have been deported from China for doing the same thing.' He began to seduce women of the streets and their slightly less unfortunate sisters, at first showering them with gifts, but then neglecting them. This was a costly way of life, and it induced him to go into the drug business. His success won him a following and his name: 'an appellation bestowed upon him by his Oriental followers in England as a mark of their admiration for his cunning'.[50]

The most developed narrative appeared in 1928, and was entitled 'The Passing Of Brilliant Chang'.[51] It portrayed him as a smart opportunist who latched onto the 1922 cocaine boom, acquiring a Rolls Royce and a flat in Park Lane from the proceeds. So far from being a sadist, he had a 'soft and impressionable heart', which caused him to carry on acceding to Freda Kempton's demands for cocaine, until fatal consequences ensued.

In Limehouse, Chang's compatriots spat at him in the streets, and barred him from their premises. Unable to settle in the rank neighbourhood, he was at a loss to know what to do. Ah Ket, the proprietor of a pak-a-pu joint, taunted him over his reluctance to risk arrest by returning to the drug trade, and dared him to pick up a consignment of cocaine that was due soon at the docks. Troubled and restless, Chang covered his Chinese silk tunic with an overcoat, and wandered into a seedy restaurant

> frequented by white women – dissipated and degraded creatures, it is true, but indisputably white. Chang's opulent years in the other end of London had inculcated passionate cravings for white women; he loathed the women of his own race, despised them for their lack of spirit, and lived only for the day when he might return to the life he loved so well.

He was in search of whisky, and through it oblivion; he met an acquaintance, 'Violet something-or-other', an alcoholic 'object of derision to all the people in Chinatown'. In his cups, he decided that as outcasts, they suited each other. He took her to live with him, but she was a difficult companion, demanding cocaine when the whisky ran out. Sometimes Chang confiscated her cocaine, but she evaded him by hiding packets around the flat. Often she forgot where she had put them, but despite Chang's warnings that she was risking his liberty, she persisted in the habit. Seeing that Violet was proving expensive to keep, Ah Ket took his opportunity, and this time persuaded Chang to become a courier. Eventually, the police visited Chang's flat again, and the hidden packets were discovered.

The moral engine of 'The Passing Of Brilliant Chang' is the interaction between two transgressive desires; Chang's lust for white women, and the women's craving for whisky or cocaine. Instead of claiming the women as victims, they are placed on the wrong side of the line, along with dope and the Chinaman. The story was not unique in attributing positive qualities to Chang. Even a positive quality could be given a negative inflection, though: '... he is the softest-hearted man in the world, and whilst he was in this country he always had a cheery word and a helping hand for those of his associates who were down on their luck; and in that fact, combined with the prospects of an easy living, lies his strength.'[52]

Perhaps the most sympathetic account appears in the autobiography of a 1920s underworld figure, who is inclined to blame biology – and the inherently flawed psychology of the Western woman – rather than morality:

> I first met the Chink in an all-night café, then existing in Gerrard Street, near Mrs. Meyrick's 'Forty-three' Club. I summed him up as a very shrewd man who, nevertheless, being an oriental, did not make sufficient allowance for the difference in the nervous make-up of westerners and his own countrymen in the matter of drug-taking, and could not foresee the hysterical lack of control English women especially would be bound to exhibit when they became addicts to cocaine – a lack of control which eventually gave the whole game away and got himself and his partner into trouble. He apparently thought he was merely giving them a new emotional 'kick' which would have no more serious after-effects than, say, sexual indulgence or drink. Later on, I believe, he became a little scared about the grip the vice exerted on most of his clients, the lengths to which they would go to appease their craving, and the disturbing effect it was having upon them. That such a state of things should come about was, I have no doubt, astonishing to this placid, philosophic oriental, whose countrymen enjoyed these indulgences as a matter of course and seemed little the worse for them.[53]

The moral, as ever, was the incompatibility of the races; Chang's 'placid, philosophic' nature recalled Cheng Huan, the mystical poet of *Broken Blossoms*, whose encounter with white femininity also had tragic results. To the more xenophobic storyteller, even spiritual refinement might be sinister. Arthur Tietjen called Chang 'an oriental mystic in the true Doctor Fu Manchu style'. Tietjen's account was written in the mid-1950s, but the passage of a generation seemed only to have hardened his racial suspicions: 'Chang possessed a strangely macabre – some said hypnotic – power to persuade women to sniff cocaine. It may well have been that he did so as a member of the yellow race to degrade white women.'[54]

Brilliant Chang was an entity that did not add up. His component elements were incompatible, his trajectory undetectable. Above all, he did not belong anywhere. He might be in Paris or he might be in Hong Kong; perhaps prosperous, perhaps impoverished. A location is equivalent to a conclusion; in its absence, his narratives carried on. He persisted as a character because the storytellers could not place him.

The Chang apocrypha, warning of his return or telling of his fate, was an essentially half-hearted affair. Apart from its factual implausibility, it lacked symbolic force. The phase of the Aftermath, half neurosis and half Dionysus, was over. Even the magazine *Pan* transformed itself from a chic partisan of youthful pleasure into a compendium of popular fiction. In the second half of the 1920s, the press was able to raise the spectre of Chang as Fu Manchu, the 'yellow spider' at the centre of a dope web. But Brilliant Chang had derived at least as much of his symbolic force as the incarnation of the Great God Pan.

The break between the early post-war years and the succeeding period was like the roughly coterminous one between silent cinema and the talkies. Like the Silent Era, the Aftermath rapidly acquired a nostalgic mystique. In the eyes of the whites, the Chinese had turned full circle, back to the turn-of-the-century Cockney John Chinaman; a 'most peaceable, inoffensive, harmless character'.[55]

With the threat neutralised, the bohemian explorers who had ventured into old Limehouse were replaced by charabancs full of tourists, whose guide would point out sites where he claimed to have seen women being drugged or attacked by Chinese men with large knives. Local residents would bang on the side of the coach and shout 'Don't listen to Tom the Liar!'[56] The new visitors were at least docile. A police surgeon, interviewed in 1934, recalled that the roughest customers had been a group led by Billie Carleton.[57]

The mythology of the drug underground persisted not only among the sightseers and the popular writers, but in personal memory. Until her death in 1991, Annie Lai was almost certainly the last surviving link with Brilliant Chang. A series of oral history interviews she recorded during the mid-1980s is the only account of its kind from within the Limehouse underworld. It describes the precarious living she scraped from selling opium and cocaine, and from prostitution.

She arrived in Limehouse in 1921, at the age of sixteen; two years later she met Yuen Lai, a professional gambler and drug dealer. They lived together until he was deported in 1928, for hitting a man over the head with an iron bar. The reason was jealousy: Yuen Lai suspected every man of being after her. One of the men she encountered was

Brilliant Chang himself. 'Yuen went after him and told him to keep away from me,' she recalled. 'The whole Chinatown used to be against this man, you see ... They pushed him out of Chinatown.'

Annie Lai thought she had met Chang on his release from prison, although he was actually deported straight away. She also believed that Billie Carleton, a 'big star', had lived in Limehouse, and that she had died in Chang's apartment: this was the reason for the Chinese community's hostility. But on matters of direct experience, the co-authors of the paper based on her interviews found her story to contain a strong degree of internal consistency.[58] There is no reason to doubt that she really did meet Brilliant Chang. Perhaps Yuen Lai's jealousy was justified, and Chang had designs on her. Either way, Annie Lai's death marks a symbolic end to the span of living memory stretching on from the days of the dope girls, just as Chang's deportation marked the symbolic end of those days themselves. And just as in the written tales, Brilliant Chang and Billie Carleton were intertwined in the imagination of the last woman who was actually there. The story demanded it.

10

FROM AFTERMATH
TO AFTERMATH

Soldiers and chorus girls had much in common. They were uniformed and drilled; simultaneously fetishised and expendable. The chorus girls were the ceremonial troopers of the army of young women. In their cohesion, their vivacity and their eroticism, they represented the dramatic crystallisation of a young female identity during the period that ran from the middle of the Great War to the middle of the 1920s.

At the same time, male identity was in crisis. It had leaped to its apotheosis in the joyous mobilisation of 1914; by 1918, it was exhausted and mutilated. Women seemed poised to inherit the fruits of peace, overthrowing the fundamental rule of patriarchy. They seemed to be disciples not of Judeo-Christian law, but of Dionysus and Pan. Soldiers returned, their purpose ended and the results of their service uncertain. Where they saw alien men who had secured modest niches in the docklands, they raged that their jobs, their houses and their women had been usurped.

As they shed their uniforms, it was men who faded into obscurity, while women became ever more vivid. And whether gaudy or sober, women had been breaching the boundaries within which they had previously seemed content. They even crossed racial lines: men of colour and young white women seemed to cleave together. It was as if alien men and women were conspiring to dispossess British manhood. The sense of a threat to the proper order of society was felt not just by shell-shocked servicemen, but by the old conservative ascendancy and its supporters as a whole.

In this state of tension, drugs presented themselves as an explanation for some of these disturbing developments, and as a way of expressing profound anxieties about the social order as a whole. Alien in nature, dope was invested with magical properties by being prohibited. Existing in marginal zones of society where conventional boundaries were unstable, it was understood as the agent which dissolved these boundaries, rather than as a symptom of instability. And with the prospect of drug-induced sexual contact across race lines came the threat of racial degeneration. These were the days in which Marie Stopes stamped her contraceptive caps with the brand name 'Racial', as though to create a eugenic amulet.

Many more elements contributed to the dope drama: nightlife, dancing, jazz, the appetite for instant thrills, the desire to be brilliant; the urge to forget, to deny, to dissemble. In sum, dope was a birth-pang of modernity. As Thomas Burke observed, 'the real significance of that saturnalia of the twenties is that it was our welcome to the new century.'[1]

During this inaugural phase, young womanhood acquired an extraordinarily distinct identity; as image, as object of desire, as fetish, as problem, and as the agent of modernity. The consequent feminisation of drugs, especially cocaine, was equally marked. The circumstances were unique: a society only enters modernity once. But the Dope Girls did not entirely vanish forever. They re-emerged, in strikingly similar form, after the Second World War.

Illegal drug use did not die out altogether in the mid-1920s, either as a fact or as a subject of alarms in the media, but its salience was negligible. Official monitoring indicated very low levels of drug use for the rest of the inter-war period. During the Second World War, however, an underground club scene was reborn. It embraced black seamen and GIs, a new generation of jazz musicians, and new drugs, such as cannabis and benzedrine.[2] After the war ended, these clubs became the crucible of the 'bop rebellion'. They were mongrel milieux, attracting jazzmen, West Indians, restless suburban youths shaking off the torpor of their office jobs, young women in black with a novel and feline air of independence.

The authorities had noted the wartime return of opium, brought by Chinese seamen, and a post-war rise in cannabis seizures. In 1947, the statutory report to the United Nations linked the latter to 'the coloured seamen of the East End and the clubs frequented by Negro theatrical performers and others in the West End clubs of London'.[3] Both opium and cannabis were considered to be safely contained within racial bounds until 1950, when information received from an arrested ship's steward led to a raid on Club Eleven, in Soho. Ronnie Scott was playing a Charlie Parker tune when he opened his eyes to see a policeman in front of him, too late to dispose of the cocaine in his wallet. Three months later, the Paramount Dance Hall in the Tottenham Court Road was also raided, and its 500 patrons searched. The prejudices of the police were confirmed by the discovery of twenty packets of hemp – cannabis – and several knives on the floor, along with a large number of contraceptives in the Ladies. The men were 'mainly coloured and the girls white': the picture was complete.[4]

The commentaries of the 1950s leaned to a pseudo-scientific tack. The 'Young Girls Who Smoke Doped Cigarettes' of a *Daily Telegraph* headline were identified as an epidemiological bridging group from black to white, from margin to majority.

> Home Office inspectors ... are satisfied ... that for the moment the smoking of these 'reefer' cigarettes is confined mainly to young girls of the type who became camp followers when American troops in large numbers were stationed here during the war ... The danger, of course, is that they may become confirmed addicts and spread the habit among girls and boys in their home districts.

The parallel with fears that 'camp followers' would spread venereal disease among the general population is obvious.

Science, it was confidently believed, could illuminate the mysterious processes that had baffled the people of the Great War's Aftermath. 'Is there a link between dope and hot jazz dancing – apart from the fact that coloured men who peddle reefers can meet susceptible teen-agers at the jazz clubs?' asked Chapman Pincher.

> Yes, there is scientific evidence for a much stronger link which involves the basic nature of the human brain.
>
> Reefers and rhythm seem to be directly connected with the minute electric 'waves' continually generated by the brain surface.
>
> When the rhythm of the music synchronises with the rhythm of the 'brainwaves' the jazz fans experience an almost compulsive urge to move their bodies in sympathy. Dope may help the brain to 'tune in' to the rhythm more sharply, thereby heightening the ecstasy of the dance.[6]

Teenagers were to the second aftermath of world war what young women were to the first. Once again, youth was a worry, though the anxieties did not focus quite so heavily on the feminine this time. Once again, there was a sense of external threat, but this time the men of colour that aroused fear were exclusively black, rather than black and yellow. The spectre of the yellow peril had been replaced by the red menace – as conspiratorial and ruthless as its predecessor, but actually existing and armed with atomic bombs. As well as the drug scare, newspapers of 1951 also warned of the prevalence of communist sympathies among teenage schoolgirls.[7]

The two themes were even combined, in the same way that commentaries in the earlier age had alleged drug trafficking to be a German plot. At the end of a monograph expounding the dangers of cannabis, one author suggested that it might have been used to brainwash the victims of Soviet show trials, and that the Soviets might dope bread with cannabis preparations 'to condition the mentality of a whole population'. Elsewhere he had asserted that cannabis, as well as causing violent crime and sex perversion, led to paranoia and grandiose delusions.[8]

Behind these contemporary variations, however, the stories of the 1950s drug flap stood directly in the traditions of their predecessors – though direct comparison, stylistically speaking, does the prose of the prefab concrete age no favours.

'In a corner five coloured musicians, brows perspiring, played bebop music with extraordinary fervour.' – *'The band crashed out a really good foxtrot.'*

'I watched the dancing ... I counted 28 coloured men and some 30 white girls. None of the girls looked more than 25.' – *'Round us danced the same old sickening crowd of under-sized aliens, blue about the chin and greasy, the same predominating type of girl, young, thin, underdressed, perpetually seized with hysterical laughter, ogling, foolish.'*

'Girls and coloured partners danced with an abandon – a savagery almost – which was both fascinating and embarrassing. From a doorway came a coloured man, flinging away the end of a strange cigarette. He danced peculiar convulsions on his own, then bounced to a table and held out shimmering arms to a girl.' – *'I heard several girls call out "Hello!" and, looking towards the stairhead, I saw a Chinaman ... A young girl ran up to him, held her arms out, he clasped her closely to him, and off they danced.'*

'We went outside. I had seen enough of my first bebop club, its coloured peddlers, its half-crazed uncaring girls.' – *'Outside, in the cool, refreshing air of Monday morning, the pale light of a new day was colouring London with the faint tints of dawn ... in the sleeping city were millions of people ... happily ignorant of the beastliness and the squalor, the foolishness and the wickedness which live in the small heart of man.'*[9]

Many of the locales were the same. As well as Soho and the dockland areas, the black district that still survived in the western hinterland of Tottenham Court Road was also known as a gathering-place of drug dealers. In the sepia and cream 1950s, the black habitués of the quarter made a sartorial splash. 'A number wore coloured shirts outside their trousers. Others, elaborately tailored drape suits with broad rimmed hats and startling ties,' recalled Raymond Thorp, a white drugtaker of the time. 'Their loud voices and unexpected outbursts of childish pleasure, worried a lot of folk. But those I had met around the jazz clubs I found kindly, simple, and anxious to please.'[10]

Robert Fabian took a similarly patronising line. Describing the Twilight Club, behind Gerrard Street, where cannabis 'hangs in the air like the taste of sin' and the band plays 'bewitching rhythms', he protests that 'It is not the fault of the coloured boys that this is one of the most dangerous clubs in London ... They have brains of children, can only dimly know the cruel harm they do to the 'teen-age girls who dance with them and try thrilled puffs at those harmless-looking, crude pungent marijuana cigarettes.' Partly as a result of American propaganda of the 1930s, partly because of its perception as an agent that facilitated contact between coloured men and young white women, cannabis was widely seen as worse than heroin or cocaine. Raymond Thorp was said to have kicked the 'white' drugs – so called for their colour – on his own, but to require medical assistance for the hemp. Fabian was not out of step with common opinion when he declared that of all the drugs that had been introduced to London, 'this new marijuana menace is becoming the worst and most diabolical in the history of Metropolitan crime!'[11]

Other self-appointed experts on the underworld, such as Arthur Tietjen, used the drug issue to bang a more straightforward anti-immigrant drum.

> In their flamboyant suits, shirts and ties, these coloured loungers who never worked, but drew their unemployment pay, enhanced their income by peddling 'reefers'. Their chief victims are white girls who, craving excitement, haunt the 'hot' jazz spots in the underground dens in Soho and off the Tottenham Court Road that are frequented by negroes. It is a fact that the coloured instrumentalists in the bands in these places are often 'under the influence' of the drug which keeps them going and stimulates them in their fantastic jive session.[12]

Derek Agnew, Raymond Thorp's ghost-writer, added an afterword to the addict's confessions in which he proposed imprisonment as a substitute for immigration control:

> Thousands of these immigrants are pouring into Britain every year. A majority of them smoke hemp. They do not leave their vice at home – they bring it with them. And the blunt truth is that numbers of them take perverted satisfaction from 'lighting up' a white girl. I know. I have watched it happen. And it is a horrible sight!
>
> We cannot stop them entering Britain. We can at least put them out of society's way for a long, long time, once they have been convicted of drug offences.

The shift of emphasis towards black men and immigration brings these drug narratives closer to today's political and social concerns. But the stories of the 1950s are closer to those of the 1920s than to the present. To a large extent, they shared assumptions about sex, racial differences, and inter-racial contact. In both periods, illicit drugtaking was a minor, focal metropolitan phenomenon that cast a shadow out of proportion to its actual size. So was 'coloured' settlement.

In the intervening decades, the racist rhetoric so fundamental to the dope narrative has been stifled by the establishment of a dominant ideology based on the profession of racial equality. Sexual morality has undergone a shift of geological proportions. Illegal drug use goes on in the most sedate of towns. Drugs still have a massive and peculiar symbolic force, however. In complex social situations, they are eagerly identified as cause rather than symptom. And anxieties about drugs are still about much more than drugs.

The system of beliefs underpinning the drug issue dates back, for the most part, no farther than the 1960s – though it might be noted that the legal and medical regime designed to control illegal drug use remains essentially the one established in the 1920s. The history of illegal drug use in this country divides into two eras; the modern one beginning around 1960. Up to then, drugtaking was interpreted according to the paradigm that evolved at the beginning of the Jazz Age. As late as 1956, Arthur Tietjen was still using Brilliant Chang to back his racist arguments about contemporary men of colour.

In that respect, the subsequent disappearance of Brilliant Chang and Billie Carleton from popular memory, like mummies exposed to modern air, can be taken as a welcome mark of progress. Now, passing beyond the very farthest limits of living memory, they deserve to be remembered again.

NOTES

Introduction

1. Courtwright, David T., *Dark Paradise: Opiate Use In America Before 1940*, Harvard University Press, Cambridge, Massachusetts 1982, p78. The following account of the history of drugs in the United States is derived from this source.
2. The stereotype has remained perennial. After Los Angeles police officers were videotaped beating Rodney King, an unarmed motorist, one of them claimed in his defence that he thought King looked as though he was under the influence of PCP. 'PCP's a dangerous drug,' said Sergeant Stacey Koon. 'It's kinda like a policeman's nightmare, that the individual under it is super-strong, that they have more or less a one-track mind, they exhibit super-strength. And they equate it with a monster.' (*Observer*, 3 May 1992) Koon also claimed in a book manuscript that King's 'sexually suggestive' motions induced the fear of 'a Mandingo sexual encounter' in a female officer (*Sunday Times*, 17 May 1992). The policemen's acquittal triggered rioting in which 58 people died.
3. Report of Committee on the Acquirement of Drug Habits (*American Journal of Pharmacy*, no.75 (1903), pp474-87), quoted in Grinspoon, L. and Bakalar, J.B., *Cocaine: A Drug and its Social Evolution*, Basic Books, New York 1985. The Committee was set up after the Vice-President of the American Pharmaceutical Association raised the issue of 'Negro cocainists' in 1901.
4. 'Soldier's Heart: Literary Men, Literary Women, and the Great War', p207, in Higonnet, M.R. *et al.*, *Behind the Lines: Gender And the Two World Wars*, Yale University Press, New Haven 1987.
5. Stevenson, John, *British Society 1914-45*, Penguin, London 1984, pp80, 82-5.
6. Cf Grinspoon, *op.cit.*, Ch.2: both in the United States and Europe, cocaine use was especially common 'in the regions where the fringes of high society overlap with the fringes of bohemia and the lower middle-class'.
7. Berridge, Virginia, 'The Origins of the English Drug "Scene", 1890-1930', *Medical History*, 1988, no.32, pp51-64. The most notorious example was Aleister Crowley, author of *Diary of a Drug Fiend*, (Collins, London 1922) Abacus, London 1979.
8. *Observer*, 16 March 1919.
9. Public Record Office, HO45 11599 433067.
10. *Sunday Pictorial*, 1 December 1918.
11. The expression 'dope girl' is from an *Evening News* article of 13 March 1922, p3, headlined 'A Cocaine Victim At 17 – Dazzling Change In A Nightclub Girl – A Terrible Picture'. (It also appears in Crowley, *op.cit.*, p182.)
12. See Kohn, Marek, *Narcomania*, Faber and Faber, London 1987.
13. *Empire News*, 19 November 1922; *John Bull*, 22 September 1923.
14 Kohn, *op.cit.*

Chapter 1

1. *The Stage*, 18 July 1901, 25 July 1901; *Daily Mail*, 20 July 1901, *Reynolds's Newspaper*, 21 July 1901.
2. Quoted in *Daily Mail*, 22 July 1901.
3. Dr John Henry, personal communication; also Anglin, Lise, *Cocaine: A Selection of Annotated Papers From 1880 to 1984 Concerning Health Effects*, Addiction Research Foundation, Toronto 1985; Chiang, William, and Goldfrank, Lewis, 'The Medical Complications of Drug Abuse', *Medical Journal of Australia*, no.152, 15 January 1990, pp83-8; Goldfrank, Lewis R., and Hoffman, Robert S., 'The Cardiovascular Effects of Cocaine', *Annals of Emergency Medicine*, no.20, February 1991, pp165-75; Spivey, William H., Euerle, Brian, 'Neurological Complications of Cocaine Abuse', *Annals of Emergency Medicine*, no.19, December 1990, pp1422-8.
4. *Daily Mail*, 10 August 1901.
5. *British Medical Journal*, 22 February 1902, p473; quoted in Stein, S.D., *International Diplomacy, State Administrators and Narcotics Control: The Origins of a Social Problem*, Gower (for London School of Economics), Aldershot 1985, p100.
6. Ng, Kwee Choo, *The Chinese in London*, Oxford University Press, Oxford 1968.
7. *East London Advertiser*, 28 December 1907.
8. *John Bull*, 6 May 1922.
9. *The Times*, 8 April 1919.
10. *Reynolds's Newspaper*, 26 January 1919; *The Times*, 26 May 1911, 1 June 1911, 1 July 1911; *News of the World*, 4 June 1911.
11. *Daily News*, 24 January 1919; *News of the World*, 26 January 1919.

Chapter 2

1. Burke, Leda (David Garnett), *Dope-Darling*, T. Werner Laurie, London 1919.
2. Stevenson, *op.cit.*, p50.
3. Machen, Arthur, in Brangham, Godfrey and Jarrett, Nigel (eds), *The Day's Portion*, Village Publishing, Pontypool 1991, pp40-7.
4. Haste, Cate, *Keep The Home Fires Burning*, Allen Lane, London 1977.
5. *Ibid.*, p108; *Weekly Dispatch*, 16 May 1915.
6. *Ibid.*; Holmes, Colin, *John Bull's Island: Immigration and British Society, 1871-1971*, Macmillan Education, London 1988; *John Bull*, 15 May 1915; Panayi, Panikos, *The Weekend Guardian*, 5-6 August 1989. Horatio Bottomley was eventually convicted of fraud in connection with a 'Victory Bond' scheme which he used *John Bull* to promote, and was sentenced to seven years' penal servitude in 1922.
7. MacDonagh, Michael, *In London During the Great War*, Eyre & Spottiswoode, London 1935, pp85-6.
8. Macdonagh, *op.cit.*
9. Burke, Thomas, *London in my Time*, Rich & Cowan, London 1934.
10. Stevenson, *op.cit.*, p71.

11. *New Statesman*, 21 November 1914.
12. *The Times*, 13, 15 October, 8, 19, 20 November 1915; Stevenson, *op.cit.*; Bishop, James, *The Illustrated London News Social History of the First World War*, Angus & Robertson, London 1982.
13. *Evening News*, 29 December 1915.
14. *Evening News*, 3 January 1916, p5.
15. Public Record Office MEPO2 1698; *Umpire*, 12 March 1916.
16. Willis, W.N., *White Slaves of London*, Anglo-Eastern Publishing Co., London 1912. White slavery emerged as a topic of concern in 1879-80, after the discovery of a traffic in English women to Belgium, and its exposure in the *Pall Mall Gazette* (cf Mort, Frank, *Dangerous Sexualities: Medico-Moral Politics in England Since 1830*, Routledge & Kegan Paul, London 1987, pp126-7). See also Bishop, Cecil, *Women and Crime*, Chatto & Windus, London 1931, Ch VII: 'The traffic in drugs and the traffic in women are closely allied.' (p144)
17. *Daily Express*, 18 December 1918: 'Cocaine In Cigarettes – How Thousands Of Men Are 'Doped' And Robbed ...' "The cocaine cigarette traffic is undoubtedly the most terrible enemy which the troops have to face in London at the present time," said an Army officer.' The *News of the World* ran the story on 22 December 1918, under the headline 'Doped Cigarettes – Used As An Aid To Rob Our Soldier-Heroes'. YMCA officials were cited; the report spoke of a 'cocaine cigarette syndicate'.
18. Public Record Office HO45 10500 119609.
19. Ziegler, Philip, *Diana Cooper*, Hamish Hamilton, London 1981, p55.
20. Ibid.
21. Cooper, Diana, *The Rainbow Comes and Goes* (Autobiography), Michael Russell, Salisbury 1979, p224.
22. Berridge, Virginia, 'War Conditions and Narcotics Control: The Passing of Defence of the Realm Act Regulation 40B', *Journal of Social Policy*, vol.7, no.3, pp285-304; 'Drugs and Social Policy: The Establishment of Drug Control in Britain 1900-30', *British Journal of Addiction*, no.79, 1984, pp17-29.
23. *The Times*, 12 February 1916.
24. *Daily Mail*, 11 February 1916; *Folkestone Herald*, 12 February 1916.
25. *The Times*, 5 February 1916; Public Record Office DPP4 50.
26. *Daily Chronicle*, 19 July 1916: 'The Cocaine Habit', by Dr C.W. Saleeby, p4; 'Sale Of Cocaine To Soldiers On Leave' and accompanying background article, p5.
27. Courtwright, *op.cit.*
28. Chester, *op.cit.*, p71.
29. Public Record Office HO45 10813 312966.
30. 19 July 1916.
31. 13 June 1916.
32. *Daily Chronicle*, 19 July 1916.
33. Nor did Jews come to be strongly associated with the drug traffic in subsequent stages of the drug panic. They did, however, have a minor place in the folklore: see, for example, Felstead, Sidney Theodore, *The Underworld of London*, John Murray, London 1923, pp270-2.
34. 23 July 1916. For another comment on ether, see the *Daily Express*, 16

December 1918, which, after the end of hostilities, could affirm that the *Sturm-Truppen* attacking 'stolid Tommies' found that 'though cold and drenched and starved, the same brave man, with steadfast will and cool courage, faced and beat to his death the drug-driven hero of a moment.'

35. Berridge, *op.cit.*
36. Public Record Office HO45 10500 119609.

Chapter 3

1. Gilbert, Sandra M., 'Soldier's Heart: Literary Men, Literary Women, and the Great War', p207, in Higonnet, M.R. et al., *Behind the Lines: Gender and The Two World Wars*, Yale University Press, New Haven 1987.
2. Graves, Robert, *Goodbye to All That*, (Jonathan Cape, London 1929), Penguin, London 1960, pp188-91.
3. Aldington, Richard, *Death of a Hero*, (Chatto & Windus, London 1929), Hogarth Press, London 1984, p18.
4. Hirschfeld, Magnus, *Sexual History of the World War*, Panurge, New York 1934, p64.
5. Fischer, H.C., and Dubois, E.X., *Sexual Life During the World War*, Francis Aldor, London 1937, p161.
6. Aldington, *op.cit.*, pp253-4.
7. *Ibid.*, p244.
8. Fischer and Dubois, *op.cit.*, pp104-5.
9. *Ibid.*, pp70-1.
10. Aldington, *op.cit.*, p24.
11. Brittain, Vera, *Testament of Youth*, Victor Gollancz, London (1933) 1979, p578.
12. *The Collected Short Stories: Volume Two*, Heinemann, London 1973, pp334-46.
13. Graves, Robert, *The Greek Myths*, Penguin, London 1960.
14. *Weekly Dispatch*, 3 June 1917.
15. Fischer and Dubois, *op.cit.*, p473.
16. 'The Invisible Flâneur', *New Left Review*, no.191, January/February 1992, pp90-110.
17. See Gavin Weightman and Steve Humphries, *The Making of Modern London*, Sidgwick & Jackson, London 1984, p23.
18. Fischer and Dubois, *op.cit.*, pp108-9.
19. Ronell, Avital, *Crack Wars: Literature Addiction Mania*, University of Nebraska Press, Lincoln 1992, p162.
20. F.W. Hirst, *The Consequences of the War to Great Britain*, (1934), quoted in Mannheim, H., *Social Aspects of Crime in England Between the Wars*, Allen & Unwin, London 1940.
21. Lawrence, *op.cit.*
22. Mannheim, *op.cit.* The complete survey results are as follows:

Occupation	1921	1929-35
Domestic servants	10	7
Dressmakers etc.	17	68
Clerical workers	3	5

Shop assistants	–	3
Chorus girls, etc.	8	13
Waitresses	2	39
Married women	7	16
No occupation	2	9
Prostitute	1	1
Miscellaneous	9	4

23. Flexner, Abraham, *Prostitution in Europe*, Century, New York 1914, pp14-15. On the Continent, registration of prostitutes made the identification of the 'professional' prostitute easier. Surveys supported the idea that, as well as women exclusively engaged in prostitution, a large number of women in the low-paid, casual sector combined selling sexual services with other occupations. Flexner quotes a study made in Mannheim, *op.cit.*, between 1892 and 1901, which found that 316 of 594 prostitutes also worked as waitresses, laundresses, seamstresses, actresses etc. In Hanover 139 of 330 prostitutes were 'professional'; the rest working in shops, bars, domestic service, or the theatre. A Munich survey of 2574 prostitutes enumerated 721 domestic servants, 608 waitresses or barmaids, 250 factory workers, 246 seamstresses, 60 women connected with the stage, 52 laundresses, and 40 dressmakers.
24. See, for example, Gardiner, James, *Gaby Deslys: A Fatal Attraction*, Sidgwick & Jackson, London 1986.
25. Flexner, *op.cit.*, p87.
26. *News of the World*, 15 December 1918.
27. Fischer and Dubois, *op.cit.*, Ch.10; Hirschfeld, *op.cit.*, Ch.3.

Chapter 4

1. Ng, *op.cit.*
2. May, J.P., 'The Chinese in Britain, 1860-1914', in Colin Holmes (ed.), *Immigrants and Minorities in British Society*, Allen & Unwin, London 1978.
3. Burke, Thomas, *Limehouse Nights*, *Daily Express* Fiction Library, London [no date].
4. *Ibid.*
5. Rohmer, Sax, *Dope: A Story of Chinatown and the Drug Traffic*, Cassell, London 1919, p178.
6. *Empire News*, 1 June 1919, 'Yellow Men Charm White Women'.
7. James, E.O., 'The Church In China Town', *East London Church Chronicle* XXXII, no.2, Midsummer 1920 (held in the Tower Hamlets Borough Library Local History Collection).
8. May, *op.cit.*
9. Thorogood, Horace, *East of Aldgate*, Allen & Unwin, London 1935, p146.
10. 5 October 1920.
11. 27 May 1923.
12. Cancellor, H.L., *The Life of a London Beak*, Hurst & Blackett, London 1930. Like Horace Thorogood, cited above, Cancellor's main animus was against the Jews. He claimed that, during the war, they were only

interested in profiting from the indigenous population, and that they trampled women and children in their rush to take cover from air raids. For a magistrate, he showed an unusual fondness for appeasement, in his defence of the lenient sentences passed after the 'Lusitania riots' (q.v.); he argued that stiff sentences would have provoked further disorder.

13. *Evening News*, 4, 6, 7 October 1920.
14. *Illustrated Sunday Herald*, 30 April 1922.
15. James, *op.cit.*; Ng, *op.cit.*; Mrs Rose Maudesley (interviewed by author); Walter Dunsford (Museum of London: Docklands Oral History Project, 85/593); Tower Hamlets Borough Library Local History Collection cuttings (*East London Advertiser*, 26 April 1919; unattributed, 10 March 1923).
    The Tower Hamlets collection also contains examples of pai-ke-p'iao papers, and a copy of *Odd Jobs*, by Pearl Binder, Harrap, London 1935. Claimed by its author to be factually based, this book includes 'Pukka Poo', the story of a white woman who falls into prostitution, and ends up living with a pai-ke-p'iao agent in Limehouse.
16. *Evening News*, 6 October 1920.
17. *Evening News*, 5 October 1920. This article, headed 'White Girls 'Hypnotised' By Yellow Men', was accompanied by the 'Yellow Perils' editorial cited above.
18. *East End News*, 15 July 1924.
19. Chester, *op.cit.*, pp272-5.
20. *Daily Express*, 1 October 1920.
21. Parssinen, *op.cit.*, p147.
22. *Ibid.*, p90.
23. *Ibid.*; Berridge, Virginia, 'East End Opium Dens and Narcotic Use in Britain, *The London Journal*, vol.4, no.1, pp3-28; Berridge, Virginia and Edwards, Griffith, *Opium and the People*, Allen Lane, London 1981.
24. Berridge, 'East End Opium Dens', *op.cit.*
25. *Daily Telegraph*, 3 October 1916.
26. *Empire News*, 5 February 1928.
27. *Sunday Pictorial*, 29 December 1918.
28. *Evening News*, 5 October 1920; *East End News*, 18 January 1921.
29. May, *op.cit.*; Waller, P.J., *History Today*, September 1985.
30. E.g., *East End News*, 12, 15 May 1908; 26 May 1919.
31. *Umpire*, 4 June 1916.
32. May, *op.cit.*
33. *Maritime Review*, 8 July 1911.
34. 19 September 1916, included in Public Record Office HO45 24683.
35. Parssinen, *op.cit.*, Ch.10.
36. Public Record Office HO45 24683 311604.
37. *Empire News*, 4 December 1921.

Chapter 5

1. *World's Pictorial News*, 22 March 1925.
2. *News of the World*, 6 April 1919.
3. *Empire News*, 26 July 1925.

4. *Daily Sketch*, 28 November 1918; *News of the World*, 1 December 1918.
5. *Empire News*, 26 July 1925; Cochran, Charles B., *Secrets of a Showman*, Heinemann, London 1925.
6. *News of the World*, 26 January 1919.
7. *The Times*, 1 March 1919.
8. *Daily Mirror*, 24 January 1919; *The Times*, 15 February 1919.
9. *The Times*, 4 December 1918.
10. *News of the World*, 19 January 1919.
11. *Daily Graphic*, 24 January 1919.
12. *Empire News*, 12 August 1928. See also Lawrence, Gertrude, *A Star Danced*, Doubleday, New York 1945, and Lillie, Beatrice, *Every Other Inch a Lady*, W.H. Allen, London 1973: in these accounts, Lillie and Lawrence, rather than Lillie and Carleton, were the partners in crime. Lillie remained friends with Carleton, however; she was one of the most frequent visitors to Carleton's flat in the period shortly before her death (*Daily Telegraph*, 4 December 1918).
13. *Tatler*, 26 September 1917.
14. *Tatler*, 16 February 1916.
15. *Tatler*, 1 March 1916.
16. Compton, Fay, *Rosemary: Some Remembrances*, Alston Rivers, London 1926.
17. *The Times*, 3 January 1919.
18. *The Times*, 24 January 1919.
19. *Daily Graphic*, 3 January 1919.
20. *The Times*, 19 February 1919.
21. *Daily Telegraph*, 24 January 1919.
22. *Daily Mirror*, 24 January 1919.
23. *Daily Graphic*, 17 January 1919.
24. *The Times*, 3, 24 January 1919.
25. *Empire News*, 23 February 1919.
26. *News of the World*, 26 January 1919.
27. *The Times*, 13 December 1918; *Daily Mirror*, 24 January 1919.
28. *News of the World*, 19 January 1919.
29. *The Times*, 13 December 1918.
30. *The Times*, 15 February 1919.
31. *The Times*, 3 January 1919.
32. *The Times*, 8 April 1919.
33. *Empire News*, 23 February 1919; *The Times*, 13 December 1918.
34. *News of the World*, 6 April 1919.
35. *Reynolds's News*, 12 January 1919.
36. *Daily Sketch*, 28 November 1918.
37. *Daily Telegraph*, 28 November 1918.
38. *News of the World*, 19 January 1919.
39. *The Times*, 13 December 1918, 24 January 1919.
40. *News of the World*, 23 February 1919.
41. *News of the World*, 15 December 1918, 19 January 1919; *The Times*, 1, 24 January 1919.
42. *The Times*, 1 January 1919; Daily Mail, 24 January 1919.
43. *Daily Sketch*; *The Times*, 28 November 1918.

44. *The Times*, 4 December 1918, 3 January 1919; *News of the World*, 8
    December 1918; *Reynolds's News*, 5 January 1919.

Chapter 6

1. *The Times*, 17 January 1919; *News of the World*, 6 April 1919.
2. *News of the World*, 26 January 1919.
3. *News of the World*, 15 December 1918, 6 April 1919.
4. *Empire News*, 27 April, 4 May 1919.
5. *The Times*, 30 November 1918.
6. *News of the World*, 1 December 1918.
7. *The Times*, 13 December 1918.
8. *News of the World*, 15 December 1918; Oddie, Samuel Ingleby, *Inquest*,
    Hutchinson, London 1941.
9. *News of the World*, 15 December 1918.
10. Wyles, Lilian, *A Woman at Scotland Yard*, Faber and Faber, London 1951.
11. *Daily Sketch*, 21 December 1918.
12. *Daily Mail*, 24 January 1919.
13. Courtwright, David T., *Dark Paradise: Opiate Addiction in America
    Before 1940*, Harvard University Press, Cambridge, Massachusetts 1982;
    Courtwright, David T., Joseph, Herman and Des Jarlais, Don, *Addicts
    Who Survived: An Oral History of Narcotic Use in America, 1923-1965*,
    University of Tennessee Press, Knoxville 1989.
14. *The Times*, 21 December 1918.
15. *The Times*, 15 February 1919.
16. Douglas, Mary, *Purity and Danger*, Ark, London 1984.
17. *Empire News*, 11 May 1919.
18. *Daily Telegraph*, 13 December 1918.
19. *Daily Telegraph*, 17 January 1919.
20. *Kinematograph & Lantern Weekly*, 12 December 1918.
21. Reported in *Sunday Pictorial*, 23 February 1919.
22. *The Times*, 8 March 1919.
23. *Empire News*, 8 June 1919.
24. *Daily Telegraph*, 17 January 1919; *Empire News*, 6 February 1919.
25. *News of the World*, 26 January 1919; *Daily Mirror*, 24 January 1919.
26. *News of the World*, 26 January 1919; *The Times*, 24 January 1919.
27. Public Record Office Calendar of Indictments, CRIM 5 10.
28. *The Times*, 24 January 1919.
29. *The Times*, 8 February 1919.
30. *Daily Telegraph*, *The Times*, 5 April 1919; see also *The Times*, 8 March, 3,
    4 April 1919; *News of the World*, 9 March 1919.
31. *The Times*, 8 April 1919.
32. I am greatly indebted to Dr John Henry, Consultant Physician at the
    National Poisons Unit, Guy's Hospital, and Mr John Ramsey, Head of
    Toxicology at St. George's Hospital Medical School, for discussing the
    forensic aspects of the Billie Carleton case with me. Both these experts felt
    that the most likely cause of death was veronal. The evidence they had to
    go on is thin, however, and I should stress that their views were based on
    my verbal and written presentation of the case. Although these discussions

inform my treatment of the question, any errors are mine alone.
33. Unattributed cutting from Mander & Mitchenson Collection, 1 March 1919.
34. *The Times*, 8 March 1919.
35. *News of the World*, 5 January 1919.
36. *The Times*, 4 December 1918, 17 January 1919, 5 April 1919.
37. *Daily Express*, 31 December 1917; Spurling, Hilary, *Ivy When Young: The Early Life of Ivy Compton-Burnett 1884-1919*, Victor Gollancz, London 1974, pp253-6.
38. Oddie, *op.cit.*
39. *News of the World*, 26 January 1919.
40. *The Times*, 15 February, 8 April 1919; *News of the World*, 6 April 1919.
41. As note 33.
42. *News of the World*, 19 January 1919.
43. Anglin, *op.cit.*
44. *The Times*, 24 January 1919.
45. *News of the World*, 6 April 1919.
46. *The Times*, 8 April 1919.
47. *Daily Mirror*, 26 February, 11 June 1986.

Chapter 7

1. *Daily Express*, 7, 9, 16 December 1918.
2. *Daily Express*, 9 December 1918.
3. *Daily Express*, 16 December 1918.
4. *Daily Mail*, 16 December 1918.
5. *Empire News*, 23 January 1921.
6. *Empire News*, 19 January 1919.
7. *The Times*, 8 April 1919.
8. Low, Rachael, *The History of the British Film 1914-18*, Allen & Unwin, London 1950, p140.
9. *Kinematograph & Lantern Weekly*, 19 December 1919.
10. *The Stage*, 30 January 1919.
11. Gish, Lillian, with Ann Pinchot, *Lillian Gish: The Movies, Mr Griffith and Me*, W.H. Allen, London 1969.
12. Andrew, Dudley, *Film in the Aura of Art*, Princetown University Press, Princetown, NJ 1984, Ch.2, 'Broken Blossoms: The Vulnerable Text and the Marketing of Masochism'.
13. Rohmer, *op.cit.*
14. Enright, D.J, introduction to *The Mystery of Dr Fu-Manchu*, J.M. Dent, London 1985.
15. *News of the World*, 1 December 1918.
16. *Sunday Pictorial*, 1 December 1918.
17. *News of the World*, 15 December 1918.
18. *World's Pictorial News*, 7 January 1922.
19. *Empire News*, 26 July 1925; Cochran, Charles B., *Secrets of a Showman*, Heinemann, London 1925.
20. *Empire News*, 2 January 1921.
21. *World's Pictorial News*, 22 March 1925.

22. *Empire News*, 1 August 1920.
23. Garber, Marjorie, *Vested Interests: Cross-Dressing and Cultural Anxiety*, Routledge, New York 1992.
24. *Empire News*, 27 February 1927.
25. Unattributed cutting from Mander & Mitchenson Collection, December 1931.
26. Wearing, J.P., *The London Stage 1890-1930: A Calendar of Plays and Players*, Scarecrow Press, Metuchen, NJ and London 1981-90.
27. *News of the World*, 6 April 1919.
28. *The Times*, 5 April 1919; *Empire News*, 15 June 1919.
29. Parssinen, *op.cit.*, p172; *The Times*, 30 July 1922.
30. *Empire News*, *World's Pictorial News*, 31 May 1925.
31. Unattributed cutting from Mander & Mitchenson Collection, November 1956. Rather than the usual work of imagination, this piece appears to have been sloppily compiled from reliable sources, giving rise to a number of inaccuracies in detail.
32. *Daily Express*, Obituaries 005460 (British Library, Colindale); including *The People*, 2 May, 14 May ('Confessions Of A Broken Butterfly'), 4, 11 June 1933; Paul, Brenda Irene Isabelle Frances Teresa Dean, *My First Life*, John Long, London 1935; Bing Spear, interviewed by author.
33. *Empire News*, 27 June 1926; 'Fallen Stars, No.3', Mander & Mitchenson cutting, November 1956 (*op.cit.*).
34. Finlayson, Iain, *Tangier: City of the Dream*, Harper Collins, London 1992; Green, Michelle, *The Dream at the End of the World: Paul Bowles and the Literary Renegades in Tangier*, Harper Collins, New York 1991.
35. Maugham, Robin, *Escape From the Shadows*, Hodder & Stoughton, London 1972, p206.
36. Finlayson, *op.cit.*, p302.

Chapter 8

1. *Tatler*, 15 January 1919.
2. *Observer*, 16 March 1919.
3. Blythe, Ronald, *The Age of Illusion: Glimpses of Britain Between the Wars, 1919-1940*, Oxford University Press, Oxford 1983.
4. Meyrick, Kate, *Secrets of the 43*, John Long, London 1933.
5. *Empire News*, 11, 18 January, 2 February 1920.
6. *Ibid.*
7. *Empire News*, 27 January, 3 February 1929.
8. *Empire News*, 23 May 1926.
9. *Sunday Express* 7 May 1922; *Empire News*, 30 April 1922.
10. *Evening News*, 7 March 1922.
11. *Evening News*, 17 April 1922.
12. *Daily Express*, 18 April 1922; *Illustrated Police News*, 20 April 1922; *People*, 30 April 1922.
13. *Evening News*, 16 January 1922; *World's Pictorial News*, 21 January 1922.
14. *People*, 23 April 1922.
15. *Ibid.*
16. *People*, 12 March 1922.

17. *World's Pictorial News*, 22 April 1922.
18. *People*, 23 April 1922.
19. *Ibid.*; *Daily Express*, 11 April 1924.
20. *Ibid.*
21. *Reynolds's News*, 30 April 1922.
22. *Daily Express*, 18 April 1926; *Empire News*, 18 April 1926.
23. *People*, 23 April 1922.
24. *Empire News*, 12 March 1922.
25. *World's Pictorial News*, 29 April 1922; *Reynolds's News*, 30 April 1922.
26. *Empire News*, 30 April 1922.
27. *Daily Express*, 10 March 1922.
28. *Sunday Express*, 30 April 1922.
29. *Daily Express*, 14 March 1922.
30. *Evening News*, 25, 27 April 1922.
31. *Evening News*, 24 February 1922.
32. *Evening News*, 14 March 1922.
33. *Evening News*, 20 April 1922.
34. *Evening News*, 13 March 1922.
35. *Evening News*, 30 April 1922.
36. Public Record Office HO45 11252 432253.
37. *Daily Express*, 10 March 1922.
38. *World's Pictorial News*, 15 April 1922; see also May, Betty, *Tiger-Woman*, (Duckworth, London 1929) Cedric Chivers, Portway, Bath 1972.
39. *Illustrated Sunday Herald*, 19 March 1922.
40. *Evening News*, 17 March 1922.
41. *Daily Express*, 4 May 1922 (source for other *Daily Express* references in this section, except where otherwise stated).
42. Public Record Office HO45 11599 433067 (source for other references in this section, except where otherwise stated).
43. *Evening News*, 3 May 1922; *World's Pictorial News*, 13 May 1922.
44. *The Film Renter & Moving Picture News*, 13 May 1922.
45. *Bioscope*, 11 May 1922.
46. *Daily Express*, 3 May 1922.
47. Public Record Office HO45 11599 433067.
48. Anger, Kenneth, *Hollywood Babylon*, Dell, New York 1981.
49. Blythe, *op.cit.*
50. Crisp, Quentin, *The Naked Civil Servant*, Fontana, Glasgow 1977.
51. Laver, James, quoted in Montgomery, John, *The Twenties*, Allen & Unwin, London 1957.
52. *Illustrated Sunday Herald*, 26 March 1922.
53. Bland, Lucy, 'In the Name of Protection: The Policing of Women in the First World War', in Brophy, Julia and Smart, Carol (eds), *Women in Law: Explorations in Law, Family and Sexuality*, Routledge & Kegan Paul, London 1985.
54. Lock, Joan, *The British Policewoman: Her Story*, Robert Hale, London 1979; Wyles, Lilian, *A Woman at Scotland Yard*, Faber and Faber, London 1951.
55. *The Times*, 8 April 1922.

56. *Illustrated Police News*, 30 March 1922; *Sunday Express*, 26 February 1922.
57. *Sunday Express*, 21 May 1922.
58. *Daily Express*, 2 May 1922.
59. *Illustrated Police News*, 18 May 1922.
60. Public Record Office MEPO 3 420; *Daily Express*, *The Times*, 3 April 1922.
61. *Daily Express*, 3 May 1922.
62. *Empire News*, 30 April 1922.
63. *Sunday Express*, 27 August 1922; *Empire News*, 27 August, 12 November 1922.
64. *Illustrated Sunday Herald*, 26 November 1922; *Illustrated Police News*, 30 November 1922.
65. *Empire News*, 26 November 1922.
66. *Empire News*, 10 December 1922.
67. *World's Pictorial News*, 2 December 1922.
68. *Illustrated Police News*, 30 November 1922; *World's Pictorial News*, 25 November 1922.
69. *Empire News*, 3 December 1922.
70. *Illustrated Sunday Herald*, 26 November 1922.
71. Leed, Eric J., *No Man's Land: Combat and Identity in World War I*, Cambridge University Press, London 1979; Stevenson, *op.cit.*
72. Leed, *op.cit.*
73. Fryer, Peter, *Staying Power: The History of Black People in Britain*, Pluto Press, London 1984.
74. Dickens, Charles, *The Mystery of Edwin Drood*, Penguin, London 1974.

Chapter 9

1. Except where otherwise indicated, the sources of information on Edgar Manning are Public Record Office files MEPO3 424 and CRIM4 1424.
2. Allen, Trevor, *Underworld: The Biography of Charles Brooks, Criminal*, Newnes, London 1931, p233.
3. Harrison, Richard, *Whitehall 1212*, Jarrolds, Norwich 1947.
4. John Dudley, for instance, a former bomber crewman arrested on cocaine charges by Walter Burmby (*Empire News*, 3 April 1921); or John Hall, an airman found dead of a morphine overdose at the Imperial Hotel in Russell Square (*Empire News*, 23 January 1921). At Hall's inquest, the pathologist Sir Bernard Spilsbury said that morphine-taking had not been uncommon among wartime fliers. Another man reported to have used morphine while in the Royal Flying Corps was Ronald True, who killed a woman and was found to be criminally insane (*World's Pictorial News*, 29 April 1922).
5. *Daily Chronicle*, 27 January 1922.
6. *Empire News*, 20 November 1921.
7. *Evening News*, 7 May 1922; Reynolds's *News 4, 11 June 1922*.
8. *Evening News*, 28 April 1922.
9. *Evening News*, 30 July 1922.

10. *Ibid.*
11. *Ibid.*, and 24 September 1922; *The Times*, 18 September 1922.
12. *News of the World*, 2 July 1923.
13. *World's Pictorial News*, 28 February 1926.
14. 'Black Devil and White Girls', *John Bull*, 22 September 1923.
15. *News of the World*, 16 March 1919.
16. *Empire News*, 16 June 1918.
17. *John Bull*, 7 July 1923.
18. Fabian, Robert, *London After Dark*, Naldrett, Kingswood, Surrey 1955, p36. Fabian claimed the credit for obtaining information that led to Manning's imprisonment, in 1923 and again in 1929. The official papers make no mention of him, however.
19. *Empire News*, 27 July 1924.
20. *Daily Express*, 11 April 1924.
21. *Ibid.*
22. Parssinen, *op.cit.*; *Empire News*, 2 December 1922.
23. *Daily Express*, 11 April 1924; *World's Pictorial News*, 17 May 1924.
24. *Empire News*, 27 May, 3 June 1923; *Evening News, 10 April 1924*.
25. *Empire News*, 2 March 1924.
26. *Empire News*, 9 March 1924. A woman more forthright in claiming intimacy with Chang was Lily Rumble, alias Brentano, of Pennyfields. After being arrested at the Princess Louise pub, in Holborn, where she was seen with associates known as Big Vi and Brixton Peggy, she received a six-month sentence for offering to supply cocaine. She said she supposed that people had been saying she was involved with cocaine because 'I am living with the Chinaman, Bill Chang', whose own court case had come up a couple of weeks before. (*People*, 27 April, 4 May 1924.)
27. *Daily Express*, 11 April 1924.
28. *Ibid.*
29. *Empire News*, 13 April 1924; World's Pictorial *News, 10 May 1924*.
30. *World's Pictorial News*, 26 April 1924.
31. *Empire News*, 9 March 1924.
32. *World's Pictorial News*, 26 April 1924.
33. *Empire News*, 5 September 1926.
34. Parssinen, *op.cit.*
35. Brittain, *op.cit.*, p11.
36. *Daily Express*, 11 April 1924.
37. *World's Pictorial News*, 17 May 1924.
38. *Empire News*, *World's Pictorial News*, 19 April 1925; *Empire News*, 14 March 1926.
39. *John Bull*, 13 February 1926; *Empire News*, 14 March 1926.
40. *Empire News*, 22 May 1927.
41. *Empire News*, 11, 25 September 1927.
42. *World's Pictorial News*, 2 October 1927.
43. *World's Pictorial News*, 11 November 1928.
44. *Empire News*, 21 July 1929.
45. *Empire News*, 8 September 1929.
46. *News of the World*, 15 September 1929.

47. Allen, *op.cit.*; Davis, Val, *Phenomena in Crime*, John Long, London [no date].
48. *Isle of Wight County Press*, 14 February 1931; *News of the World*, 22 February 1931.
49. Chester, *op.cit.*; see also Thorogood, *op.cit.*
50. *World's Pictorial News*, 19 April 1924.
51. *People*, 29 July 1928.
52. *Empire News*, 22 May 1927.
53. Allen, *op.cit.*, p222.
54. Tietjen, Arthur, *Soho: London's Vicious Circle*, Allan Wingate, London 1956, p25.
55. Wade, George A., 'The Cockney John Chinaman', *English Illustrated Magazine*, vol.23, no.202, July 1900.
56. Cockney John Chinaman, TV documentary, made by Orientations, 1987; also *Daily Mirror*, 27 May 1935; and Thorogood, *op.cit.*
57. *Daily Sketch*, 3 May 1934.
58. Lai, Annie, Little, Bob and Little, Pippa, 'Chinatown Annie: The East End Opium Trade 1920-35: The Story of a Woman Opium Dealer', *Oral History Journal*, vol.14, no.1, Spring 1986, pp18-30. The quotations are from unpublished transcript.

Chapter 10

1. Burke, Thomas, *London in my Time*, Rich & Cowan, London 1934.
2. Fordham, John, *Let's Join Hands and Contact the Living: Ronnie Scott and his Club*, Elm Tree, London 1986.
3. Spear, H.B., 'The Growth of Heroin Addiction in the United Kingdom', *British Journal of Addiction*, vol.64, no.2, 1969, pp245-55.
4. Lyle, George, 'Dangerous Drug Traffic in London', *British Journal of Addiction*, vol.50, no.1, 1953, pp47-55.
5. *Daily Telegraph*, 28 August 1951.
6. *Daily Express*, 26 November 1951.
7. Hopkins, Harry, *The New Look: A Social History of the Forties and Fifties*, Secker & Warburg, London 1964, pp264-5.
8. Johnson, Donald McI., *Indian Hemp: A Social Menace*, Christopher Johnson, London 1952.
9. *Ibid.* (quotation from *Sunday Graphic*, 16 September 1951); *Daily Express*, 14 March 1922 (italics).
10. Thorp, Raymond, *Viper: The Confessions of a Drug Addict*, Robert Hale, London 1956.
11. Fabian, *op.cit.*, p26.
12. Tietjen, *op.cit.*, p22.

INDEX